T0371636

Explainable Artificial Intelligence for Autonomous Vehicles

Explainable AI for Autonomous Vehicles: Concepts, Challenges, and Applications is a comprehensive guide to developing and applying explainable artificial intelligence (XAI) in the context of autonomous vehicles. It begins with an introduction to XAI and its importance in developing autonomous vehicles. It also provides an overview of the challenges and limitations of traditional black-box AI models and how XAI can help address these challenges by providing transparency and interpretability in the decision-making process of autonomous vehicles. The book then covers the state-of-the-art techniques and methods for XAI in autonomous vehicles, including model-agnostic approaches, post-hoc explanations, and local and global interpretability techniques. It also discusses the challenges and applications of XAI in autonomous vehicles, such as enhancing safety and reliability, improving user trust and acceptance, and enhancing overall system performance. Ethical and social considerations are also addressed in the book, such as the impact of XAI on user privacy and autonomy and the potential for bias and discrimination in XAI-based systems. Furthermore, the book provides insights into future directions and emerging trends in XAI for autonomous vehicles, such as integrating XAI with other advanced technologies like machine learning and blockchain and the potential for XAI to enable new applications and services in the autonomous vehicle industry. Overall, the book aims to provide a comprehensive understanding of XAI and its applications in autonomous vehicles to help readers develop effective XAI solutions that can enhance autonomous vehicle systems' safety, reliability, and performance while improving user trust and acceptance.

This book:

- Discusses authentication mechanisms for camera access, encryption protocols for data protection, and access control measures for camera systems.
- Showcases challenges such as integration with existing systems, privacy, and security concerns while implementing explainable artificial intelligence in autonomous vehicles.

- Covers explainable artificial intelligence for resource management, optimization, adaptive control, and decision-making.
- Explains important topics such as vehicle-to-vehicle (V2V) communication, vehicle-to-infrastructure (V2I) communication, remote monitoring, and control.
- Emphasizes enhancing safety, reliability, overall system performance, and improving user trust in autonomous vehicles.

The book is intended to provide researchers, engineers, and practitioners with a comprehensive understanding of XAI's key concepts, challenges, and applications in the context of autonomous vehicles. It is primarily written for senior undergraduate, graduate students, and academic researchers in the fields of electrical engineering, electronics and communication engineering, computer science and engineering, information technology, and automotive engineering.

Explainable AI (XAI) for Engineering Applications
Series Editors
Aditya Khamparia and Deepak Gupta

Explainable AI (XAI) has developed as a subfield of Artificial Intelligence, focussing on exposing complex AI models to humans in a systematic and interpretable manner. This area explores, discusses the steps and models involved in making intelligent decisions. This series will cover the working behavior and explains the ability of powerful algorithms such as neural networks, ensemble methods including random forests, and other similar algorithms to sacrifice transparency and explainability for power, performance, and accuracy in different engineering applications relates to the real world. Aimed at graduate students, academic researchers and professionals, the proposed series will focus key topics including XAI techniques for engineering applications, Explainable AI for Deep Neural Network Predictions, Explainable AI for Machine learning Predictions, XAI driven recommendation systems for Automobile and Manufacturing Industries, and Explainable AI for Autonomous Vehicles.

Deep Learning in Gaming and Animations
Principles and Applications
Vikas Chaudhary, Moolchand Sharma, Prerna Sharma and Deevyankar Agarwal

Artificial Intelligence for Solar Photovoltaic Systems
Approaches, Methodologies and Technologies
Bhavnesh Kumar, Bhanu Pratap and Vivek Shrivastava

Smart Distributed Embedded Systems for Healthcare Applications
Preeti Nagrath, Jafar A. Alzubi, Bhawna Singla, Joel J. P. C. Rodrigues and A.K. Verma

Medical Data Analysis and Processing using Explainable Artificial Intelligence
Edited by Om Prakash Jena, Mrutyunjaya Panda and Utku Kose

For more information about this series, please visit: *www.routledge.com/ Explainable-AI-XAI-for-Engineering-Applications/book-series/CRCEAIFEA*

Explainable Artificial Intelligence for Autonomous Vehicles

Concepts, Challenges, and Applications

Edited by
Kamal Malik, Moolchand Sharma,
Suman Deswal, Umesh Gupta,
Deevyankar Agarwal,
and Yahya Obaid Bakheet Al Shamsi

CRC Press
Taylor & Francis Group
Boca Raton London New York

CRC Press is an imprint of the
Taylor & Francis Group, an **Informa** business

Dedication

*Dr. Kamal Malik would like to dedicate this book to her father,
Sh. Ashwani Malik, her mother, Smt. Shakuntla Malik and her brother,
Dr. Shiv Malik, for their constant support and motivation; she would
also like to give my special thanks to the publisher and her other co-
editors for believing in her abilities. Above all, a humble thanks to the
Almighty for this accomplishment.*

*Mr. Moolchand Sharma would like to dedicate this book to his father,
Sh. Naresh Kumar Sharma and his mother, Smt. Rambati Sharma for
their constant support and motivation, and his family members, including
his wife, Ms. Pratibha Sharma, and son, Dhairya Sharma. He also thank
the publisher and his other co-editors for believing in his abilities.*

*Dr. Suman Deswal would like to dedicate this book to her father Late
Sh. V D Deswal and Mother Smt. Ratni Deswal, who taught her to
never give up, her husband, Mr. Vinod Gulia, and daughters, Laisha and
Kyna, for always loving and supporting her in every endeavor of life. She
also thanks the publisher and co-editors who believed in her capabilities.*

*Dr. Umesh Gupta would like to dedicate this book to his mother, Smt.
Prabha Gupta, his father, Sh. Mahesh Chandra Gupta, for their constant
support and motivation, and his family members, including his wife,
Ms. Umang Agarwal, and his son, Avaya Gupta. He also thank the
publisher and his other co-editors for believing in his abilities. Before
beginning and after finishing his endeavor, he must appreciate the
Almighty God, who provides me with the means to succeed.*

Dr. Deevyankar Agarwal would like to dedicate this book to his father, Sh. Anil Kumar Agarwal, his mother, Smt. Sunita Agarwal, his wife, Ms. Aparna Agarwal, and his son, Jai Agarwal, for their constant support and motivation. He would also like to give his special thanks to the publisher and his other co-editors for having faith in his abilities.

Dr. Yahya Obaid Bakheet Al Shamsi would like to dedicate this book to his father and mother for their constant support, prayers, and motivation. He would also like to give his special thanks to the publisher and his co-editors for their collaboration and mutual support.

Contents

Preface xv
About the editors xvii
List of contributors xx

1 **Autonomous vehicles** 1

RASHMI KUMARI, SUBHRANIL DAS, ABHISHEK THAKUR,
ANKIT KUMAR AND RAGHWENDRA KISHORE SINGH

1.1 *Introduction 1*
1.2 *Importance of artificial intelligence (AI) in autonomous*
vehicles 3
1.3 *AI-driven decision making 6*
1.4 *AI techniques and deep learning algorithms 9*
1.5 *Sensor fusion and data integration in autonomous*
vehicles 12
1.6 *Perception system in autonomous vehicles 15*
1.7 *Human-AI interaction in autonomous vehicles 16*
1.8 *Safety and reliability in AI-driven autonomous*
vehicles 17
1.9 *Conclusion 20*
References 20

2 **Explainable artificial intelligence: fundamentals,**
approaches, challenges, XAI evaluation, and validation 25

MANOJ KUMAR MAHTO

2.1 *Fundamentals of XAI 25*
2.2 *Introduction to explainable artificial intelligence 26*
2.3 *XAI and its significance 26*
2.4 *Key concepts in explainability 27*

2.4.1   *Model transparency* 28
2.4.2   *Interpretability vs. transparency* 28
2.4.3   *Trustworthiness* 28
2.5   *Approaches to developing XAI models* 29
2.6   *Model transparency* 30
2.6.1   *Transparent models in XAI* 30
2.6.2   *Limitations and use cases* 30
2.7   *Rule-based systems* 31
2.7.1   *Rule-based approaches to XAI* 31
2.7.2   *Scalability and complexity* 32
2.8   *Feature importance analysis* 32
2.8.1   *Shap and lime methods* 32
2.8.2   *Applications in various domains* 33
2.9   *Visualization techniques* 33
2.9.1   *Visualizing model decisions* 34
2.9.2   *Practical implementations* 34
2.10   *Challenges of implementing XAI in autonomous vehicles* 34
2.11   *Trade-Offs between performance and explainability* 35
2.11.1   *Balancing act: performance vs. interpretability* 36
2.11.2   *Strategies for achieving balance* 36
2.12   *Handling uncertainty* 37
2.12.1   *Uncertainty in autonomous vehicle context* 37
2.12.2   *Probabilistic models and uncertainty management* 38
2.13   *Safety and reliability* 38
2.13.1   *Safety considerations in XAI* 38
2.13.2   *Integration of safety mechanisms* 39
2.14   *Human-AI interaction* 39
2.14.1   *Designing user-friendly XAI interfaces* 40
2.14.2   *Ensuring positive user experience* 40
2.15   *XAI evaluation and validation* 40
2.16   *Metrics for evaluating explainability* 41
2.16.1   *Measuring fidelity, comprehensibility, and trustworthiness* 42
2.16.2   *Tailoring metrics to specific use cases* 42
2.17   *User studies* 43
2.17.1   *Conducting user-centric XAI evaluations* 43
2.17.2   *Methodologies and best practices* 43
2.18   *Simulation and testing* 44
2.18.1   *Simulated environments for XAI validation* 44
2.18.2   *Real-world testing scenarios* 45
2.19   *Regulatory compliance* 45

2.19.1 *Regulatory frameworks for XAI integration 46*
2.19.2 *Industry standards and guidelines 46*
2.20   Conclusion *46*
References 47

3   **Explainable artificial intelligence in autonomous
    vehicles: prospects and future direction**   **50**
MANARELDEEN AHMED, ZEINAB E. AHMED, AND RASHID A. SAEED

3.1   *Introduction 50*
3.2   *Current state of XAI in autonomous vehicles 52*
       3.2.1   *Autonomous vehicles 52*
       3.2.2   *Explainable artificial intelligence (XAI) 53*
       3.2.3   *Case studies of XAI techniques in autonomous
               vehicles 54*
3.3   *Challenges and limitations of XAI in autonomous vehicles 61*
3.4   *Future trends in XAI for autonomous vehicles 64*
3.5   *Conclusion 65*
References 66

4   **XAI applications in autonomous vehicles**   **73**
LINA E. ALATABANI AND RASHID A. SAEED

4.1   *Introduction 73*
4.2   *Background and review of related work 74*
       4.2.1   *XAI method for convolutional neural networks in
               self-driving cars 74*
       4.2.2   *The internet of vehicles structure and need for
               XAI-IDS 76*
       4.2.3   *XAI frameworks 76*
       4.2.4   *Practical implementation of XAI-based models 76*
4.3   *Internet of vehicles (IoV) network architecture 77*
       4.3.1   *Autonomous vehicle components and design 79*
       4.3.2   *Applications and services 84*
       4.3.3   *Current issues 85*
4.4   *XAI methods and algorithms 86*
       4.4.1   *XAI methods can be sub-divided into four categories 86*
       4.4.2   *XAI algorithms in autonomous vehicles 88*
4.5   *XAI models to improve overall system performance 92*
4.6   *Discussion 94*
4.7   *Conclusion 95*
References 95

5 Emerging applications and future scope of internet
   of vehicles for smart cities: a survey   100
   JYOTI SHARMA, MANISH BHARDWAJ, AND NEELAM CHANTOLA

   5.1   Introduction 100
   5.2   Layered architecture of IoV 106
   5.3   Literature survey 107
         5.3.1   Applications of IoV in smart cities 108
   5.4   Issues and challenges of IoV 110
   5.5   Future scope of IoV 111
   5.6   Conclusion 112
   References 112

6 Future issues and challenges of internet of
   vehicles: a survey   116
   MANISH BHARDWAJ, SUMIT KUMAR SHARMA, NITIN KUMAR,
   AND SHWETA ROY

   6.1   Introduction 116
   6.2   Literature survey 119
   6.3   IoV ecosystem 121
   6.4   Internet of vehicles applications 124
   6.5   Summarized challenges and future research directions 126
   6.6   Conclusion 130
   References 130

7 Feature designing and security considerations in electrical
   vehicles utilizing explainable AI   134
   MANDEEP KAUR AND VINAYAK GOEL

   7.1   Feature designing for smart electrical vehicles 134
   7.2   Explainable recommendations and decision support 137
         7.2.1   Building trust through explainable
                 recommendations 140
   7.3   Addressing user concerns and misconceptions 140
         7.3.1   User education and training 140
         7.3.2   Continuous improvement and feedback 141
         7.3.3   User feedback and iterative design 141
         7.3.4   Importance of user feedback 141
         7.3.5   Gathering user feedback 142
         7.3.6   Surveys and questionnaires 142
         7.3.7   User interviews and focus groups 142
         7.3.8   User testing and observations 142

7.4   Online communities and social media 143
         7.4.1   Incorporating explainable AI in user
                  feedback 144
         7.4.2   Safety considerations in smart cars 144
         7.4.3   Importance of safety in smart cars 144
         7.4.4   Safety challenges in smart cars 144
         7.4.5   Explainable AI for safety in smart cars 145
         7.4.6   Decision explanation 145
         7.4.7   Error detection and diagnosis 145
         7.4.8   Safety validation and certification 145
         7.4.9   Privacy and data protection 145
         7.4.10   Collaborative safety 146
         7.4.11   Human-machine interaction for safety 146
         7.4.12   Security challenges in smart cars 146
         7.4.13   Cybersecurity risks 147
         7.4.14   Data privacy and protection 147
         7.4.15   Malicious attacks on AI systems 147
         7.4.16   Supply chain security 148
         7.4.17   Over-the-air updates 148
         7.4.18   XAI for security enhancement 148
         7.4.19   Explainable AI for safety and security 149
         7.4.20   Enhancing safety with explainable AI 149
         7.4.21   Real-time risk assessment 149
         7.4.22   Error detection and diagnosis 149
         7.4.23   Safety-critical decision support 149
         7.4.24   Strengthening security with explainable AI 150
         7.4.25   Intrusion detection and prevention 150
         7.4.26   Vulnerability assessment 150
         7.4.27   Adversarial attack detection 150
         7.4.28   Regulatory compliance and accountability 150
         7.4.29   Compliance with safety standards 151
         7.4.30   Ethical decision-making 151
         7.4.31   Accountability and liability 151
         7.4.32   Importance of privacy and data protection
                  in smart cars 152
         7.4.33   Privacy challenges in smart cars 152
         7.4.34   Role of explainable AI in privacy
                  and data protection 153
         7.4.35   Challenges in implementing XAI for privacy
                  and data protection 154
References 155

8 **Feature detection and feature visualization in smart cars
utilizing explainable AI**   **158**

MANDEEP KAUR AND VINAYAK GOEL

8.1 *Introduction 158*
   8.1.1 *Feature visualization 158*
   8.1.2 *Benefits of feature importance and feature
      visualization 159*
   8.1.3 *Challenges and limitations 160*
   8.1.4 *Local explanations and counterfactuals 161*
   8.1.5 *Local explanations 161*
   8.1.6 *Counterfactuals 161*
   8.1.7 *Benefits and applications 162*
   8.1.8 *Model-agnostic explanations 163*
   8.1.9 *Understanding model-agnostic explanations 163*
   8.1.10 *Techniques for model-agnostic explanations 163*
   8.1.11 *Global explanations 164*
   8.1.12 *Local explanations 164*
   8.1.13 *Application of model-agnostic explanations
      in smart cars 164*
   8.1.14 *Safety and decision-making 165*
   8.1.15 *Regulatory compliance and accountability 165*
   8.1.16 *User experience and trust 165*
   8.1.17 *Rule extraction and rule sets 166*
   8.1.18 *Rule extraction techniques 166*
   8.1.19 *Rule sets for decision-making 166*
   8.1.20 *Benefits and limitations of rule extraction
      and rule sets 167*
References 168

Index   171

Preface

We are delighted to launch our book entitled *Explainable AI for Autonomous Vehicles: Concepts, Challenges, and Applications* under the book series Explainable AI (XAI) for Engineering Applications, CRC Press, Taylor & Francis Group. It is a comprehensive guide to developing and applying explainable artificial intelligence (XAI) in the context of autonomous vehicles. The book is intended for researchers, engineers, and practitioners interested in enhancing the safety, reliability, and performance of autonomous vehicles while also improving user trust and acceptance of these systems. It begins with an introduction to XAI and its importance in developing autonomous vehicles. It also provides an overview of the challenges and limitations of traditional black-box AI models and how XAI can help address these challenges by providing transparency and interpretability in the decision-making process of autonomous vehicles. It is a valuable source of knowledge for researchers, engineers, practitioners, and graduate and doctoral students working in the same field. It will also be helpful for faculty members of graduate schools and universities. Around 25 full-length chapters have been received. Amongst these manuscripts, eight chapters have been included in this volume. All the chapters submitted were peer-reviewed by at least two independent reviewers and provided with a detailed review proforma. The comments from the reviewers were communicated to the authors, who incorporated the suggestions in their revised manuscripts. The recommendations from two reviewers were considered while selecting chapters for inclusion in the volume. The exhaustiveness of the review process is evident, given the large number of articles received addressing a wide range of research areas. The stringent review process ensured that each published chapter met rigorous academic and scientific standards.

We would also like to thank the authors of the published chapters for adhering to the schedule and incorporating the review comments. We extend my heartfelt acknowledgment to the authors, peer reviewers, committee members, and production staff whose diligent work shaped this volume. We especially want to thank our dedicated peer reviewers who volunteered for the arduous and tedious step of quality checking and critiquing the submitted chapters.

Kamal Malik, Moolchand Sharma, Suman Deswal,
Umesh Gupta, Deevyankar Agarwal,
Yahya Obaid Bakheet Al Shamsi

About the editors

Kamal Malik is currently working as a Professor in CSE in the School of Engineering and Technology at CTU Ludhiana, Punjab, India. She has published scientific research publications in reputed international journals, including SCI and Scopus-indexed journals such as *Ad Hoc & Senior Wireless Networks, 50, Engineering, Technology and Applied Sciences Research, Journals of Advanced Research in Engineering, Research Journal of Applied Sciences of Engineering & Technology (RJASET-Maxwell Sciences), SSRN-Electronic Journal, Design Engineering, Indian Journal of Science and Technology (IJST), International Journal of Computer Applications (IJCA)*, and many more. She has also attended many national and international conferences of repute, like Springer and Elsevier in India. Her major research areas are Artificial Intelligence, Machine Learning and Deep Learning, Data Analytics, Computational Neurosciences, and bio-inspired computing. She has more than 13 years of rich academic and research experience. She has guided three research scholars and is currently guiding eight research scholars at CT University, Ludhiana. She has worked in renowned institutes and universities, like RIMT Mandigobindgarh, Maharishi Markandeshwar University, Mullana, and GNA University, Phagwara. She has also chaired various sessions in Springer and Elsevier. She has been awarded the preeminent researcher award from the Green Thinkerz Society at CII, Chandigarh. She completed her Doctor of Philosophy in Computer Science from IKGPTU Kapurthala in 2017 and her master's and bachelor's from Kurukshetra University, Kurukshetra, in 2009 and 2006, respectively.

Moolchand Sharma is currently an Assistant Professor in the Department of Computer Science and Engineering at the Maharaja Agrasen Institute of Technology, GGSIPU Delhi. He has published scientific research publications in reputed international journals and conferences, including SCI-indexed and Scopus-indexed journals such as *Expert Systems* (Wiley), *Cognitive Systems Research* (Elsevier), *Physical Communication* (Elsevier), *Journal of Electronic Imaging* (SPIE), *Intelligent Decision Technologies: An International Journal*,

Cyber-Physical Systems (Taylor & Francis Group), *International Journal of Image & Graphics* (World Scientific), *International Journal of Innovative Computing and Applications* (Inderscience), and *Innovative Computing and Communication Journal* (scientific peer-reviewed journal). He has authored/co-authored chapters with international publishers like Elsevier, Wiley, and De Gruyter. He has authored/edited four books with a national/international level publisher (CRC Press, Bhavya Publications). His research areas include Artificial Intelligence, Nature-Inspired Computing, Security in Cloud Computing, Machine Learning, and Search Engine Optimization. He is associated with various professional bodies like IEEE, ISTE, IAENG, ICSES, UACEE, Internet Society, and has a life membership with the Universal-Inovators research lab, etc. He possesses teaching experience of more than nine years. He is the co-convener of the ICICC, DOSCI, ICDAM, and ICCCN Springer Scopus-indexed conference series and ICCRDA-2020 Scopus-indexed IOP Material Science & Engineering conference series. He is also the organizer and co-convener of the International Conference on Innovations and Ideas towards Patents (ICIIP) series. He is also an advisory and TPC committee member of the ICCIDS-2022 Elsevier SSRN Conference. He is a reviewer of many reputed journals for Springer, Elsevier, IEEE, Wiley, Taylor & Francis Group, IJEECS, World Scientific Journal, and many Springer conferences. He also served as a session chair in many international springer conferences. He is a doctoral researcher at DCR University of Science & Technology, Haryana. He completed his postgraduate in 2012 at SRM University, NCR Campus, Ghaziabad, and graduated in 2010 from KNGD MODI ENGG College, GBTU.

Suman Deswal holds a Ph.D. from DCR University of Science & Technology, Murthal, India. She completed her M. Tech (CSE) from Kurukshetra University, Kurukshetra, India, and B. Tech (Computer Science & Engg.) from CR State College of Engg., Murthal, India, in 2009 and 1998, respectively. She has 18 years of teaching experience and works as a Professor in the Department of Computer Science and Engineering at DCR University of Science and Technology, Murthal, India. Her research areas include wireless networks, heterogeneous networks, distributed systems, Machine Learning, and Bioinformatics. She has many research papers to her credit in reputed journals, including SCI-indexed and Scopus-indexed journals and conferences. She is also a reviewer of many reputed journals like Springer, Elsevier, IEEE, Wiley, and International IEEE, and Springer conferences.

Umesh Gupta is currently an Associate Professor at the School of Computer Science Engineering and Technology at Bennett University, Times of India Group, Greater Noida, Uttar Pradesh, India. He received a Doctor of Philosophy (Ph.D.) (Machine Learning) from the National Institute of Technology, Arunachal Pradesh, India. He was awarded a gold medal for his Master of Engineering (M.E.) from the National Institute of Technical Teachers Training and Research (NITTTR), Chandigarh, India, and Bachelor of Technology (B.Tech.) from Dr. APJ, Abdul Kalam Technical University, Lucknow, India. His research interests include SVM, ELM, RVFL, machine learning, and deep learning approaches. He has published over 35 referred journal and conference papers of international repute. His scientific research has been published in reputable international journals and conferences, including SCI-indexed and Scopus-indexed journals like *Applied Soft Computing* (Elsevier) and *Applied Intelligence* (Springer), each of which is a peer-reviewed journal. His publications have more than 158 citations with an h-index of 8 and an i10-index of 8 on Google Scholar as of March 1, 2023. He is a senior Member of IEEE (SMIEEE) and an active member of ACM, CSTA, and other scientific societies. He also reviewed papers for many scientific journals and conferences in the US and abroad. He led sessions at the Sixth International Conference (ICICC-2023), the Third International Conference on Data Analytics and Management (ICDAM 2023), the Third International Conference on Computing and Communication Networks (ICCCN 2022), and other international conferences, like Springer ETTIS 2022 and 2023. He is currently supervising two Ph.D. students. He is the co-principal investigator (co-PI) of two major research projects. He published three patents in the years 2021–2023. He also published four book chapters with Springer, CRC.

Deevyankar Agarwal is a lecturer at the University of Technology and Applied Sciences in Muscat, Oman. He works in the Engineering Department, EEE Section (Computer Engineering). He has 22 years of teaching and research experience. He is currently a doctoral researcher at the University of Valladolid, Spain. He has written several research papers that have been published in Springer, Elsevier, and Taylor & Francis international journals. Also, he has published various papers in IEEE international conferences and national conferences. He is a reviewer for Springer's Journal and for many IEEE conferences. He has also served as a session chair in many international Springer conferences. His research areas include the optimization of algorithms in Artificial Intelligence, Deep Learning, and Machine Learning for the healthcare sector.

Yahya Obaid Bakheet Al Shamsi is working as the Dean of Engineering at the University of Technology and Applied Sciences in Muscat, Oman. He has 25 years of teaching and research experience. He got his PhD from the University of Bath, Department of Architecture and Civil Engineering, UK. He has published various research papers in the international journals of Springer and Elsevier. He is a reviewer for Springer's Journal and for many IEEE conferences. He has also served as a session chair in many international Springer conferences.

Contributors

Manareldeen Ahmed
Department of Electrical and
   Electronic Engineering
Omdurman Islamic University
Sudan

Zeinab E. Ahmed
Department of Electrical and
   Computer Engineering
International Islamic University
Malaysia

Lina E. Alatabani
Department of Data
   Communications & Network
   Engineering
Faculty of Telecommunications
Future University
Khartoum, Sudan

Manish Bhardwaj
Department of Computer Science
   and Information Technology
KIET Group of Institutions
Delhi-NCR, Ghaziabad, India

Neelam Chantola
Department of Applied Sciences
KIET Group of Institutions
Delhi-NCR, Ghaziabad, India

Subhranil Das
School of Business, Faculty of
   Business and Leadership
MIT World Peace University
Pune, India

Vinayak Goel
Liverpool John Moores University
Liverpool, UK

Mandeep Kaur
CT University
Ludhiana, India

Ankit Kumar
Department of Electrical and
   Electronics Engineering
BIT Mesra
Ranchi, India

Nitin Kumar
Department of Information
   Technology
KIET Group of Institutions
Delhi-NCR, Ghaziabad, India

Rashmi Kumari
Bennett University
Greater Noida, Uttar Pradesh,
   India

Manoj Kumar Mahto
Vignan Institute of Technology and
    Science
Deshmukhi, Hyderabad, Telangana,
    India

Shweta Roy
Department of Computer
    Science and Information
    Technology
KIET Group of Institutions
Delhi-NCR, Ghaziabad,
    India

Rashid A. Saeed
Department of Computer
    Engineering
College of Computers and
    Information Technology, Taif
    University
Saudi Arabia

Jyoti Sharma
Department of Information
    Technology
KIET Group of Institutions
Delhi-NCR, Ghaziabad, India

Sumit Kumar Sharma
Department of Information
    Technology
KIET Group of Institutions
Delhi-NCR, Ghaziabad, India

Raghwendra Kishore Singh
National Institute of Technology
Jameshedpur, India

Abhishek Thakur
Department of Electrical and
    Electronics Engineering
BIT Mesra
Ranchi, India

Chapter 1

Autonomous vehicles

Rashmi Kumari, Subhranil Das, Abhishek Thakur, Ankit Kumar and Raghwendra Kishore Singh

1.1 INTRODUCTION

Autonomous vehicles, also known as self-driving cars, are automobiles equipped with advanced technologies and Artificial Intelligence (AI) that allow them to navigate and operate without the need for human intervention [1, 2]. These vehicles have the capability to perceive their environment, make decisions, and control their movements based on sensory inputs and pre-programmed algorithms, enabling them to drive and interact with other road users autonomously. Autonomous vehicles use a combination of sensors, such as cameras, Light Detection and Ranging (LiDAR), Radio Detection and Ranging (RADAR), and Ultrasonic Sensors (US), to gather real-time data about their surroundings. The data is processed by onboard computers using AI-based algorithms to interpret the environment, identify obstacles, and make driving decisions.

The Society of Automotive Engineers (SAE) has defined a classification system to categorize autonomous vehicles based on their level of autonomy. The levels range from Level 0 (no automation) to Level 5 (full automation), with Level 5 indicating a vehicle capable of complete, fully autonomous operation without any human input or intervention, as shown in Figure 1.1 [3].

Figure 1.1 shows the different levels of Automation in the industry of Autonomous Vehicles. The levels of autonomy, as defined by the Society of Automotive Engineers (SAE) in standard J3016, are a classification system used to describe the extent of automation in vehicles, particularly with respect to their capability to operate without human intervention. The SAE J3016 standard provides a common framework for categorizing autonomous driving capabilities, ensuring clear communication among industry stakeholders and the public about the level of automation a vehicle possesses. There are six levels of autonomy in the SAE J3016 classification, ranging from Level 0 to Level 5, each representing increasing levels of automation [4].

Level 0: (No Automation/Human-Only Control) At Level 0, the controlling of the vehicle is executed by a human driver, with no automation features. The driver is responsible for all aspects of driving, including

DOI: 10.1201/9781003502432-1

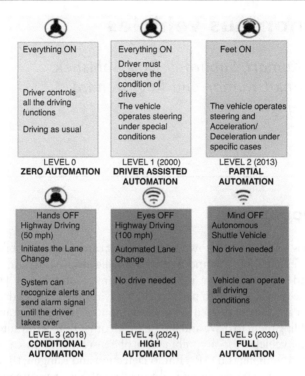

Figure 1.1 Six levels of autonomous driving according to SAEJ3016.

acceleration, braking, and steering. This level may include basic warning systems, such as lane departure warnings or forward collision warnings, but these are only intended to alert the driver and do not actively intervene in driving tasks.

Level 1: (Driver Assistance/Partial Automation) At Level 1, vehicles have certain driving assistance features that can control either the steering or the acceleration/deceleration, but not both simultaneously. An example of Level 1 automation is adaptive cruise control, which can automatically adjust the vehicle's speed to maintain a safe following distance from the vehicle ahead.

Level 2: (Partial Automation) At Level 2, the vehicle can simultaneously control steering and acceleration/deceleration under certain conditions. The system can handle tasks like lane-keeping and adaptive cruise control, allowing the driver to take their hands off the steering wheel and feet off the pedals, but the driver must remain engaged.

Level 3: (Conditional Automation) At Level 3, the vehicle can handle all aspects of driving without constant human supervision, but the driver must be ready to take over when the system requests, such as in complex or unexpected situations. The transition from Level 3 to Level 4 automation is a critical boundary, as Level 4 no longer requires human intervention in most circumstances.

Level 4: (**High Automation**) At Level 4, vehicles are highly automated and can operate without human intervention in predefined operational design domains (ODDs). Within the defined ODD, Level 4 vehicles can handle all driving tasks, including navigating complex city traffic or adverse weather conditions, without the need for human control or supervision.

Level 5: (**Full Automation**) Level 5 represents the highest level of automation, where the vehicle is fully autonomous and capable of performing all driving tasks under any conditions and without human input or intervention. There is no requirement for a human driver in a Level 5 vehicle. Level 5 autonomy enables driverless mobility and is a significant step toward fully realizing the potential of autonomous vehicles in revolutionizing transportation.

1.2 IMPORTANCE OF ARTIFICIAL INTELLIGENCE (AI) IN AUTONOMOUS VEHICLES

AI (Artificial Intelligence) is crucial for self-driving cars due to its ability to process vast amounts of data, learn from it, make informed decisions, and adapt to dynamic environments [5–9]. Several key reasons illustrate why AI is essential for the successful development and deployment of self-driving cars:

1. **Real-time Perception and Decision-Making:** Self-driving cars need to perceive their surroundings continuously, analyze complex sensory data from various sensors, and make instant decisions. AI algorithms, such as computer vision and machine learning, enable the vehicle to understand the environment, recognize objects (like pedestrians, vehicles, and traffic signs), and respond appropriately to changes in real time.

2. **Handling Uncertainties:** Driving on roads is unpredictable, with constantly changing traffic patterns, weather conditions, and unexpected events. AI's ability to handle uncertainties and ambiguous situations is vital for autonomous vehicles to operate safely and efficiently. Machine learning and probabilistic algorithms enable self-driving cars to make probabilistic assessments and adapt to varying scenarios.

3. **Learning from Data:** Autonomous vehicles gather enormous amounts of data during their operations. AI enables these vehicles to learn from the data they collect, improving their driving performance over time. This iterative learning process allows self-driving cars to become more skilled and responsive with each driving experience.

4. **Decision-Making in Complex Scenarios:** Driving involves complex decision-making, often involving ethical considerations and trade-offs. For example, an autonomous vehicle may need to decide between avoiding a collision with an obstacle by swerving into another lane or maintaining its course, possibly leading to a collision. AI algorithms can be designed to weigh different factors and make decisions that prioritize safety and follow legal and ethical guidelines.

5. **Sensor Fusion and Integration:** Autonomous vehicles utilize multiple sensors to gather data from their surroundings. AI plays a critical role in fusing and integrating this data. Sensor fusion allows the vehicle to cross-verify information from different sources, enhancing reliability and reducing the likelihood of false positives or negatives.
6. **Predictive Analysis and Planning:** AI-based predictive analytics can anticipate potential hazards and events, helping the self-driving car to plan its actions accordingly. Predictive planning considers the behavior of other road users, potential road obstacles, and traffic conditions to optimize the vehicle's driving path and enhance safety.
7. **Efficient Energy Management:** AI can optimize energy consumption in AVs, leading to improved fuel efficiency and range. AI algorithms can analyze driving patterns, road conditions, and traffic flow to suggest optimal speeds and routes that reduce energy consumption.
8. **Continuous Improvement and Remote Updates:** AI enables self-driving cars to receive over-the-air updates, which can enhance their performance, fix bugs, and adapt to new regulations. This ability to continuously improve the driving capabilities of autonomous vehicles is crucial for keeping them up-to-date and safe.

The advantages of applying AI in the context of autonomous vehicles are as follows:

1. **Safety Improvement:** One of the primary advantages of AI in self-driving cars is its potential to enhance road safety. AI algorithms can process data from various sensors in real-time, detecting and responding to potential hazards faster than human drivers. As a result, the accidents are reduced to a great extent, which are mainly caused by humans.
2. **Efficient Decision-Making:** AI-driven decision-making in autonomous vehicles is based on complex algorithms and vast amounts of data analysis. This enables self-driving cars to make well-informed decisions in challenging situations, such as navigating through heavy traffic or handling unexpected road conditions.
3. **Traffic Flow Optimization:** AI can optimize traffic flow by coordinating self-driving cars to avoid congestion and reduce traffic jams. This ability to communicate and cooperate between autonomous vehicles can lead to more efficient use of road space and smoother traffic flow, ultimately reducing travel time and fuel consumption.
4. **Accessibility and Mobility:** Autonomous vehicles have the potential to improve accessibility and mobility for individuals who cannot drive, such as the elderly or people with disabilities. AI-driven self-driving cars can provide independent transportation options to those who may have been limited by traditional means of transportation.

5. **Reduced Emissions:** AI can optimize driving patterns and energy consumption, leading to more fuel-efficient driving and reduced emissions. In the case of electric vehicles, AI can optimize battery usage, extending the range and promoting greener transportation.
6. **Improved Productivity:** Self-driving cars can free up valuable time for passengers during their commutes, as they no longer need to focus on driving. This opens up opportunities for increased productivity, such as working, reading, or relaxing while being transported.

There are certain limitations to the application of AI in different applications used in the autonomous vehicles industry, which are listed as follows:

1. **Technological Limitations:** Despite significant advancements in AI, achieving full autonomy remains a challenging problem. Self-driving cars must operate in diverse and dynamic environments with countless variables, making it difficult to predict and account for all scenarios.
2. **Ethical and Moral Dilemmas:** Autonomous vehicles may face ethical dilemmas in certain situations, such as choosing between minimizing harm to the vehicle's occupants and avoiding harm to pedestrians or other road users. Resolving these ethical challenges is a difficult task and requires societal consensus.
3. **Legal and Regulatory Challenges:** The deployment of autonomous vehicles raises numerous legal and regulatory issues. Determining liability in the event of accidents, establishing safety standards, and adapting existing traffic laws for autonomous vehicles are some of the complex legal challenges.
4. **Data Privacy and Security:** Self-driving cars generate and collect massive amounts of data about their surroundings and passengers. Ensuring data privacy and safeguarding against cyber threats and hacking attempts are crucial for maintaining public trust in autonomous vehicle technology.
5. **Adverse Weather Conditions:** Inclement weather conditions, such as heavy rain, snow, or fog, can negatively impact the performance of sensors used in autonomous vehicles, affecting their ability to perceive the environment accurately.
6. **Cost and Infrastructure:** The development and integration of AI systems in autonomous vehicles can be costly. Additionally, creating a reliable and interconnected infrastructure to support autonomous driving is a significant challenge that requires substantial investment.
7. **Acceptance and Trust:** Convincing the public about the safety and reliability of autonomous vehicles is essential for their widespread adoption. Building trust and acceptance among potential users and stakeholders is critical to the success of self-driving technology.

Despite these limitations, ongoing research, advancements in AI, and collaboration among industry stakeholders, regulators, and researchers are continuously addressing these challenges to realize the full potential of autonomous vehicles and make them a safe and viable transportation option for the future.

1.3 AI-DRIVEN DECISION MAKING

Making accurate decisions necessitates a comprehensive understanding of the nearby surroundings. Conventional methods like heuristics and numerical optimization have proven insufficient in simulating all potential situations. However, DL techniques have emerged as powerful solutions that are capable of real-time decision-making in complex scenarios. Li et al. [10] successfully employed Convolutional Neural Networks (CNNs) to replicate human drivers' decision-making processes by extracting information from road scene images. Gallardo et al. [11] also demonstrated the effectiveness of CNNs, specifically utilizing the AlexNet architecture proposed by Krizhevsky et al. [12] for decision-making in autonomous vehicles based on environmental cues. Addressing the challenging task of lane-changing maneuvers, Xie et al. [13] proposed an approach employing Long Short-Term Memory (LSTM) to model interactions between autonomous vehicles and other vehicles on the road, as shown in Figure 1.2.

Given the complexity of lane-changing and emergency situations, accurate systems that consider surrounding vehicles' movements are crucial. Liu et al. [14] devised a Deep Neural Network (DNN) based method, leveraging drivers' historical experiences and Vehicle to Vehicle (V2V) information, to execute precise lane-changing maneuvers. Additionally, Strickland et al. [15] introduced a Bayesian Convolutional LSTM approach to avoid collisions in emergency scenarios. This method processes data to steer clear of potential collisions effectively. Moreover, Wang et al. [16] proposed a system using Region-based Convolutional Neural Networks (R-CNN) to guide autonomous vehicles at roundabouts. Their system enables informed decisions, such as entering or waiting, when approaching roundabouts. The comparative analysis of different AI-integrated autonomous vehicles is shown in Table 1.1.

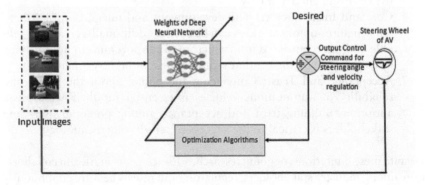

Figure 1.2 Schematic representation of decision making in AVs.

Table 1.1 Comparative Analysis of XAI Applications in Autonomous Vehicles

Reference	Year	Publication	Short Survey	In-Depth Survey	Deep Learning/ Reinforcement Learning	Safety System	AI Hardware Deployment	Sensor Fusion System
Mahadev et al. [17]	2018	ACM	✓		✓	✓		
Q Rao and J. Frotunki [18]	2018	ACM	✓		✓		✓	
Haboucha, et al. [19]	2017	IEEE	✓				✓	✓
AM Nascimento et al. [20]	2019	IEEE		✓	✓	✓	✓	
Thadeshwar et al. [21]	2020	IEEE		✓	✓		✓	✓
Y Ma et al. [22]	2020	IEEE		✓	✓		✓	✓
S. Grigarsse [23]	2020	Wiley		✓	✓			✓
S. Das and SK Mishra [24]	2020	Springer			✓			
C Medrano-Berum et al. [25]	2021	Taylor & Francis			✓			
X Di and R Shi [26]	2021	Elsevier		✓	✓	✓		
S. Gupta et al. [27]	2021	Elsevier		✓	✓			
F. Ding et al. [28]	2021	IEEE		✓	✓	✓✓	✓	
M. Tammvee et al. [29]	2021	Springer			✓	✓		✓
Vartika et al. [30]	2021	Springer		✓	✓		✓	
S Das and R Kumari [31]	2021	IOP			✓	✓	✓	
M. Singh et al. [32]	2022	IEEE			✓		✓	
C Kim et al. [33]	2022	Springer	✓		✓	✓		

Table 1.2 Summary of Various DL Methods for Scene Understanding in AVs

Reference	Year	Publication	Dataset	Proposed Method	Learning	Hardware	Condition of Traffic
Sless et al. [37]	2019	IEEE	NuScenes Dataset	Occupancy grid mapping	Unsupervised	Titan X GPU	Semi-Urban
Diu et al. [38]	2020	Springer	Foggy Zurich Database	Curriculum Model Adaptation (CMA)	Unsupervised	Nvidia EVGA GeForce GTX TITAN X GPU	Adverse Traffic condition
Huang et al. [39]	2021	IEEE	CoRL2017	End to End Deep Learning	Supervised	Titan X GPU	Urban
Divya et al. [40]	2021	IEEE	India Driving Dataset	Domain Adaptation (DA)	Unsupervised	Not reported	Urban
Andreas et al. [41]	2021	IEEE	KITTI odometry	Multi-modal	Supervised	Nvidia Geforce GTX	Semi-urban
M. Singh et al. [32]	2022	IEEE	KITTI	Fuzzy Logic Controller	Supervised	Nvidia EVGA GeForce GTX TITAN X GPU	Semi-urban
Sundar et al. [42]	2022	Springer	KITTI	3D CNN and Pedestrian Detection Algorithm	Supervised	Titan X GPU	Urban
Nousias et al. [43]	2023	IEEE	KITTI	Vector Quantization	Unsupervised	Not reported	Urban

1.4 AI TECHNIQUES AND DEEP LEARNING ALGORITHMS

Autonomous driving is revolutionizing the automotive industry, and at the heart of this transformation lie several critical Artificial Intelligence (AI) techniques. These techniques work in tandem to enable self-driving vehicles to navigate the complexities of real-world environments while ensuring safety and efficiency.

Computer vision plays a fundamental role in autonomous driving by processing visual data captured through onboard cameras. This technique allows vehicles to detect and recognize objects, pedestrians, traffic signs, and lane markings, providing crucial input for decision-making. Complementing computer vision, machine learning, and deep learning algorithms analyze vast amounts of data to learn patterns, identify potential hazards, and make informed driving decisions in real-time. These AI methods enable vehicles to adapt to diverse driving scenarios and continuously improve their performance through data-driven learning. Sensor fusion integrates data from LiDAR and RADAR. This multidimensional perception enhances the vehicle's awareness, allowing it to precisely detect and track objects, map the surroundings, and navigate safely. Localization and mapping algorithms further contribute to autonomous driving by providing precise vehicle positioning and building detailed maps of the environment. With a clear understanding of its location and surroundings, the autonomous vehicle can plan safe and efficient routes while remaining aware of obstacles and the road layout. Path planning and decision-making algorithms form the next layer of AI techniques, empowering self-driving cars in real-time. These algorithms evaluate the conditions of traffic and potential obstacles that comply with traffic rules. By selecting the optimal trajectory, the autonomous vehicle can navigate complex road scenarios with confidence. Additionally, reinforcement learning serves as a valuable tool in autonomous driving, enabling vehicles to learn from their experiences. Through trial and error, the vehicle refines its decision-making process, continually improving its response to uncertain or challenging situations, as shown in Figure 1.3.

In this section, DL-based approaches have been reviewed to address the various tasks of AVs, as shown in Figure 1.4.

Over the past two decades, remarkable advancements in Deep Learning (DL) techniques have propelled the scene-understanding field forward. These advancements have paved the way for AVs to benefit from accurate and vital information about the driving environment. AVs now leverage a diverse range of sensors, including LiDAR, cameras, and RADAR, to obtain precise and crucial data that enhances their understanding of the surroundings. Accurate recognition and extraction of main road information are pivotal for AVs to discern and identify essential road elements. Leveraging the remarkable capabilities of DL, it becomes feasible to achieve a high level of accuracy. The power of DL empowers AVs with the necessary tools to navigate and comprehend the road environment with heightened precision and reliability. Accurate and real-time detection of surrounding objects, encompassing other road users, assumes utmost importance and becomes a critical requirement for AVs. The different DL methods are summarized in Table 1.2.

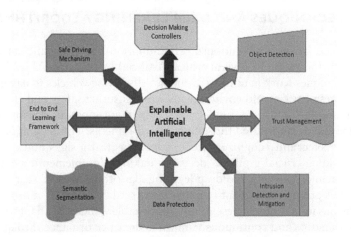

Figure 1.3 Overview of XAI algorithms applicable to different areas of AVs.

Figure 1.4 Schematic diagram for the various categories of XAI in AV.

Following scene understanding, motion planning emerges as a primary task for AV. Traditional approaches, including Dijkstra Algorithm [34], A* [35], and State lattice algorithms [36], applied to various optimization techniques to address motion planning challenges, as shown in Table 1.3.

From the table, these algorithms exhibit slow performance in extensive areas, rendering them unsuitable for real-time applications. As a result,

Table 1.3 Summary of Motion Planning Methods for Different Applications in AVs

Reference	Year	Publication	Dataset	Proposed Architecture	Learning	Hardware	Environment
Manjari et al. [32]	2020	IEEE	Not Mentioned	FLC Controller	Supervised Learning	NVDIA RTX 3090	Urban
Hang et al. [44]	2020	IEEE	CuLane Dataset	Model Predictive Controller (MPC)	Supervised Learning	Not reported	Traffic Conditions
Peng et al. [45]	2021	MDPI	CuLane	SAA	Unsupervised Learning	NVDIA RTX 3090	Traffic
Zhang et al. [46]	2022	MDPI	Lane Detection Dataset (CuLane-I)	GMRES	Supervised Learning	Not reported	Urban
Li et al. [47]	2022	IEEE	CuLane	Dynamic Enhanced Framework—APF	Unsupervised Learning	Nvidia EVGA GeForce GTX TITAN X GPU	Traffic Condition
Shi et al. [48]	2023	Springer	CuLane	Rank Privacy reward Function	Reinforcement Learning	AMD Threadripper PRO 3975WX CPU	Urban

researchers have sought alternative solutions, such as employing DL-based techniques [42–46], to overcome the limitations of traditional approaches and achieve more efficient and real-time motion planning capabilities for AVs. Building a universal motion planning system, particularly in real-time, poses challenges because of the intricate nature of traffic situations. The unpredictability and complexity of road users' behavior makes it particularly difficult to create a comprehensive and reliable model for motion planning. For secure navigation to the destination, AVs must analyze sensor-collected data to detect obstacles. However, recent advancements in DL techniques have demonstrated their real-time decision-making capabilities, particularly in complex environments, revolutionizing the field of autonomous driving.

1.5 SENSOR FUSION AND DATA INTEGRATION IN AUTONOMOUS VEHICLES

Sensor fusion and data integration are critical aspects of AVs that enable them to build a comprehensive understanding. Autonomous vehicles are equipped with various sensors, such as cameras, LiDAR, RADAR, ultrasonic sensors, and GPS, each providing unique data about the environment. Sensor fusion and data integration involve combining information from these different sensors to create a coherent representation.

Sensor fusion involves the process of merging data from multiple sensors to create a more robust and reliable perception of the environment. Each sensor has its strengths and limitations. For example, cameras are excellent at recognizing objects and reading road signs, but they may struggle in low-light conditions. LiDAR can provide precise 3D point cloud data, but it may have difficulties in heavy rain or snow. RADAR is proficient in detecting the velocity of objects but may lack detailed information about their shape. Ultrasonic sensors are useful for short-range obstacle detection but have limited coverage. By fusing the data from these sensors, AVs can compensate for individual sensor shortcomings and obtain a more comprehensive and accurate view of the environment.

Data integration involves not only combining sensor data but also incorporating other relevant information, such as maps, traffic data, and historical driving patterns. For example, GPS data can help AVs with localization and positioning, while maps provide information about road layouts and speed limits. Traffic data can assist with real-time route planning, and historical driving patterns can help predict and anticipate the behavior of other road users. A summary of the sensor fusion and data integration methods is provided in what follows.

Sriram et al. [49] present a novel approach for sensor fusion, integrating LiDAR and Camera sensors to create a robust drivable road detection system. In this study, we employ edge detection and color-based segmentation techniques to generate binary lane images from camera sensor input. Subsequently, we employ the RANSAC algorithm to fit line models to the binary images, effectively identifying lane markings. However, challenges arise in urban settings where single-side lane markings or even the absence of lane markings prevail. In such instances, the existing drivable road detection system may exhibit limitations, lacking the ability to define the road's boundaries accurately for safe vehicle navigation. To address these limitations, our proposed sensor fusion method combines LiDAR sensor data with camera images, enhancing the system's ability to determine a trajectory for secure travel. This hybrid approach proves highly effective across various urban road scenarios, accommodating diverse conditions such as roads with dual lane markings, single-side lanes adjacent to curbs, and roads bordered by curbs on both sides. By leveraging the complementary strengths of LiDAR and Camera sensors, our algorithm ensures reliable and precise performance, contributing to enhanced road safety and improved navigation within complex urban environments.

Cao et al. [50] introduced a systematic approach to process multi-LiDAR data, encompassing a sequence of steps that includes three main processes: clustering, filtering, and classification. While detecting the obstacle precision mainly effects on filtering of different noises and object clustering. This study presents an innovative filtering algorithm that is embedded in the multi-LiDAR framework. Specifically, the filtering methodology generally relies on the occupancy rates derived from sparse "feature seeds" in each search space. Concurrently, DBSCAN algorithm is further refined by an adaptive algorithm for enhancing the accuracy of detection during clustering. The amalgamation of AS-DBSCAN with the proposed OR-based filtering further contributes to robust and precise obstacle detection. To substantiate these advancements, two new tests are incorporated, including indoor perception and an on-road test using AV. The efficacy of the proposed approach is validated by the results of real-time experiment findings, which establish a relevant solution.

In Rawashdeh et al. [51], the challenge of detecting drivable paths under adverse weather conditions, even on roads covered with snow, has been addressed. Accurate detection of drivable paths is of paramount importance for ensuring the safe autonomous operation of passenger vehicles. Unfavorable weather conditions pose a significant challenge to the perception system. To tackle this issue, a novel approach involving CNN-based multi-modal sensor fusion is employed for path detection. Specifically, a new network based on encoder-decoder is introduced, facilitating the fusion of camera, LiDAR, and Radar data. This innovative fusion technique aims to counteract the asymmetric degradation of individual sensors. The model's training and evaluation were conducted using a subset of the DENSE dataset, meticulously labeled with manual annotations. The performance of the model was assessed using a range of diverse metrics.

The research discussed by Yifang et al. [22] explores the utilization of dynamic Gaussian processes, focusing specifically on applications related to occupancy mapping and predicting navigable paths for autonomous vehicles within the field of view (FOV) of radar sensors. The innovation of Gaussian occupancy mapping is its reduced dependency on copious training data, presenting an enticing alternative to data-intensive deep learning approaches. The proposed methodology intricately fine-tunes parameters (including variational and kernel-based aspects) of the Gaussian process. This fine-tuning is achieved through the stochastic selection of functional points (referred to as pseudo inputs) and the calibration of threshold values. Rigorous experimentation across varied environmental conditions, encompassing diverse road and traffic scenarios, as well as a range of weather and illumination contexts, substantiates the efficacy of the proposed approach. Notably, the technique adeptly identifies a navigable route for autonomous vehicles, even in challenging weather conditions. Additionally, its attractiveness is amplified by its utilization of a cost-efficient setup and its capability to cover substantial distances effectively. In reference by Duraisamy et al. [52] the research utilizes a deep learning architecture to differentiate between drivable areas and obstacles within images. Through the application of semantic segmentation, the architecture undertakes the dual task of region classification and clustering. Moreover, the research introduces a ground segmentation method that capitalizes on LiDAR data to enhance the precision of drivable region classification. This innovative ground segmentation technique partitions regions into smaller units and deploys an adaptive likelihood estimation-based ground fitting approach. To consolidate outcomes and refine drivable region classification, a novel late fusion approach is proposed, optimizing the amalgamation of both methodologies. The comprehensive fusion architecture is seamlessly integrated into the Robot Operating System (ROS) framework. Notably, on the RELLIS3D dataset, the semantic segmentation component attains a commendable mean accuracy of 84.3%. Interestingly, the study reveals that certain regions initially misclassified by the semantic segmentation model are effectively rectified through LiDAR-based ground segmentation. Consequently, the proposed fusion methodology yields an improved depiction of the drivable regions, substantiating the effectiveness of the integrated approach.

From the studies discussed previously, it can be observed that with the integration of sensor fusion and real-time data, autonomous vehicles can effectively perceive the environment, recognize obstacles, detect lane markings, identify other road users, and interpret complex traffic scenarios. This rich and integrated data enables AVs to make critical decisions, such as determining the vehicle's trajectory, controlling acceleration and braking, and avoiding collisions or unsafe situations. By combining the strengths of different sensors and integrating various data sources, sensor fusion, and data integration play a pivotal role in making autonomous driving safer, more reliable, and capable of navigating diverse and dynamic real-world driving conditions.

1.6 PERCEPTION SYSTEM IN AUTONOMOUS VEHICLES

The perception system in AVs is a crucial component responsible for gathering and processing data from various sensors to build a comprehensive understanding of the surrounding environment. Its primary goal is to enable the AV to "perceive" the world as a human driver would, allowing it to make informed decisions and safely navigate through complex and dynamic road scenarios. The perception system typically integrates data from cameras, LiDAR, RADAR, ultrasonic sensors, and GPS. Each sensor provides different types of information about the environment, such as visual images, 3D point clouds, velocity, and distance measurements. Sensor fusion techniques are employed to combine and reconcile data from these disparate sources, creating a more robust and accurate representation of the environment, as shown in Figure 1.5.

Computer vision is a fundamental component of the perception system, responsible for processing visual data captured by cameras. Computer vision algorithms can detect and recognize various objects, such as traffic signs, traffic lights, lane markings, and road boundaries. This information

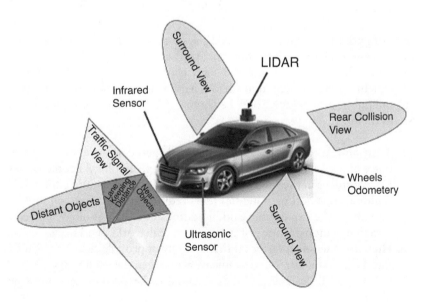

Figure 1.5 Perception system in AV.

is critical for understanding the vehicle's surroundings and making decisions about navigation, lane-keeping, and avoiding obstacles. LiDAR and RADAR sensors contribute to the perception system by providing detailed information about the 3D structure of the environment and detecting the distance and velocity of objects. LiDAR generates a point cloud representing the shapes and positions of surrounding objects, while RADAR measures the time taken for radio waves to bounce off objects, enabling the estimation of distance and relative speed. Ultrasonic Sensors (US) are commonly used for short-range obstacle detection, aiding the AV in maneuvering in tight spaces or during parking. GPS data is integrated to provide the vehicle's global position and support localization, helping the AV to know its position on the map accurately.

The perception system processes the data from all these sensors in real time and continuously updates the vehicle's perception of the environment. Using advanced algorithms, machine learning, and deep learning techniques, the perception system can identify and track objects, predict their future movements, and assess potential hazards and risks on the road. The accuracy and reliability of the perception system are critical for safe autonomous driving. Any errors or misinterpretations in the perception of the environment can lead to incorrect decisions, potentially resulting in accidents. Therefore, extensive testing, validation, and redundancy measures are implemented to ensure the perception system's robustness.

1.7 HUMAN-AI INTERACTION IN AUTONOMOUS VEHICLES

Human factors in autonomous driving systems refer to the considerations and challenges related to how humans interact with and respond to autonomous vehicles (AVs). Despite the increasing autonomy of AVs, human involvement remains essential in various aspects of their deployment, operation, and public acceptance. Some key human factors in autonomous driving systems include:

1. **Trust and Acceptance:** Trust is a crucial factor influencing the acceptance and adoption of autonomous driving technology. People need to feel confident in the safety and reliability of AVs to embrace them fully. Building trust among potential users requires transparent communication about the capabilities and limitations of the technology, as well as effective demonstrations of its safety in real-world conditions.

2. **Human-Machine Interface (HMI):** AVs must provide clear and intuitive interfaces to facilitate communication between the vehicle and its occupants. A well-designed HMI is essential to keep passengers informed about the vehicle's status, upcoming maneuvers, and any potential handover of control between the human driver and the autonomous system.

3. **Handover of Control:** The transition of control between human drivers and autonomous systems (known as handover) poses unique challenges. Ensuring a smooth and safe handover is critical to avoid confusion, disengagement errors, and potential accidents. AVs must provide sufficient warning and information to human drivers when they need to take back control.

4. **Situational Awareness:** Although AVs can handle most driving tasks, humans may still need to be vigilant in adverse weather, complex urban environments, or construction zones. Maintaining situational awareness and being prepared to take control when needed is crucial.

5. **Human Behavior Prediction:** AVs must be able to predict and respond appropriately to human behavior, such as pedestrian crossings, unpredictable actions of other drivers, or gestures indicating the intention to cross the road.

6. **Ethical Decision-Making:** Autonomous driving systems may encounter complex ethical dilemmas, such as deciding between minimizing harm to the vehicle's occupants and avoiding harm to pedestrians or other road users. Addressing these ethical challenges requires careful consideration and societal consensus.

7. **User Training and Education:** Training and education programs are essential to ensure that human drivers and passengers understand how to interact with AVs safely. Education can also help users grasp the capabilities and limitations of the technology, enhancing their confidence and decision-making while using autonomous driving systems.

8. **Legal and Regulatory Considerations:** The legal and regulatory frameworks surrounding autonomous driving need to account for human factors, such as liability in the event of accidents involving AVs, licensing requirements for human drivers in autonomous vehicles, and standards for the safety and performance of autonomous systems.

Addressing these human factors is vital to fostering public acceptance, ensuring safe interaction, and facilitating the smooth integration of autonomous driving systems into our transportation ecosystem. As technology continues to advance, understanding and addressing the human factors involved in autonomous driving will remain a crucial area of research and development.

1.8 SAFETY AND RELIABILITY IN AI-DRIVEN AUTONOMOUS VEHICLES

Over the past ten years, vehicles plying the roads have led to a surge in traffic accidents, posing significant challenges for public safety and society. Human error, characterized by inappropriate judgments, distractions, and fatigue, often contributes to these accidents, resulting in fatalities and mishaps. In light of this pressing issue, AVs offer potential solutions for enhancing the

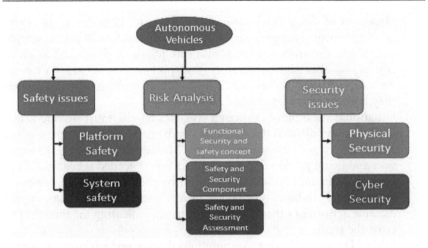

Figure 1.6 Safety and reliability issues in AVs.

safety of vehicles by employing advanced technologies such as ECU, path planning, GPS, 3D mapping, and LiDAR. However, ensuring safety and security remains a complex undertaking in the domain of AVs, necessitating further research contributions to overcome these challenges successfully, as shown in Figure 1.6.

The security aspect of AVs focuses on protecting the vehicle from intentional attacks, while safety is concerned with safeguarding the vehicle against accidental failures. AVs equipped with multiple sensors can anticipate potential attack conditions and respond proactively. Through integration with advanced technologies like AI/ML, Internet of Things (IoT), and Big Data analysis, AVs can detect and avoid both deliberate attacks and accidents by adjusting their trajectory accordingly. To ensure operational security in AV, ISO 26262 has been established. This standard aligns with the IEC 61508 series of measures and addresses specific requirements for electrical systems. Additionally, SAE J3061 defines the operational security for conventional vehicles. SAE J3061 delineates a structural framework for the security lifecycle of cyber-physical vehicle systems, facilitating an interface between the phases of cybersecurity and safety, thereby harmonizing the integration of vehicle security and safety. Nonetheless, this standard does not provide explicit guidance on the effective amalgamation of security and safety analyses. In scholarly discourse, scholars have undertaken the task of addressing the complexities associated with aligning cyber-physical systems, aiming to bridge the gap between security and safety considerations. Each tier of driving automation presents distinct prerequisites for safety and operation, with varying levels encountering an escalating array of potential challenges, hazards, and risks. To ensure functional safety and the evaluation of failures, the Hazard Analysis and Risk Assessment (HARA) process is strategically employed following the standardized guidelines stipulated in ISO 26262. Building on this foundation, the authors have proposed a HARA technique tailored to Level 4 autonomous vehicles. This approach utilizes Automotive Safety Integrity Levels (ASILs) in a recursive manner to establish precise safety objectives for vehicles. The incorporation of ASILs plays a pivotal role in evaluating hazards or threats specific to AVs, serving as a critical reference point. Furthermore, in a related study to classify and identify potential threats to the system, a threat model called STRIDE was employed.

In recent years, researchers have increasingly turned to deep learning techniques to improve the safety of autonomous driving systems. One prominent area of exploration is the application of DL to safety, particularly with regard to two essential aspects: understanding the potential consequences of errors and comprehending the broader implications of the system's behavior [42]. By harnessing the capabilities of deep learning algorithms, autonomous vehicles can learn from vast amounts of data and develop a more comprehensive understanding of various scenarios, enabling them to make more informed decisions and mitigate potential risks effectively. A notable study [33] demonstrates the utilization of CN for pedestrian detection, a critical task for ensuring road safety. The system's objective is not only to identify pedestrians accurately but also to maintain a safe distance from the detected objects. Upon detecting a pedestrian, the autonomous vehicle adjusts its speed and engages the braking system as necessary to prevent potential accidents. This showcases how deep learning technologies can contribute to enhancing the AV's perception and response capabilities, thereby promoting safer interactions with the environment.

Safety considerations in autonomous driving encompass various aspects, including the management of epistemic uncertainty, risk assessment, and mitigating harm resulting from unintended consequences [40]. Kothandaraman et al.'s study highlights the significance of addressing uncertainties and potential risks that arise during the operation of autonomous vehicles. Moreover, the authors conducted an analysis to optimize the training cost function, exploring ways to minimize potential risks while training deep learning models and ensuring a robust and safe learning process. However, as the field of autonomous driving progresses, challenges related to the adoption of machine-learning approaches remain. In Yifang et al. [22], the authors emphasize the importance of addressing the potential for harmful and unintended behavior in artificial intelligence systems, particularly in the context of autonomous vehicles. The study identifies and categorizes accidental risks into five research problems, shedding light on areas that require focused attention to ensure safety and reliability in autonomous driving. Furthermore, the amount of data generated by autonomous vehicles is a significant consideration [21]. These vehicles generate vast quantities of data regularly, with data collection reaching the scale of petabytes. This emphasizes the importance of robust data management and processing systems to extract valuable insights and ensure the safe and efficient operation of autonomous vehicles.

The integration of DL techniques in autonomous driving holds immense promise for improving safety and mitigating risks. Understanding the potential consequences of errors, enhancing perception capabilities through CNNs, managing uncertainties, and addressing accidental risks are vital aspects of advancing the safety of autonomous vehicles on our roads. As the research in this field progresses, addressing these challenges and optimizing data utilization will be crucial in realizing the full potential of autonomous driving for a safer and more efficient transportation system.

1.9 CONCLUSION

The synthesis of extensive research in the realm of autonomous vehicles has illuminated notable progress in perception systems, the integration of artificial intelligence, safety protocols, and the consideration of human elements. By merging sensor data, leveraging AI-driven decision-making, and implementing robust safety mechanisms, autonomous vehicles have demonstrated enhanced capabilities in navigating diverse environments and intricate scenarios while prioritizing dependability and security. The focal point on user-centered design principles underscores the importance of user acceptance, trust, and seamless human-machine interaction. This collective advancement holds the potential to reshape transportation, ushering in a future characterized by safer, more efficient, and sustainable mobility solutions, all while fundamentally influencing societal and urban landscapes. Collaboration among researchers, industry stakeholders, and policymakers remains pivotal in steering this transformative journey forward.

REFERENCES

[1] Ebert, Christof, Michael Weyrich, and Hannes Vietz. *AI-Based Testing for Autonomous Vehicles*. No. 2023–01–1228. SAE Technical Paper, 2023.

[2] Karnati, Akshitha, and Devanshi Mehta. "Artificial intelligence in self driving cars: Applications, implications and challenges." *Ushus Journal of Business Management* 21, no. 4 (2022).

[3] Guntrum, Laura Gianna, Sebastian Schwartz, and Christian Reuter. "Dual-use technologies in the context of autonomous driving: An empirical case study from Germany." *Zeitschrift für Außen-und Sicherheitspolitik* 16, no. 1 (2023): 53–77.

[4] Ma, Yifang, Zhenyu Wang, Hong Yang, and Lin Yang. "Artificial intelligence applications in the development of autonomous vehicles: A survey." *IEEE/CAA Journal of Automatica Sinica* 7, no. 2 (2020): 315–329.

[5] Das, Subhranil, Rashmi Kumari, and S. Deepak Kumar. "A review on applications of simultaneous localization and mapping method in autonomous vehicles." *Advances in Interdisciplinary Engineering: Select Proceedings of FLAME 2020* (2021): 367–375.

[6] Das, Subhranil, and Rashmi Kumari. "Application of horizontal projection lines in detecting vehicle license plate." In *2020 International Conference on Smart Electronics and Communication (ICOSEC)*, IEEE, pp. 1–6, 2020.

[7] Das, Subhranil, P. Arvind, Sourav Chakraborty, Rashmi Kumari, and S. Deepak Kumar. "IoT based solar smart tackle free AGVs for industry 4.0." In *International Conference on Internet of Things and Connected Technologies*, pp. 1–7. Springer International Publishing, 2020.

[8] Das, Subhranil, and Rashmi Kumari. "Application of extended Hough transform technique for stationary images in vehicle license plate." In *2021 6th International Conference for Convergence in Technology (I2CT)*, pp. 1–4. IEEE, 2021.

[9] Das, Subhranil, and Rashmi Kumari. "Online training of identifying characters present in vehicle license plate." In *2021 4th Biennial International Conference on Nascent Technologies in Engineering (ICNTE)*, pp. 1–6. IEEE, 2021.

[10] Li, L., K. Ota, and M. Dong. "Humanlike driving: Empirical decision-making system for autonomous vehicles." *IEEE Transactions on Vehicular Technology* 67, no. 8 (2018): 6814–6823. https://doi.org/10.1109/TVT.2018.2822762

[11] Gallardo, Nicolas, Nicholas Gamez, Paul Rad, and Mo Jamshidi. "Autonomous decision making for a driver-less car." In *2017 12th System of Systems Engineering Conference (SoSE)*, pp. 1–6. IEEE, 2017.

[12] Krizhevsky, Alex, Ilya Sutskever, and Geoffrey E. Hinton. "Imagenet classification with deep convolutional neural networks." *Advances in Neural Information Processing Systems* 25 (2012).

[13] Xie, Dong-Fan, Zhe-Zhe Fang, Bin Jia, and Zhengbing He. "A data-driven lane-changing model based on deep learning." *Transportation Research Part C: Emerging Technologies* 106 (2019): 41–60.

[14] Li, Dong, Dongbin Zhao, Qichao Zhang, and Yaran Chen. "Reinforcement learning and deep learning based lateral control for autonomous driving." *arXiv preprint arXiv:1810.12778* (2018).

[15] Strickland, Mark, Georgios Fainekos, and Heni Ben Amor. "Deep predictive models for collision risk assessment in autonomous driving." In *2018 IEEE International Conference on Robotics and Automation (ICRA)*, pp. 4685–4692. IEEE, 2018.

[16] Wang, Huanjie, Shihua Yuan, Mengyu Guo, Ching-Yao Chan, Xueyuan Li, and Wei Lan. "Tactical driving decisions of unmanned ground vehicles in complex highway environments: A deep reinforcement learning approach." *Proceedings of the Institution of Mechanical Engineers, Part D: Journal of Automobile Engineering* 235, no. 4 (2021): 1113–1127.

[17] Mahadevan, Karthik, Sowmya Somanath, and Ehud Sharlin. "Can interfaces facilitate communication in autonomous vehicle-pedestrian interaction?." In *Companion of the 2018 ACM/IEEE International Conference on Human-Robot Interaction (HRI '18)*, pp. 309–310. Association for Computing Machinery, 2018. https://doi.org/10.1145/3173386.3176909

[18] Rao, Qing, and Jelena Frtunikj. "Deep learning for self-driving cars: Chances and challenges." In *Proceedings of the 1st International Workshop on Software engineering for AI in Autonomous Systems (SEFAIS '18)*, pp. 35–38. Association for Computing Machinery, 2018. https://doi.org/10.1145/3194085.3194087

[19] Haboucha, Chana J., Robert Ishaq, and Yoram Shiftan. "User preferences regarding autonomous vehicles." *Transportation Research Part C: Emerging Technologies* 78 (2017): 37–49.

[20] Nascimento, Alexandre Moreira, Lucio Flavio Vismari, Caroline Bianca Santos Tancredi Molina, Paulo Sergio Cugnasca, Joao Batista Camargo, Jorge Rady de Almeida, Rafia Inam, Elena Fersman, Maria Valeria Marquezini, and Alberto Yukinobu Hata. "A systematic literature review about the impact of artificial intelligence on autonomous vehicle safety." *IEEE Transactions on Intelligent Transportation Systems* 21, no. 12 (2019): 4928–4946.

[21] Thadeshwar, Hiral, Vinit Shah, Mahek Jain, Rujata Chaudhari, and Vishal Badgujar. "Artificial intelligence based self-driving car." In *2020 4th International Conference on Computer, Communication and Signal Processing (ICCCSP)*, IEEE, pp. 1–5, 2020.

[22] Ma, Yifang, Zhenyu Wang, Hong Yang, and Lin Yang. "Artificial intelligence applications in the development of autonomous vehicles: A survey." *IEEE/CAA Journal of Automatica Sinica* 7, no. 2 (2020): 315–329.

[23] Grigorescu, Sorin, Bogdan Trasnea, Tiberiu Cocias, and Gigel Macesanu. "A survey of deep learning techniques for autonomous driving." *Journal of Field Robotics* 37, no. 3 (2020): 362–386.

[24] Das, Subhranil, and Sudhansu Kumar Mishra. "Collision avoidance and path planning for mobile robots based on state estimation approach." *Journal of Intelligent & Fuzzy Systems* Preprint (2023): 1–12.

[25] Medrano-Berumen, Christopher, and Mustafa İlhan Akbaş. "Validation of decision-making in artificial intelligence-based autonomous vehicles." *Journal of Information and Telecommunication* 5, no. 1 (2021): 83–103.

[26] Di, Xuan, and Rongye Shi. "A survey on autonomous vehicle control in the era of mixed-autonomy: From physics-based to AI-guided driving policy learning." *Transportation Research Part C: emerging Technologies* 125 (2021): 103008.

[27] Gupta, Savyasachi, Dhananjai Chand, and Ilaiah Kavati. "Computer vision based animal collision avoidance framework for autonomous vehicles." In *Computer Vision and Image Processing: 5th International Conference, CVIP 2020, Prayagraj, India, December 4–6, 2020, Revised Selected Papers, Part III 5*, Springer, pp. 237–248, 2021.

[28] Ding, Feng, Keping Yu, Zonghua Gu, Xiangjun Li, and Yunqing Shi. "Perceptual enhancement for autonomous vehicles: Restoring visually degraded images for context prediction via adversarial training." *IEEE Transactions on Intelligent Transportation Systems* 23, no. 7 (2021): 9430–9441.

[29] Tammvee, Martin, and Gholamreza Anbarjafari. "Human activity recognition-based path planning for autonomous vehicles." *Signal, Image and Video Processing* 15, no. 4 (2021): 809–816.

[30] Vartika, Vagisha, Swati Singh, Subhranil Das, Sudhansu Kumar Mishra, and Sitanshu Sekhar Sahu. "A review on intelligent PID controllers in autonomous vehicle." *Advances in Smart Grid Automation and Industry 4.0: Select Proceedings of ICETSGAI4. 0* (2021): 391–399.

[31] Das, Subhranil, and Rashmi Kumari. "Real time implementation of square path tracing by autonomous mobile robot." *Journal of Physics: Conference Series* 1831, no. 1 (2021): 012011.

[32] Singh, Manjari, Subhranil Das, and Sudhansu Kumar Mishra. "Static obstacles avoidance in autonomous ground vehicle using fuzzy logic controller." In *2020 International Conference for Emerging Technology (INCET)*, pp. 1–6. IEEE, 2020.

[33] Kim, Cheol-jin, Myung-jae Lee, Kyu-hong Hwang, and Young-guk Ha. "End-to-end deep learning-based autonomous driving control for high-speed environment." *The Journal of Supercomputing* 78, no. 2 (2022): 1961–1982.

[34] Wang, Huijuan, Yuan Yu, and Quanbo Yuan. "Application of Dijkstra algorithm in robot path-planning." In *2011 Second International Conference on Mechanic Automation and Control Engineering*, IEEE, pp. 1067–1069, 2011.

[35] Tang, Gang, Congqiang Tang, Christophe Claramunt, Xiong Hu, and Peipei Zhou. "Geometric A-star algorithm: An improved A-star algorithm for AGV path planning in a port environment." *IEEE Access* 9 (2021): 59196–59210.

[36] Zhang, Chaoyong, Duanfeng Chu, Shidong Liu, Zejian Deng, Chaozhong Wu, and Xiaocong Su. "Trajectory planning and tracking for autonomous vehicle based on state lattice and model predictive control." *IEEE Intelligent Transportation Systems Magazine* 11, no. 2 (2019): 29–40.

[37] Sless, Liat, Bat El Shlomo, Gilad Cohen, and Shaul Oron. "Road scene understanding by occupancy grid learning from sparse radar clusters using semantic segmentation." In *Proceedings of the IEEE/CVF International Conference on Computer Vision Workshops (ICCVW)*, pp. 867–875. IEEE, 2019.

[38] Dai, Dengxin, Christos Sakaridis, Simon Hecker, and Luc Van Gool. "Curriculum model adaptation with synthetic and real data for semantic foggy scene understanding." *International Journal of Computer Vision* 128 (2020): 1182–1204.

[39] Huang, Zhiyu, Chen Lv, Yang Xing, and Jingda Wu. "Multi-modal sensor fusion-based deep neural network for end-to-end autonomous driving with scene understanding." *IEEE Sensors Journal* 21, no. 10 (2020): 11781–11790.

[40] Kothandaraman, Divya, Rohan Chandra, and Dinesh Manocha. "BoMuDANet: unsupervised adaptation for visual scene understanding in unstructured driving environments." In *2021 IEEE/CVF International Conference on Computer Vision Workshops (ICCVW)*, pp. 3966–3975. IEEE, 2021. https://doi.org/10.1109/ICCVW54120.2021.00442

[41] Papandreou, Andreas, Andreas Kloukiniotis, Aris Lalos, and Konstantinos Moustakas. "Deep multi-modal data analysis and fusion for robust scene understanding in CAVs." In *2021 IEEE 23rd International Workshop on Multimedia Signal Processing (MMSP)*, IEEE, pp. 1–6, 2021.

[42] Iftikhar, Sundas, Muhammad Asim, Zuping Zhang, and Ahmed A. Abd El-Latif. "Advance generalization technique through 3D CNN to overcome the

false positives pedestrian in autonomous vehicles." *Telecommunication Systems* 80, no. 4 (2022): 545–557.

[43] Nousias, Stavros, Erion-Vasilis Pikoulis, Christos Mavrokefalidis, and Aris S. Lalos. "Accelerating deep neural networks for efficient scene understanding in multi-modal automotive applications." *IEEE Access* 11 (2023): 28208–28221.

[44] Hang, Peng, Chen Lv, Chao Huang, Jiacheng Cai, Zhongxu Hu, and Yang Xing. "An integrated framework of decision making and motion planning for autonomous vehicles considering social behaviors." *IEEE Transactions on Vehicular Technology* 69, no. 12 (2020): 14458–14469.

[45] Peng, Bo, Dexin Yu, Huxing Zhou, Xue Xiao, and Chen Xie. "A motion planning method for automated vehicles in dynamic traffic scenarios." *Symmetry* 14, no. 2 (2022): 208.

[46] Zhang, Yuxiang, Jiachen Wang, Jidong Lv, Bingzhao Gao, Hongqing Chu, and Xiaoxiang Na. "Computational efficient motion planning method for automated vehicles considering dynamic obstacle avoidance and traffic interaction." *Sensors* 22, no. 19 (2022): 7397.

[47] Li, Hongcai, Wenjie Liu, Chao Yang, Weida Wang, Tianqi Qie, and Changle Xiang. "An optimization-based path planning approach for autonomous vehicles using the DynEFWA-artificial potential field." *IEEE Transactions on Intelligent Vehicles* 7, no. 2 (2021): 263–272.

[48] Shi, Y., C. Shen, H. Wei, and K. Zhang. Receding horizon optimization for integrated path planning and tracking control of an AUV. In *Advanced Model Predictive Control for Autonomous Marine Vehicles*, pp. 29–48. Springer International Publishing, 2023.

[49] Raguraman, Sriram Jayachandran, and Jungme Park. "Intelligent drivable area detection system using camera and lidar sensor for autonomous vehicle." In *2020 IEEE International Conference on Electro Information Technology (EIT)*, IEEE, pp. 429–436, 2020.

[50] Cao, Mingcong, and Junmin Wang. "Obstacle detection for autonomous driving vehicles with multi-lidar sensor fusion." *Journal of Dynamic Systems, Measurement, and Control* 142, no. 2 (2020): 021007.

[51] Rawashdeh, Nathir A., Jeremy P. Bos, and Nader J. Abu-Alrub. "Drivable path detection using CNN sensor fusion for autonomous driving in the snow." In *Autonomous Systems: Sensors, Processing, and Security for Vehicles and Infrastructure 2021*, vol. 11748, pp. 36–45. SPIE, 2021.

[52] Duraisamy, Palmani, and Sudha Natarajan. "Multi-sensor fusion based off-road drivable region detection and Its ROS implementation." In *2023 International Conference on Wireless Communications Signal Processing and Networking (WiSPNET)*, IEEE, pp. 1–5, 2023.

Chapter 2

Explainable artificial intelligence

Fundamentals, Approaches, Challenges, XAI Evaluation, and Validation

Manoj Kumar Mahto

2.1 FUNDAMENTALS OF XAI

Fundamentals of Explainable Artificial Intelligence (XAI) encompass essential principles that form the bedrock of transparent and interpretable AI systems. XAI seeks to bridge the gap between the opaque nature of complex AI algorithms and the need for human understanding and trust in AI-driven decision-making. As Doshi-Velez and Kim (2017) pointed out, XAI revolves around the concept of model transparency, which involves making AI models more comprehensible and interpretable. Transparency in AI can be achieved through various means, including rule-based systems, feature importance analysis, and visualization techniques (Ribeiro et al., 2016; Lundberg and Lee, 2017). Rule-based systems encode decision rules in a human-readable format, making the reasoning behind AI decisions explicit and intuitive. Feature importance analysis methods, such as SHAP (SHapley Additive exPlanations) and LIME (Local Interpretable Model-agnostic Explanations), provide insights into the relative importance of input features in driving model predictions (Lundberg and Lee, 2017). Visualization techniques, such as saliency maps and activation maximization, transform complex model behavior into visual representations that are more accessible to human operators (Ribeiro et al., 2016).

Furthermore, the concept of trustworthiness in AI models emphasizes the need for reliability, robustness, and the ability to provide explanations that align with human reasoning (Adadi and Berrada, 2018). Trustworthy AI is not merely about transparency but also about ensuring that AI systems perform reliably in diverse and dynamic environments, such as autonomous vehicles operating in unpredictable traffic scenarios. These fundamental principles lay the foundation for the development and implementation of XAI, particularly in complex domains such as autonomous vehicles, where the stakes are high and human safety and trust are paramount.

DOI: 10.1201/9781003502432-2

2.2 INTRODUCTION TO EXPLAINABLE ARTIFICIAL INTELLIGENCE

The concept of Explainable Artificial Intelligence (XAI) has gained significant traction in recent years as AI systems are increasingly integrated into various aspects of society. XAI addresses the inherent opacity of complex AI models, providing a means to understand, interpret, and trust the decisions made by AI systems. As articulated by Doshi-Velez and Kim (2017), XAI seeks to move beyond black-box AI, which often hinders the comprehension of how and why AI arrives at specific outcomes. It encompasses a range of techniques and approaches designed to make AI algorithms more transparent and their decision processes more accessible to human understanding. XAI is not a singular methodology but rather a broad field encompassing diverse strategies, including model transparency, rule-based systems, feature importance analysis, and visualization techniques (Ribeiro et al., 2016; Lundberg and Lee, 2017). These techniques aim to shed light on the inner workings of AI systems, ultimately fostering trust and accountability, which are crucial for the responsible adoption of AI technologies in applications ranging from healthcare to autonomous vehicles.

2.3 XAI AND ITS SIGNIFICANCE

Defining Explainable Artificial Intelligence (XAI) is pivotal in comprehending its significance in contemporary AI research and application domains. XAI can be understood as the set of techniques and methodologies aimed at making AI systems transparent, interpretable, and accountable for their

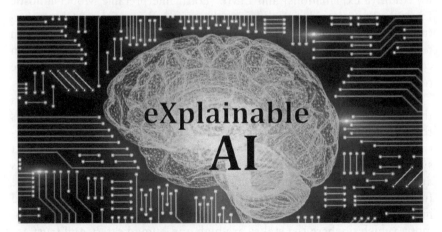

Figure 2.1 Explainable Artificial Intelligence.

decision-making processes. In the words of Doshi-Velez and Kim (2017), XAI represents a paradigm shift from treating AI models as inscrutable black boxes to developing AI systems that provide human-understandable explanations for their outputs. This shift is of paramount importance, particularly in critical domains such as healthcare (Caruana et al., 2015) and autonomous vehicles (Rudin, 2019), where AI systems are entrusted with making high-stakes decisions. By enabling humans to comprehend the rationale behind AI decisions, XAI enhances not only transparency but also trust, fostering user confidence in AI technologies and facilitating their responsible integration into society.

2.4 KEY CONCEPTS IN EXPLAINABILITY

Key concepts in the realm of explainability provide a foundational understanding of how Explainable Artificial Intelligence (XAI) operates and why it is pivotal in AI systems. Model transparency, as highlighted by Doshi-Velez and Kim (2017), represents the core concept involving the disclosure of an AI model's inner workings in a human-understandable manner. Transparency serves as a basis for the comprehensibility of AI systems, allowing stakeholders to scrutinize and trust the decision-making process. Alongside transparency, the distinction between interpretability and transparency, as articulated by Lipton (2016), is fundamental. Interpretability refers to the ease with which a human can discern and predict the behavior of a model, whereas transparency centers on revealing the model's mechanisms. This differentiation underscores the multifaceted nature of XAI, where methods can

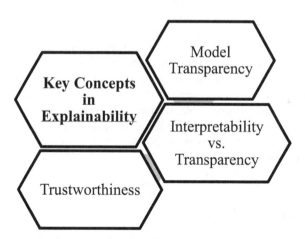

Figure 2.2 Key concepts in explainability.

focus on making models interpretable, transparent, or both. Understanding these key concepts lays the groundwork for the application of XAI across domains, including healthcare (Caruana et al., 2015) and autonomous vehicles (Ribeiro et al., 2016).

2.4.1 Model transparency

Model transparency stands as a pivotal concept in the realm of Explainable Artificial Intelligence (XAI). It involves the process of making AI models comprehensible and interpretable to humans. As articulated by Lipton (2016), transparent models allow individuals to gain insight into the decision-making processes of complex algorithms. This transparency is achieved by revealing the inner workings of AI models, enabling stakeholders to understand why a particular decision was made. Transparency plays a critical role in enhancing trust, especially in high-stakes applications such as healthcare (Caruana et al., 2015) and autonomous vehicles (Ribeiro et al., 2016). When AI models are transparent, users can scrutinize and validate the decision logic, leading to greater confidence in the technology. Consequently, model transparency serves as a foundational concept in the pursuit of responsible and trustworthy AI.

2.4.2 Interpretability vs. transparency

The distinction between interpretability and transparency in Explainable Artificial Intelligence (XAI) is pivotal to understanding how AI systems can be made more comprehensible. As elucidated by Lipton (2016), interpretability relates to the ease with which a human can discern and predict the behavior of a model. In essence, it focuses on whether an individual can grasp the rationale behind a model's decisions, even if the model itself remains complex. In contrast, transparency, as defined by Doshi-Velez and Kim (2017), centers on revealing the inner mechanisms and decision processes of an AI model in a human-understandable manner. This difference highlights the multifaceted nature of XAI approaches, where methods can aim to make models interpretable, transparent, or both. This nuanced understanding is vital, especially in fields like healthcare (Caruana et al., 2015) and autonomous vehicles (Ribeiro et al., 2016), where striking the right balance between interpretability and transparency can determine the usability and trustworthiness of AI systems.

2.4.3 Trustworthiness

Trustworthiness is a fundamental concept in Explainable Artificial Intelligence (XAI) that transcends mere transparency and interpretability. As emphasized by Adadi and Berrada (2018), trustworthiness goes beyond revealing how AI models work; it embodies the assurance that AI systems can be relied upon to make decisions that align with human values and expectations. In contexts where AI influences critical outcomes, such as healthcare (Caruana et al., 2015) and autonomous vehicles (Ribeiro et al., 2016), trustworthiness is paramount. Trustworthy AI systems exhibit not only transparency but also reliability and robustness. They provide explanations that are not only comprehensible but also consistent with human reasoning. In essence, trustworthiness fosters confidence in AI technologies, facilitating their responsible adoption and integration into society.

2.5 APPROACHES TO DEVELOPING XAI MODELS

Various approaches are employed in the development of Explainable Artificial Intelligence (XAI) models, all with the overarching goal of making AI systems more transparent and interpretable. Model transparency, one such approach, involves simplifying complex machine learning models, rendering their internal mechanisms more accessible to human understanding (Ribeiro et al., 2016). Rule-based systems, as discussed by Carvalho and Freitas (2019), offer another avenue where decision rules are explicitly represented, making the reasoning behind AI decisions explicit and intuitive. Feature importance analysis, including methods like SHAP (SHapley Additive exPlanations) and LIME (Local Interpretable Model-agnostic Explanations), is pivotal for discerning the relative importance of input features in model predictions (Lundberg and Lee, 2017). Visualization techniques, such as saliency maps and activation maximization, provide intuitive visual representations of model behavior, enabling stakeholders to explore and understand AI model outputs

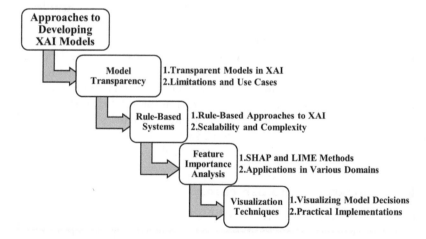

Figure 2.3 Approaches to developing XAI.

(Ribeiro et al., 2016). These diverse approaches collectively contribute to the advancement of XAI, offering a range of tools and methodologies to enhance model transparency and interpretability across various domains.

2.6 MODEL TRANSPARENCY

Model transparency is a central concept in the pursuit of Explainable Artificial Intelligence (XAI). It refers to the extent to which the inner workings of an AI model are made comprehensible and interpretable to human users. As articulated by Ribeiro et al. (2016), transparent models aim to bridge the gap between complex machine learning algorithms and human understanding by revealing how a model arrives at its decisions. This transparency is essential for building trust in AI systems, as it allows users to scrutinize and validate the decision-making process. Transparent models often involve the simplification of complex models or the representation of decision rules in a human-readable format (Carvalho and Freitas, 2019). By offering transparency, AI systems can provide stakeholders with insights into the logic and reasoning behind their outputs, ultimately fostering trust and facilitating the responsible adoption of AI technologies across various domains.

2.6.1 Transparent models in XAI

Transparent models play a pivotal role in the field of Explainable Artificial Intelligence (XAI). These models are designed to be inherently interpretable, enabling humans to comprehend their decision-making processes easily. As emphasized by Ribeiro et al. (2016), transparent models provide a direct and intuitive understanding of how inputs are transformed into outputs, making the decision rationale explicit. Examples of transparent models include decision trees, linear regression, and logistic regression, which inherently offer a high level of interpretability due to their simple and structured nature. Such models have been widely used in various applications, including healthcare (Caruana et al., 2015) and finance (Lipton, 2016), where the need for clear, comprehensible decision-making processes is paramount. While transparent models offer a clear advantage in terms of interpretability, they may have limitations in capturing complex relationships present in data. Thus, the choice of model transparency must consider the trade-off between simplicity and the complexity required for accurate modeling in a given context.

2.6.2 Limitations and use cases

While transparent models are valued for their inherent interpretability, it's essential to recognize their limitations and consider appropriate use cases. Transparent models, such as decision trees and linear regression, excel in scenarios where the underlying data relationships are relatively simple and can be adequately captured by a straightforward model. However, these models may struggle when dealing with highly complex data and intricate patterns. As pointed out by Lipton (2016), in use cases where data relationships are nonlinear or involve a multitude of interacting factors, transparent models may not offer the required predictive accuracy. In such situations, more complex and non-transparent models, such as deep neural networks, might be necessary. Therefore, the choice of model transparency must be context-specific, balancing the need for interpretable decision-making with the complexity of the data and the accuracy requirements of the application.

2.7 RULE-BASED SYSTEMS

Rule-based systems represent a notable approach within the realm of Explainable Artificial Intelligence (XAI) that seeks to enhance interpretability by making decision rules explicit. These systems encode decision rules in a human-readable format, allowing for a clear understanding of how inputs lead to specific outputs. As outlined by Carvalho and Freitas (2019), rule-based systems are particularly valuable when the decision process can be articulated through a set of logical conditions and actions. These systems have found extensive use in domains where transparency and interpretability are paramount, such as healthcare (Holzinger et al., 2019). In medical diagnosis, for example, rule-based systems can provide clear, comprehensible explanations for the basis of a diagnosis or treatment recommendation, making them a valuable tool for both healthcare practitioners and patients. However, it's important to acknowledge that rule-based systems may face scalability challenges when dealing with complex, high-dimensional data, and they might not capture subtle nonlinear relationships present in some datasets.

2.7.1 Rule-based approaches to XAI

Rule-based approaches stand as a cornerstone in the pursuit of Explainable Artificial Intelligence (XAI) by explicitly encoding decision rules in a human-interpretable format. These approaches, as highlighted by Carvalho and Freitas (2019), offer a structured way to make AI models transparent and interpretable. Rule-based models often consist of "if-then" statements, where specific conditions are defined and corresponding actions or decisions are prescribed. This explicit representation allows for clear insight into how inputs are processed and decisions are made. Rule-based systems have been widely employed in various applications, including healthcare (Holzinger et al., 2019), where the need for transparent and accountable decision-making is critical. These systems are particularly valuable when the decision process can be expressed as a series of logical rules, providing both experts and end-users with a comprehensible explanation of AI-generated decisions. However, it's essential to acknowledge that rule-based approaches may have limitations when dealing with more complex and high-dimensional data, as they might not capture intricate nonlinear relationships.

2.7.2 Scalability and complexity

While rule-based approaches in Explainable Artificial Intelligence (XAI) offer transparency and interpretability benefits, they may encounter challenges related to scalability and complexity, as discussed by Carvalho and Freitas (2019). Rule-based models thrive in scenarios where decision processes can be succinctly captured through a set of logical conditions and actions. However, they may face limitations when dealing with large, high-dimensional datasets or complex, nonlinear relationships in the data. As the dimensionality and complexity of data increase, the number of rules required to represent the decision process accurately can grow exponentially, potentially leading to unwieldy rule sets that are difficult to manage and comprehend. Balancing the need for transparency with the challenges posed by scalability and complexity is a critical consideration when employing rule-based approaches in XAI, and it highlights the importance of selecting the most appropriate XAI technique for a given problem domain.

2.8 FEATURE IMPORTANCE ANALYSIS

Feature importance analysis is a pivotal approach in the realm of Explainable Artificial Intelligence (XAI) that focuses on discerning the relative significance of input features in driving model predictions. Methods such as SHAP (SHapley Additive exPlanations) and LIME (Local Interpretable Model-agnostic Explanations) are instrumental in this regard, as outlined by Lundberg and Lee (2017). These methods provide insights into the contribution of individual features to the model's output, offering a clear understanding of which factors influence a particular prediction. Feature importance analysis is invaluable in various applications, including finance and healthcare (Caruana et al., 2015), where identifying the key determinants of an outcome is critical for decision-making and model interpretability. By revealing feature importance, XAI practitioners can not only enhance the transparency of AI models but also facilitate domain experts' understanding of the decision process.

2.8.1 SHAP and LIME methods

In the domain of Feature Importance Analysis in Explainable Artificial Intelligence (XAI), two prominent methods, SHAP (SHapley Additive exPlanations) and LIME (Local Interpretable Model-agnostic Explanations), have garnered significant attention. These methods, as detailed by Lundberg and Lee (2017), offer complementary approaches to understanding the influence of input features on model predictions. SHAP, based on cooperative game theory, calculates feature importance by assigning Shapley values to each feature, reflecting their contributions to the prediction. On the other hand, LIME, introduced by Ribeiro et al. (2016), focuses on creating local surrogate models that approximate the behavior of the complex black-box model. These surrogate models are interpretable, providing insights into how changes in input features affect predictions locally. Both SHAP and LIME offer valuable tools for uncovering the black-box model's inner workings, enhancing model transparency, and fostering trust in AI systems across domains such as healthcare and finance (Caruana et al., 2015).

2.8.2 Applications in various domains

The SHAP and LIME methods for Feature Importance Analysis have found widespread applications across various domains, offering valuable insights into the workings of complex AI models. In healthcare, as demonstrated by Caruana et al. (2015), these methods have been instrumental in predicting disease risks and patient readmission rates. SHAP and LIME enable healthcare practitioners to understand which patient attributes are most influential in making critical healthcare decisions. In finance, they have been used to interpret credit scoring models, offering transparency in lending decisions (Ribeiro et al., 2016). In natural language processing and sentiment analysis, these methods have provided interpretable explanations for classifying texts or reviews (Lundberg and Lee, 2017). These applications underscore the versatility of SHAP and LIME in diverse domains, empowering stakeholders to harness the predictive power of AI models while ensuring accountability and trustworthiness.

2.9 VISUALIZATION TECHNIQUES

Visualization techniques serve as a powerful approach to Explainable Artificial Intelligence (XAI) by providing intuitive visual representations of AI model behavior. These techniques, as discussed by Ribeiro et al. (2016), include methods like saliency maps and activation maximization, which offer insights into how models process input data and arrive at predictions. Saliency maps, for instance, highlight the regions of input data that significantly influence model predictions, making it evident which aspects of an image or dataset drive the decision-making process. Activation maximization, on the other hand, allows users to visualize the features or patterns in data that trigger specific model responses, aiding in understanding what the model has learned. Such visualization techniques have proven valuable across domains such as computer vision, where interpreting deep neural networks is crucial for applications like object recognition and image segmentation. By offering interpretable visualizations, XAI empowers both experts and non-experts to comprehend AI model outputs, ultimately enhancing transparency and trustworthiness.

2.9.1 Visualizing model decisions

Visualizing model decisions is a crucial aspect of Explainable Artificial Intelligence (XAI) that empowers users to understand why an AI model makes specific predictions. Techniques for visualizing model decisions, such as saliency maps and activation maximization, have been instrumental in shedding light on the decision-making process of complex models. Saliency maps, as elucidated by Ribeiro et al. (2016), highlight the most relevant regions or features in input data, making it evident which parts of an image or dataset contribute most to a particular prediction. Activation maximization, on the other hand, allows users to visualize what a model has learned by generating inputs that maximize the activation of specific neurons or features within the model. These visualization techniques have broad applications, ranging from computer vision to natural language processing, and have been employed to explain the reasoning behind AI decisions in tasks like image classification and sentiment analysis. Visualizing model decisions not only enhances transparency but also fosters user trust, making AI systems more accountable and suitable for critical applications.

2.9.2 Practical implementations

Practical implementations of visualization techniques in Explainable Artificial Intelligence (XAI) have demonstrated their value across diverse applications. These techniques, as highlighted by Ribeiro et al. (2016), not only enhance model transparency but also facilitate model debugging and improvement. In computer vision, for instance, visualizations aid in identifying misclassifications and understanding why they occur. For medical imaging, visualization techniques have been employed to highlight regions of interest in X-rays and MRI scans, aiding radiologists in diagnosis (Litjens et al., 2017). In natural language processing, visualizing word embeddings and attention mechanisms has provided insights into how models process and interpret text data, benefiting tasks such as machine translation and sentiment analysis (Vaswani et al., 2017). Practical implementations of visualization techniques bridge the gap between the complexity of AI models and human understanding, enabling users, including domain experts and non-experts, to interact with and trust AI systems effectively.

2.10 CHALLENGES OF IMPLEMENTING XAI IN AUTONOMOUS VEHICLES

Implementing Explainable Artificial Intelligence (XAI) in autonomous vehicles presents a complex set of challenges that impact not only the technical aspects but also the societal acceptance and safety of these vehicles. One

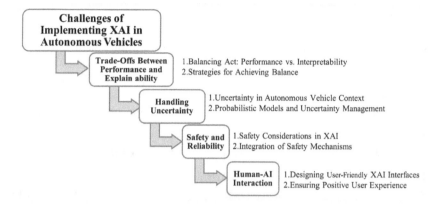

Figure 2.4 Challenges of implementing XAI in autonomous vehicles.

of the foremost challenges is ensuring the interpretability of the AI algorithms driving these vehicles. As autonomous vehicles employ sophisticated machine learning models for decision-making, making these models interpretable becomes essential for trust and accountability (Ribeiro et al., 2016). Furthermore, the challenge of real-time interpretability adds an additional layer of complexity. In safety-critical situations, it is imperative for human passengers, as well as external parties like law enforcement and accident investigators, to understand why an autonomous vehicle made a particular decision. This necessitates the development of XAI techniques that provide clear and concise explanations in real time, aligning with the dynamic nature of driving scenarios (Lipton, 2016). These challenges underscore the need for not only technical advancements in XAI but also the establishment of regulatory frameworks and standards to govern the deployment of explainable AI in autonomous vehicles.

2.11 TRADE-OFFS BETWEEN PERFORMANCE AND EXPLAINABILITY

One of the critical challenges in implementing Explainable Artificial Intelligence (XAI) in autonomous vehicles revolves around the inherent trade-offs between performance and explainability. Autonomous vehicles rely on highly complex machine learning models and neural networks to navigate and make split-second decisions in dynamic environments (Bojarski et al., 2016). These models often prioritize performance and accuracy, which can lead to their inherent opacity and limited interpretability. Striking the right balance between the need for high-performance AI algorithms and the necessity for explainability is a delicate task. As noted by Lipton (2016), there's often an inverse relationship between the complexity of AI models and their interpretability. Simplifying models for improved transparency may come at the cost of reduced predictive accuracy, potentially compromising the safety and efficiency of autonomous vehicles. Therefore, the challenge lies in developing AI systems that can maintain a high level of performance while providing comprehensible explanations for their actions—a challenge critical to ensuring the safe adoption of autonomous vehicles on our roads.

2.11.1 Balancing act: performance vs. interpretability

The implementation of Explainable Artificial Intelligence (XAI) in autonomous vehicles demands a delicate balancing act between performance and interpretability. Autonomous vehicles must meet rigorous safety and performance standards to navigate complex and dynamic environments effectively (Sun et al., 2017). Achieving the highest levels of performance often involves deploying complex machine learning models and deep neural networks. However, these models can be inherently opaque, making it challenging to provide clear explanations for their decisions. As highlighted by Lipton (2016), the trade-off between performance and interpretability is not always straightforward, as simplifying models for better transparency can lead to a loss in predictive accuracy. Striking the right balance requires a nuanced approach, where AI developers must continuously refine algorithms to ensure they remain both high-performing and explainable. Achieving this balance is critical to building trust in autonomous vehicles, as it enables passengers and external stakeholders to understand and trust the vehicle's decision-making process.

2.11.2 Strategies for achieving balance

Striking the delicate balance between performance and interpretability in autonomous vehicles necessitates the implementation of thoughtful strategies. One effective strategy is the development of hybrid AI models that combine the strengths of complex, high-performance algorithms with interpretable components. For example, ensemble models can integrate deep neural networks with decision trees or rule-based systems (Friedman et al., 2000). This approach maintains a high level of predictive accuracy while allowing for the extraction of interpretable insights. Additionally, post hoc interpretability techniques, like those mentioned by Carvalho and Freitas (2019), can be applied to complex models. These techniques generate explanations for model predictions without altering the underlying algorithms, offering a way to enhance interpretability without compromising performance. Lastly, continuous monitoring and auditing of autonomous vehicle systems, as proposed by Sun et al. (2017), can help identify potential performance-explainability trade-offs and enable iterative improvements. These strategies collectively contribute to the achievement of balance, ensuring that autonomous vehicles remain both high-performing and transparent in their decision-making processes.

2.12 HANDLING UNCERTAINTY

Handling uncertainty is a paramount challenge in implementing Explainable Artificial Intelligence (XAI) in autonomous vehicles. These vehicles operate in complex, dynamic environments where uncertainty is inherent, stemming from factors like unpredictable weather, the behavior of other road users, and sensor limitations (Alarifi et al., 2018). Ensuring that XAI systems can not only make decisions but also convey their confidence or uncertainty in those decisions is essential. Bayesian methods, as discussed by Gal et al. (2016), offer a promising approach to quantifying and managing uncertainty. Bayesian neural networks can provide probabilistic predictions, allowing autonomous vehicles to express their uncertainty in real-time decision-making. Additionally, ensemble techniques, such as bagging and bootstrapped ensembles, can be used to generate diverse model predictions and assess their agreement, aiding in the identification of uncertain scenarios (Friedman et al., 2000). Handling uncertainty is vital not only for the safe operation of autonomous vehicles but also for building trust among passengers and regulatory bodies.

2.12.1 Uncertainty in autonomous vehicle context

Uncertainty in the context of autonomous vehicles is a multifaceted challenge that encompasses various sources of unpredictability. These vehicles operate in a dynamic environment where uncertainty arises from factors such as sensor noise, ambiguous sensor inputs, and the inherently unpredictable behavior of other road users (Chen et al., 2015). Furthermore, environmental conditions, like adverse weather, can significantly affect the accuracy of perception systems, exacerbating uncertainty. To address these challenges, XAI systems in autonomous vehicles must not only make informed decisions but also quantify and communicate their degree of uncertainty. Probabilistic models, as discussed by Gal et al. (2016), offer a principled way to model uncertainty by assigning probabilities to predictions. This enables autonomous vehicles to convey when they are highly confident in their actions and when they are less certain, leading to safer and more reliable decision-making. Managing uncertainty in the context of autonomous vehicles is crucial for ensuring both safety and public trust in this transformative technology.

2.12.2 Probabilistic models and uncertainty management

Managing uncertainty in the context of autonomous vehicles necessitates the integration of probabilistic models as a fundamental strategy. These models, as highlighted by Gal et al. (2016), enable autonomous vehicles to quantify and handle uncertainty in a principled manner. Bayesian neural networks, for instance, provide a framework for estimating the uncertainty associated with predictions by assigning probability distributions to model parameters. This approach allows autonomous vehicles to express their confidence or uncertainty in real-time decision-making. Additionally, probabilistic models facilitate risk assessment, helping autonomous vehicles identify situations where uncertainty is high and take appropriate actions, such as slowing down or seeking human intervention. Managing uncertainty through probabilistic models is vital not only for safety but also for building trust among passengers and regulatory bodies, as it makes the decision-making process more transparent and accountable.

2.13 SAFETY AND RELIABILITY

Safety and reliability are paramount concerns in the integration of Explainable Artificial Intelligence (XAI) in autonomous vehicles. Ensuring the safe operation of these vehicles is not only a technical challenge but also a matter of public trust and regulatory compliance. As autonomous vehicles rely on AI algorithms to make real-time decisions in dynamic environments, the potential for unexpected behaviors and safety-critical scenarios becomes a significant concern (Sun et al., 2017). XAI plays a crucial role in addressing these concerns by providing transparent explanations for the vehicle's actions. However, it is essential to strike a balance between the need for explanations and real-time decision-making. Techniques such as real-time model explanation generation (Lipton, 2016) and rule-based systems for decision justification (Carvalho and Freitas, 2019) can contribute to the safety and reliability of autonomous vehicles by ensuring that human passengers and external stakeholders can understand and trust the vehicle's actions, even in complex and potentially hazardous situations.

2.13.1 Safety considerations in XAI

Safety considerations are of utmost importance in the deployment of Explainable Artificial Intelligence (XAI) in autonomous vehicles. As autonomous vehicles navigate complex and unpredictable environments, ensuring the safety of passengers, pedestrians, and other road users is a critical concern. XAI can contribute to safety by providing transparent insights into the decision-making process of AI algorithms (Ribeiro et al., 2016). This transparency allows for the identification and mitigation of potential risks and failure modes. Furthermore, XAI can assist in scenario-based testing and validation, as emphasized by Sun et al. (2017), enabling exhaustive testing of AI systems under various conditions. Safety considerations extend to the ability of XAI to detect and respond to adversarial attacks, which may attempt to manipulate AI algorithms. By addressing these safety considerations, XAI helps build trust in autonomous vehicles and fosters the development of robust, reliable, and accountable AI systems.

2.13.2 Integration of safety mechanisms

The integration of safety mechanisms is a critical aspect of deploying Explainable Artificial Intelligence (XAI) in autonomous vehicles. Ensuring the safety and reliability of these vehicles requires the fusion of XAI techniques with robust safety protocols. As noted by Sun et al. (2017), autonomous vehicles often incorporate multiple layers of safety, including sensor redundancy, fail-safe mechanisms, and real-time monitoring. XAI plays a pivotal role in this safety ecosystem by providing interpretable explanations for AI system decisions. These explanations allow human passengers, as well as external stakeholders like safety regulators, to understand why specific decisions are made in real time, enhancing transparency and accountability. Moreover, the integration of safety mechanisms should extend to the ability of XAI to detect and respond to anomalous or adversarial behaviors, bolstering the vehicle's resilience against potential threats. In this way, XAI serves as a key enabler in building safety-critical AI systems for autonomous vehicles, aligning technological innovation with the paramount goal of public safety.

2.14 HUMAN-AI INTERACTION

Human-AI interaction is a pivotal challenge in the implementation of Explainable Artificial Intelligence (XAI) in autonomous vehicles. Autonomous vehicles must coexist with human drivers and pedestrians, requiring a seamless interface between AI systems and human users. XAI addresses this challenge by providing comprehensible explanations for AI decisions, as highlighted by Ribeiro et al. (2016). These explanations serve as a bridge between the often complex decision-making processes of AI algorithms and human understanding, enabling passengers to trust and feel in control of autonomous vehicles. Effective human-AI interaction also involves designing user interfaces that convey XAI information intuitively and in real-time (Goodfellow et al., 2016). Moreover, XAI contributes to the establishment of clear lines of responsibility between humans and AI systems, a vital aspect of safety and accountability. The successful integration of XAI in human-AI interaction is integral to the acceptance and adoption of autonomous vehicles on a large scale, paving the way for a harmonious coexistence on our roads.

2.14.1 Designing user-friendly XAI interfaces

Designing user-friendly Explainable Artificial Intelligence (XAI) interfaces is a pivotal aspect of human-AI interaction, particularly in the context of autonomous vehicles. Effective communication between autonomous systems and human users is essential for safety and user acceptance. XAI contributes to this by offering interpretable explanations for AI decisions (Ribeiro et al., 2016). However, it's equally important to design interfaces that convey XAI information intuitively and in real time. Research by Goodfellow et al. (2016) emphasizes the importance of user-centered design principles to create interfaces that are not only informative but also easy to understand and interact with. Visualizations, natural language explanations, and real-time alerts are some of the tools that can be integrated into these interfaces. Ensuring that passengers and operators can quickly grasp the AI's reasoning enhances their trust and confidence in the autonomous vehicle's capabilities. In essence, user-friendly XAI interfaces are the bridge that connects complex AI algorithms with human users, fostering harmonious human-AI collaboration in the autonomous vehicle ecosystem.

2.14.2 Ensuring positive user experience

Ensuring a positive user experience is a paramount goal when integrating Explainable Artificial Intelligence (XAI) in autonomous vehicles. A seamless interaction between passengers and AI systems not only enhances safety but also influences user acceptance. XAI plays a pivotal role in achieving this by providing transparent explanations for AI decisions (Ribeiro et al., 2016). However, it goes beyond explanations; it's about creating an environment where users feel informed and in control. Research by Goodfellow et al. (2016) underscores the importance of designing AI interfaces that align with human cognitive processes, ensuring that information is presented in a manner that is easy to understand and act upon. Real-time feedback, context-aware alerts, and intuitive visualizations are some of the elements that contribute to a positive user experience. Moreover, feedback loops that allow users to provide input and receive responses from the AI system foster a sense of collaboration and trust. Ultimately, ensuring a positive user experience is pivotal for the widespread acceptance and adoption of autonomous vehicles, where passengers are not just passengers but active participants in the journey.

2.15 XAI EVALUATION AND VALIDATION

XAI evaluation and validation represent critical phases in the deployment of Explainable Artificial Intelligence (XAI) in autonomous vehicles. As autonomous vehicles rely on AI systems to make critical decisions, it is imperative

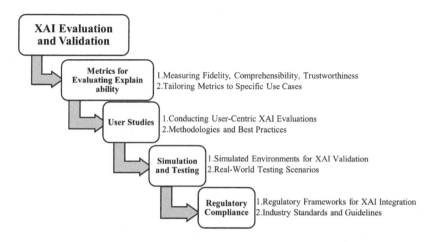

Figure 2.5 XAI evaluation and validation.

to assess the effectiveness and reliability of XAI techniques in providing comprehensible explanations for these decisions. This process often involves quantitative metrics, such as explanation fidelity and completeness, as highlighted by Ribeiro et al. (2016). Furthermore, evaluation methodologies need to consider real-world scenarios and diverse driving conditions to ensure the robustness of XAI solutions (Sun et al., 2017). Validation, on the other hand, entails ensuring that XAI systems meet regulatory standards and safety requirements, as emphasized by Alarifi et al. (2018). It's not just about producing explanations but also verifying their accuracy and utility in enhancing decision-making and trust in autonomous vehicles. By conducting rigorous evaluation and validation, we can ensure that XAI systems contribute to the safe and accountable operation of autonomous vehicles.

2.16 METRICS FOR EVALUATING EXPLAINABILITY

Evaluating the explainability of AI models is a multifaceted task, and it requires the use of various metrics and approaches. Metrics play a critical role in quantifying the quality of explanations provided by Explainable Artificial Intelligence (XAI) systems. One commonly used metric is explanation fidelity, which measures how well the explanation reflects the actual decision process of the AI model (Ribeiro et al., 2016). Another essential metric is explanation completeness, which evaluates the extent to which the explanation covers all relevant aspects of the model's decision (Doshi-Velez and Kim, 2017). Additionally, human-centric metrics, such as user satisfaction and comprehension, are crucial for assessing how well users can understand

and trust the explanations (Lage et al., 2021). Furthermore, evaluation methodologies should consider the context in which the AI system operates and how explanations impact decision-making. The selection of appropriate evaluation metrics should align with the specific goals and requirements of autonomous vehicles to ensure that XAI systems enhance safety and user trust effectively.

2.16.1 Measuring fidelity, comprehensibility, and trustworthiness

Measuring the fidelity, comprehensibility, and trustworthiness of explanations is essential for evaluating the effectiveness of Explainable Artificial Intelligence (XAI) in autonomous vehicles. Explanation fidelity, as discussed by Ribeiro et al. (2016), assesses how well the provided explanation aligns with the actual decision-making process of the AI model. This metric ensures that explanations are accurate and representative of the AI's reasoning. Comprehensibility metrics, such as those proposed by Lage et al. (2021), evaluate how easily users can understand the provided explanations. A comprehensible explanation is essential for passengers and operators of autonomous vehicles to trust and make informed decisions based on AI recommendations. Trustworthiness, as emphasized by Chen et al. (2018), measures the degree to which users rely on AI-based decisions and explanations. Collectively evaluating these three dimensions helps ensure that XAI systems enhance decision-making, safety, and user trust in the context of autonomous vehicles.

2.16.2 Tailoring metrics to specific use cases

Tailoring evaluation metrics to specific use cases is essential when assessing the effectiveness of Explainable Artificial Intelligence (XAI) in autonomous vehicles. While general metrics like explanation fidelity, comprehensibility, and trustworthiness provide a foundational framework (Ribeiro et al., 2016; Lage et al., 2021; Chen et al., 2018), it is equally important to consider the unique requirements and contexts of autonomous driving. Metrics should align with specific use cases, such as urban environments, highway driving, or off-road scenarios (Sun et al., 2017). For example, in urban environments, where safety is paramount, metrics may emphasize the ability of XAI to explain evasive maneuvers and collision avoidance strategies. In contrast, on highways, metrics could focus on the XAI system's ability to justify lane-changing decisions. By tailoring metrics to these specific contexts and use cases, we can ensure that XAI systems not only meet generic explainability criteria but also address the particular challenges and priorities of autonomous vehicle operation.

2.17 USER STUDIES

User studies represent a vital component of evaluating Explainable Artificial Intelligence (XAI) in the context of autonomous vehicles. These studies involve gathering feedback and insights from human passengers, operators, and other stakeholders who interact with AI-driven autonomous systems. Through user studies, researchers can assess the real-world impact of XAI on user trust, decision-making, and overall user experience (Chen et al., 2018). User satisfaction surveys, usability tests, and cognitive load assessments are some of the methods used to collect valuable data on how well XAI systems enhance user understanding and trust. Furthermore, user studies can help identify areas where explanations may fall short or need improvement, contributing to the iterative development of XAI solutions tailored to the unique needs and expectations of autonomous vehicle users (Lage et al., 2021). These studies are instrumental in ensuring that XAI systems are not only theoretically sound but also practical and beneficial in real-world driving scenarios.

2.17.1 Conducting user-centric XAI evaluations

Conducting user-centric evaluations is a pivotal step in assessing the effectiveness of Explainable Artificial Intelligence (XAI) in autonomous vehicles. These evaluations shift the focus from technical metrics to human-centered criteria, ensuring that XAI systems align with the needs and expectations of users in the autonomous vehicle ecosystem. User-centric evaluations often involve soliciting feedback from passengers, operators, and other stakeholders through surveys, interviews, and interactive scenarios (Chen et al., 2018). These studies not only gauge user satisfaction but also assess the comprehensibility of explanations, user trust in AI decisions, and the overall impact of XAI on user experience. By involving users in the evaluation process, researchers can identify usability issues, potential misconceptions, and areas where XAI can be enhanced to support human decision-making better (Lage et al., 2021). In sum, user-centric evaluations play a pivotal role in bridging the gap between XAI theory and practical usability, ensuring that XAI enhances safety and user trust in autonomous vehicles.

2.17.2 Methodologies and best practices

Methodologies and best practices play a crucial role in conducting effective user-centric evaluations of Explainable Artificial Intelligence (XAI) in autonomous vehicles. Establishing rigorous evaluation frameworks and protocols is essential to ensure the validity and reliability of the results. Researchers often employ a combination of qualitative and quantitative methods, such as surveys, cognitive load assessments, and usability tests, to gather comprehensive feedback from users (Chen et al., 2018). In practice, it's important to consider diverse user groups, including passengers, operators, and individuals with varying levels of technical expertise. Moreover, maintaining a focus on real-world scenarios and diverse driving conditions is essential, as highlighted by Sun et al. (2017). Best practices involve clearly defining evaluation objectives, designing realistic test scenarios, and capturing both subjective and objective measures of XAI system performance. Additionally, iterative evaluation processes allow for the continuous improvement of XAI systems based on user feedback (Lage et al., 2021). Ultimately, well-structured methodologies and best practices ensure that user-centric evaluations contribute to the development of XAI solutions that enhance user understanding, trust, and overall user experience in autonomous vehicles.

2.18 SIMULATION AND TESTING

Simulation and testing are integral components of the evaluation and validation process for Explainable Artificial Intelligence (XAI) in autonomous vehicles. Given the complex and dynamic nature of real-world driving scenarios, conducting extensive real-world testing can be costly and potentially risky. Therefore, simulation environments, as emphasized by Sun et al. (2017), offer a controlled and safe means of evaluating XAI systems under a wide range of conditions. These simulations can replicate various driving scenarios, including rare and hazardous events, allowing researchers to assess how well XAI systems perform and explain their actions in challenging situations. Moreover, simulation environments facilitate systematic testing of XAI responses to different inputs, helping to identify potential vulnerabilities and areas for improvement. Combining simulation testing with real-world testing, as advocated by Alarifi et al. (2018), provides a comprehensive validation approach that ensures XAI systems are robust, safe, and capable of delivering reliable explanations to support autonomous vehicle operation.

2.18.1 Simulated environments for XAI validation

Simulated environments play a pivotal role in the validation of Explainable Artificial Intelligence (XAI) in autonomous vehicles. These environments offer controlled and versatile settings for testing XAI systems under various scenarios, as highlighted by Sun et al. (2017). Simulated environments can replicate a wide range of driving conditions, including adverse weather, complex traffic interactions, and rare events, all of which are challenging to encounter in the real world. Additionally, simulations provide researchers with the ability to inject specific scenarios to assess how well XAI systems respond and explain their decisions. This approach helps uncover vulnerabilities and areas for improvement in a safe and cost-effective manner. Furthermore, simulated environments are instrumental in the development and fine-tuning of XAI models before their deployment in actual vehicles. By leveraging these environments, researchers can ensure that XAI systems are not only technically sound but also capable of delivering reliable explanations in the dynamic and unpredictable context of autonomous driving.

2.18.2 Real-world testing scenarios

While simulated environments are invaluable for validating Explainable Artificial Intelligence (XAI) in autonomous vehicles, real-world testing scenarios remain essential for comprehensive evaluation. Real-world scenarios introduce the unpredictability and complexity inherent to actual driving conditions, as discussed by Sun et al. (2017). They offer the opportunity to validate XAI systems in dynamic, unscripted environments where the unexpected can occur. Real-world testing allows researchers to assess how well XAI systems handle real-time data, adapt to changing road conditions, and provide explanations that are relevant and timely. Furthermore, it helps evaluate the robustness of XAI in diverse geographical regions with varying traffic patterns and infrastructure. Combining insights from both simulated and real-world testing scenarios, as suggested by Alarifi et al. (2018), provides a holistic approach to validating XAI in autonomous vehicles. It ensures that XAI systems are not only proficient in simulated scenarios but also capable of delivering consistent and reliable performance on the open road.

2.19 REGULATORY COMPLIANCE

Regulatory compliance is a critical aspect of implementing Explainable Artificial Intelligence (XAI) in autonomous vehicles. As these vehicles operate on public roads, they must adhere to a complex web of regulations and safety standards. XAI systems, which contribute to transparency and accountability, play a pivotal role in addressing these regulatory requirements. Ensuring that XAI in autonomous vehicles complies with safety and ethical standards, as emphasized by Alarifi et al. (2018), is of paramount importance. This involves not only validating the technical capabilities of XAI systems but also verifying that they meet legal and industry-specific standards. Additionally, XAI should facilitate compliance reporting, making it easier for manufacturers and operators to demonstrate adherence to regulations. By integrating XAI with robust safety and compliance mechanisms, autonomous vehicle technology providers can navigate the intricate regulatory landscape, ensuring the safe and responsible deployment of AI systems on our roads.

2.19.1 Regulatory frameworks for XAI integration

The integration of Explainable Artificial Intelligence (XAI) into autonomous vehicles necessitates a robust regulatory framework to ensure the safety and accountability of these advanced systems. As highlighted by Alarifi et al. (2018), the development and implementation of XAI in autonomous vehicles must align with evolving regulatory standards and ethical guidelines. Regulatory bodies, such as the National Highway Traffic Safety Administration (NHTSA) in the United States and their counterparts worldwide, play a crucial role in defining the rules and standards for autonomous vehicles. The integration of XAI should comply with these regulations, which often involve safety assessments, certification processes, and data transparency requirements. Moreover, industry consortia and standards organizations, such as SAE International, contribute to the development of best practices and standards specific to XAI in autonomous vehicles. A well-defined regulatory framework not only ensures the safety of autonomous vehicles but also instills confidence among consumers, regulators, and stakeholders, facilitating the responsible deployment of XAI technologies.

2.19.2 Industry standards and guidelines

Industry standards and guidelines are instrumental in shaping the integration of Explainable Artificial Intelligence (XAI) in autonomous vehicles. Organizations like SAE International and ISO have been actively involved in developing comprehensive standards that address the safety, transparency, and performance of autonomous systems, as emphasized by Alarifi et al. (2018). These standards often encompass various aspects of autonomous driving, including XAI requirements. For instance, the SAE J3016 standard defines the levels of driving automation, which influence the expectations and responsibilities of XAI systems at different automation levels. Additionally, guidelines from professional bodies, such as the Association for Computing Machinery (ACM) and the Institute of Electrical and Electronics Engineers (IEEE), contribute to ethical considerations and best practices in the development and deployment of XAI in autonomous vehicles. Adhering to these industry standards and guidelines ensures that XAI systems meet not only legal requirements but also community expectations for safe and responsible autonomous driving technology.

2.20 CONCLUSION

In the rapidly evolving landscape of autonomous vehicles, the integration of Explainable Artificial Intelligence (XAI) stands as a fundamental pillar for ensuring safety, transparency, and user trust. This chapter has explored the fundamentals of XAI, the various approaches to developing XAI models, the challenges of implementing XAI in autonomous vehicles, and the critical processes of XAI evaluation and validation. We delved into the nuances of measuring explanation fidelity, comprehensibility, and trustworthiness, highlighting the importance of tailoring evaluation metrics to specific use cases. We discussed the essential role of user studies, both in terms of conducting user-centric evaluations and following methodologies and best practices. Additionally, we underscored the significance of simulation and real-world testing scenarios, as well as the need for regulatory compliance and adherence to industry standards. As autonomous vehicles become an integral part of our transportation ecosystem, XAI emerges as the bridge that fosters harmonious human-AI collaboration, enhancing user understanding, trust, and overall user experience. With continual advancements in XAI techniques and rigorous evaluation practices, the future of autonomous vehicles is poised to be safer, more transparent, and more readily accepted by a broader spectrum of users. As we peer into the future, the prospects for XAI are promising, but challenges persist. The continued advancement of XAI techniques, the evolution of comprehensive evaluation methodologies, and the integration of XAI into regulatory frameworks are all avenues of growth. Nevertheless, the delicate equilibrium between performance and explainability, the nuances of addressing uncertainty, ensuring safety, and crafting user-friendly interfaces remain formidable obstacles. As AI continues its relentless progress, the demand for XAI solutions that enhance transparency and trust will remain steadfast. This demand will propel researchers and practitioners toward innovative solutions and frameworks that render AI more comprehensible and accessible, enriching the human-AI partnership. In summation, the integration of Explainable Artificial Intelligence in autonomous vehicles and various other domains is pivotal for the responsible and effective deployment of AI systems. It is a journey marked by perpetual innovation, collaboration, and a steadfast commitment to ensuring that AI remains a tool that empowers and enhances the human experience. As we navigate this ever-evolving landscape, one truth remains constant: the synergy between humans and AI, nurtured by XAI, has the power to reshape industries, elevate safety standards, and inspire trust in the AI-driven future that awaits us.

REFERENCES

Adadi, A., & Berrada, M. (2018). Peeking inside the black-box: A survey on explainable artificial intelligence (XAI). IEEE Access, 6, 52138–52160.

Alarifi, A., Alkahtani, M., Almazroi, A., Hu, J., & Alarifi, A. (2018). Autonomous Vehicles: Trusted by whom? A comprehensive survey on autonomous vehicle trust management systems. IEEE Transactions on Intelligent Transportation Systems, 20(8), 2917–2926.

Bojarski, M., Del Testa, D., Dworakowski, D., Firner, B., Flepp, B., Goyal, P., . . . & Zhang, X. (2016). End to end learning for self-driving cars. arXiv preprint arXiv:1604.07316.

Caruana, R., Lou, Y., Gehrke, J., Koch, P., Sturm, M., Elhadad, N., . . . & Polito, G. (2015). Intelligible models for healthcare: Predicting pneumonia risk and hospital 30-day readmission. In Proceedings of the 21th ACM SIGKDD International Conference on Knowledge Discovery and Data Mining (pp. 1721–1730).

Carvalho, A. M., & Freitas, A. A. (2019). A comprehensive survey of interpretable machine learning methods. The Journal of Machine Learning Research, 20(1), 1–77.

Chen, C., Seff, A., Kornhauser, A., & Xiao, J. (2015). DeepDriving: Learning affordance for direct perception in autonomous driving. In Proceedings of the IEEE International Conference on Computer Vision (ICCV) (pp. 2722–2730).

Chen, J., Song, L., Wainwright, M. J., & Jordan, M. I. (2018). Learning to explain: An information-theoretic perspective on model interpretation. In Proceedings of the 35th International Conference on Machine Learning (ICML '18) (pp. 883–892).

Doshi-Velez, F., & Kim, B. (2017). Towards a rigorous science of interpretable machine learning. arXiv preprint arXiv:1702.08608.

Friedman, J. H., Hastie, T., & Tibshirani, R. (2000). Additive logistic regression: A statistical view of boosting (with discussion and a rejoinder by the authors). The Annals of Statistics, 28(2), 337–407.

Gal, Y., Islam, R., & Ghahramani, Z. (2016). Deep Bayesian active learning with image data. In Proceedings of the 33rd International Conference on International Conference on Machine Learning—Volume 48 (ICML'16) (pp. 2153–2162).

Goodfellow, I., Bengio, Y., Courville, A., & Bengio, Y. (2016). Deep Learning (Vol. 1).

Holzinger, A., Langs, G., Denk, H., Zatloukal, K., & Müller, H. (2019). Causability and explainability of artificial intelligence in medicine. Wiley Interdisciplinary Reviews: Data Mining and Knowledge Discovery, 9(4), e1312.

Lage, I., Chen, E., He, J., Narayanan, M., Kim, B., Ribeiro, A., & Doshi-Velez, F. (2021). An evaluation of the human-interpretability of explanation. arXiv preprint arXiv:2104.14957.

Lipton, Z. C. (2016). The mythos of model interpretability. In Proceedings of the 2016 ICML Workshop on Human Interpretability in Machine Learning (pp. 1–5).

Litjens, G., Kooi, T., Bejnordi, B. E., Setio, A. A. A., Ciompi, F., Ghafoorian, M., . . . & Sánchez, C. I. (2017). A survey on deep learning in medical image analysis. Medical Image Analysis, 42, 60–88.

Lundberg, S. M., & Lee, S. I. (2017). A unified approach to interpreting model predictions. In Advances in Neural Information Processing Systems (pp. 4765–4774).

Ribeiro, M. T., Singh, S., & Guestrin, C. (2016). "Why should I trust you?" Explaining the predictions of any classifier. In Proceedings of the 22nd ACM SIGKDD International Conference on Knowledge Discovery and Data Mining (pp. 1135–1144).

Rudin, C. (2019). Stop explaining black box machine learning models for high stakes decisions and use interpretable models instead. Nature Machine Intelligence, 1(5), 206–215.

Sun, F., Wen, S., Li, S., & Li, J. (2017). Learning-based motion planning for autonomous vehicles: A review. IEEE Transactions on Intelligent Transportation Systems, 19(4), 1135–1145.

Vaswani, A., Shazeer, N., Parmar, N., Uszkoreit, J., Jones, L., Gomez, A. N., . . . & Kaiser, Ł. (2017). Attention is all you need. In Advances in Neural Information Processing Systems (pp. 30–38).

Chapter 3

Explainable artificial intelligence in autonomous vehicles

Prospects and Future Direction

Manareldeen Ahmed, Zeinab E. Ahmed,
and Rashid A. Saeed

3.1 INTRODUCTION

Autonomous driving (AD) has become one of the major key research directions in finding smart mobility solutions [1]. By providing safety and reliability in modern transportation systems, autonomous vehicles (AVs) are
expected to leverage transportation services such as car parking or avoiding
accidents due to human errors [2]. Figure 3.1 shows a conceptual figure of
autonomous driving cars in smart cities [3]. Vehicle-to-vehicle (V2V) technology [4–7] is used to describe the cooperation between different vehicles
in the same area. The purpose of V2V communication is to enhance vehicle
traffic and pedestrian and passenger safety. On the other hand, Vehicle to
Infrastructure (V2I) technology helps vehicles communicate with roadside
units (RSUs) [8, 9].

V2I could be very beneficial for avoiding traffic accidents or traffic jams
or accessing services on the internet, as illustrated in Figure 3.1. The number
of connected vehicles is growing, as there were 237 million in 2021, according to Statista [10]. This number is expected to reach 400 million by 2025.
The key challenges of such numbers of connected vehicles are related to the
telecommunication area and its security.

In a typical AD task, AVs generate massive amounts of multi-dimensional
data from different components such as cameras, RADAR, LIDAR, GPS,
and ultrasonic sensors. These data are required to be processed for different purposes, such as monitoring, prediction, decision-making, and control
purposes [11, 12]. Artificial intelligence (AI) techniques showed huge success
in dealing with the complexity of such AD tasks with the help of powerful hardware with certain capabilities. However, there are many challenges
regarding how much humans can interfere during decision-making. These
challenges limit the acceptance of such technologies due to their human
unexplainability.

Explainable Artificial Intelligence (XAI) is emerged to address the ambiguity inside AI algorithms. For instance, it is very challenging to get insight into
the internal mechanism of machine learning (ML) algorithms [13]. Figure 3.2

DOI: 10.1201/9781003502432-3

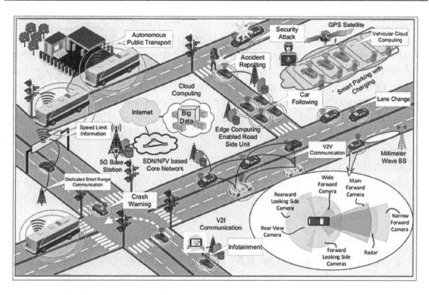

Figure 3.1 A graphical illustration of AD in a smart city [3].

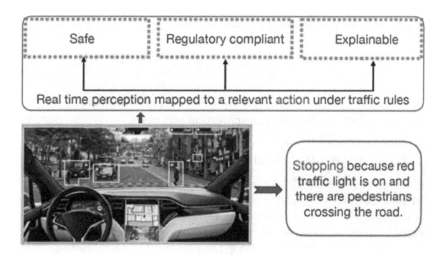

Figure 3.2 A safe, explainable, and regulatory-compliant AV [14].

shows a graphical illustration of an AV on its perception-action mapping
that is safe, explainable, and regulatory compliant. Following the traffic
rules and keeping awareness of surrounding humans and objects guarantee
safety and regulatory compliance. Moreover, justifying each action taken
ensures explainability. The text implies perception, and the another text in
the image implies the corresponding action [14].

This chapter discusses the need for explanations in AVs and presents regulations and standards related to explanations. It categorizes the different stakeholders who interact with AVs and explores various dimensions of explanations. The chapter also highlights the importance of in-vehicle user interfaces and novel interaction technologies for efficient explanation provision. It addresses the limitations and biases in current research on explanation models and provides recommendations for implementation. The chapter concludes with challenges in the explainable AV landscape and suggestions for future work.

This chapter contains four further sections. Section 2 will discuss the current State of XAI in AVs. Section 3 will report on the challenges and limitations of XAI in AVs, and Section 4 will give an idea of future trends in XAI for AVs. Finally, Section 5 offers conclusions to the discussion.

3.2 CURRENT STATE OF XAI IN AUTONOMOUS VEHICLES

This section provides a comprehensive view of the status of XAI within the AVs domain. In recent years, XAI has emerged as a crucial component in addressing the challenges associated with AVs, particularly concerning transparency and accountability. This section delves into the current advancements and developments in XAI techniques specifically tailored for AVs. It explores the ongoing research, emerging technologies, and practical applications that are shaping the landscape of XAI within this field. By examining the current state of XAI in AVs, this section offers valuable insights into how AI explainability is evolving to enhance the safety, trustworthiness, and acceptance of AVs in modern transportation systems.

3.2.1 Autonomous vehicles

Autonomous vehicles (AV) are intelligent systems that can sense their environment and make real-time driving decisions using various sensors. It's crucial to have in-vehicle interfaces that facilitate message exchange between AVs and stakeholders. This allows users to receive explanations for control and navigation decisions by querying the interface [15]. Real-time decision-making involves perception, localization, planning, and control, combining multi-modal data sources with AI-powered algorithms. It classified AVs into six automation levels—Level 0 to Level 5—that offer different degrees of automation: no automation, driving assistance, partial automation, conditional automation, high automation, and full automation [16].

The AV protocol architecture follows a structure comprising five primary stages: perception, decision-making, planning, control, and chassis integration [17]. During the perception phase, AVs depend on an array of sensors, including RADAR, LIDAR, cameras, and real-time kinetic (RTK) sensors, for environmental awareness. Recognition modules such as ADAF, control systems, and VPL modules are responsible for processing data from these sensors. In the decision-making and planning phase, this data is used to make determinations related to path planning and obstacle avoidance. The control phase handles the execution of physical control actions like steering, braking, and acceleration. Finally, the last stage entails establishing connections with the mechanical components incorporated within the chassis [17].

AVs are rapidly advancing, driven by IoT progress, fostering the growth of the Internet of Vehicles (IoV) and the Internet of Autonomous Vehicles (IoAV). These vehicles are on the verge of evolving into intelligent entities capable of local cooperation, content sharing, and potentially assuming control instead of human drivers [18]. Nonetheless, challenges related to infrastructure and security continue to exist. The fusion of artificial intelligence (AI) with edge computing, resulting in edge intelligence (EI), presents a promising solution to tackle these challenges. EI encompasses intelligent data offloading, collaboration, and on-site analysis, facilitating a vast network of billions of smart IoT devices. Achieving complete autonomy necessitates that vehicles match or surpass human perception, decision-making, and cognitive capabilities. The advent of 5G and 6G communication technologies holds the potential for highly dependable, low-latency transmissions, ensuring seamless vehicular communication. Additionally, blockchain technology, known for its transparent, immutable, and decentralized data management, can furnish AVs with a robust security framework [18].

3.2.2 Explainable artificial intelligence (XAI)

Artificial intelligence (AI) has demonstrated the potential to transform various industries, public services, and society at large, surpassing human performance in tasks such as image and speech recognition, as well as language translation [19]. Terms like transparency, interpretability, and explainability are employed to describe the opposite of the "black box" nature often associated with AI models. Transparency pertains to a model's capacity to be clear and interpretable, ensuring the development of accurate and understandable AI systems for humans [20]. Meanwhile, explainability involves the process of rendering technology or a system understandable to humans and assessing how quickly they grasp the model's conclusions [21]. Explainable AI (XAI) places its focus on devising techniques that provide explanations, aiding end-users in comprehending and effectively managing AI systems. Explainability involves providing insights to a targeted audience, such as domain experts, end-users, and modeling experts, to fulfill their needs and ensure they make sense of their domain knowledge [22]. XAI is a set of techniques and approaches aimed at making AI systems more interpretable, transparent, and accountable. There are some common categorizations of XAI [23]:

- Model-Specific Methods.
- Post Hoc Explanation Methods.
- Model-Agnostic Methods.
- Interpretable Neural Networks.
- Local vs. Global Interpretability.
- Explanations for Different Data Types.
- Human-Centric vs. Machine-Centric.

Enhancing the transparency and interpretability of AI models through model interpretation is a key focus of Explainable AI (XAI). Model-agnostic techniques, exemplified by approaches like LIME (Local Interpretable Model-Agnostic Explanations) and SHAP (SHapley Additive Explanations), delve into the relationship between input features and model outcomes without relying on specific model architectures [24]. These techniques prove particularly valuable when dealing with intricate models or decision-making processes, and they can be coupled with techniques like feature visualization and saliency mapping to offer a comprehensive insight into how a model functions and to pinpoint potential biases or errors [25].

XAI endeavors to create AI models intelligible to humans, particularly in sensitive domains such as the military, banking, and healthcare. This level of understanding is essential for domain experts who rely on precise results [26]. AI methodologies facilitate the evaluation of current knowledge, the progression of knowledge, and the development of new assumptions and theories. Researchers aspire to achieve explainability to bolster justification, control, enhancement, and discovery. The advantages of XAI encompass empowering individuals and organizations to address the adverse outcomes of automated decision-making, aiding in well-informed decision-making, uncovering and safeguarding against security vulnerabilities, aligning algorithms with human values, and elevating industry standards for AI-driven products [27]. These efforts will enhance trust among consumers and businesses in AI-powered products.

3.2.3 Case studies of XAI techniques in autonomous vehicles

Several studies in this section delve into integrating XAI techniques in AVs. They optimize vision-based autonomous driving models, enhance driver situational awareness, and bridge the gap between human-driving learning and self-driving systems. The studies also introduce datasets for evaluation and explore the potential of Blockchain and AI for AV security. Moreover, they highlight the importance of XAI in intelligent transportation, present innovative approaches for action prediction and explanations, and propose methods for improving semantic segmentation in challenging weather conditions. Applying XAI extends to decision interpretation, gaze estimation, and trust management in AVs. These studies collectively contribute to making AVs more transparent, trustworthy, and accountable in various driving scenarios.

Li *et al.* presented an optimized model for vision-based AD, focusing on detecting objects and predicting pedestrian intentions in traffic scenes [28]. It uses YOLOv4, incorporates a refined Part Affinity Fields approach, integrates explainable artificial intelligence, creates an extensive self-driving dataset, and constructs a high-accuracy end-to-end system. The results achieved a 74% reduction in parameters and a 2.6% improvement in detection precision. This paper [29] proposed a two-phase pipeline for enhancing driver situational awareness in Level 3 AD. GazeMobileNet model achieves state-of-the-art gaze vector estimation performance. The proposed method improves zone classification accuracy and robustness. This model achieves accuracies of 75.67% and 83.08% for attention zone estimation under various capture conditions, surpassing previous research. This study explored the gap between human-driving learning methods and self-driving systems [30]. It proposed a novel approach that incorporates human guidance into AV control, learning to summarize visual observations, predict actions, and adjust controls [31]. The proposed method, combining human advice with semantic representation, outperforms the previous methods in control prediction and explanation generation, resulting in more interpretable visual explanations. The Berkeley DeepDrive eXplanation (BDD-X) dataset, a new driving dataset featuring human explanations shown in Figure 3.3, is being evaluated for its effectiveness [32].

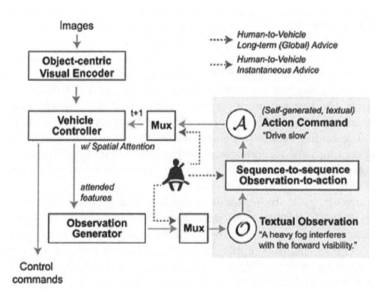

Figure 3.3 BDD-X Dataset.

AVs offer benefits like increased safety and reduced energy consumption, but these have security and privacy issues. Combining Blockchain and AI could provide strong protection against malicious attacks [33]. AI can optimize Blockchain construction, while Blockchain provides data immutability and trust mechanisms. This paper explored the potential application of Blockchain and AI solutions for AV security, identifying security and privacy threats, reviewing recent literature, and highlighting limitations and challenges. This paper [34] addressed the challenges of implementing AI in support of Automated Guided Vehicles (AGV) within smart internal logistics systems for agile manufacturing. The navigation system must be tailored to industrial environments with high interaction with other systems and human staff. AI's challenges differ from those of other smart manufacturing areas, and the paper systematizes these challenges and discusses promising AI methods for AGV-based internal logistics systems.

Automated navigation technology plays a crucial role in intelligent transportation and smart city systems. XAI aims to streamline decision-making processes in AVs, enhancing trust in AI-based solutions. Madhav and Tyagi [35] conducted a comparative analysis between XAI simulations and vehicular smart systems, emphasizing noteworthy advancements. The study introduced visual explanatory techniques and an intrusion detection classifier, yielding substantial improvements over existing research. The study proposed a post-processing mathematical framework to improve the accuracy of stereo vision in generating high-density depth values for AD [36]. The framework uses prior information from a deep learning-based U-Net model to refine the depth achieved, making it explainable and applicable to depth maps generated by any stereo vision algorithm. The framework's results show improvements in stereo depth generation accuracy.

Keneni et al. investigated the explanation of autonomous system decisions using an Unmanned Aerial Vehicle (UAV) [37]. It achieved a simulation using 15 fuzzy rules, considering weather conditions and enemies. It created two ANFIS models, one for the weather zone and the other for distance from the enemy. The best optimization is generating six fuzzy rules for the Sugeno model, which are easily comprehensible and maintain acceptable RMSE values. The findings show promising results for integrating ANFIS models with upcoming UAV technologies to make UAVs more transparent, understandable, and trustworthy. AD has gained popularity because of its potential benefits, including increased safety, traffic efficiency, and fuel economy [26]. However, most studies focus on limited data sets or fully automated environments. To address these issues, an XAI Federated Deep Reinforcement Learning (RL) model improves trajectory decisions for newcomer AVs. The model uses XAI to compute the contribution of each vehicle's features, ensuring trustworthiness. Experiments show this model outperforms benchmark solutions like Deep Q-Network and Random Selection [38].

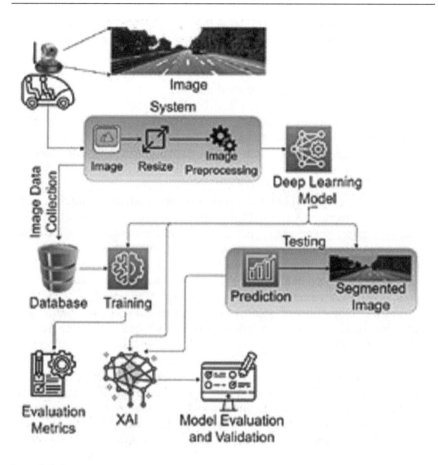

Figure 3.4 Semantic segmentation with XAI.

AVs are increasingly using AI to reduce driver stress and improve learning [39]. XAI techniques help developers understand the intricate workings of deep learning models, also known as black box models. The authors focused on how AVs can detect and segment the road using deep learning models, achieving high IoU scores [39]. Figure 3.4 illustrates the system model integration of XAI for model explanation, which includes semantic segmentation of an input frame.

Soares et al. proposed a new self-organizing neuro-fuzzy approach for self-driving cars, combining explainable self-organizing architecture and density-based feature selection methods [40]. The approach classifies action states from different self-driving conditions, providing humans with understandable IF . . . THEN rules. The density-based feature selection method ranks feature densities, creating individualized subsets per class. Experiments on a

Ford Motor Company dataset validated the approach's accuracy and showed it could surpass competitors. In Rjoub et al. [41], a trust-aware approach to AV selection, incorporating the Local Interpretable Model-Agnostic Explanations (LIME) method and One-Shot Federated Learning, was proposed. This method outperforms the standard approach in terms of both accuracy and reliability, demonstrating the effectiveness of trust metrics in AV selection in federated learning systems.

Bellotti *et al.* proposed a framework for understanding autonomous agent decision-making in a highway simulation environment [42]. Data analysis includes episode timeline, frame-by-frame, and aggregated statistical analysis. Motivators include longitudinal gap, lane position, and last-frame patterns. Attention and SHAP values are differentiated, reflecting the neural network's architecture. Xu et al. [43] presented a multi-task formulation for action prediction and explanations of AD. The authors proposed a CNN architecture that combines reasoning about action-inducing objects and global scene context. They also present a large dataset annotated for both driving commands and explanations. The experiments show that the generation of explanations improves decision-making for actions, and both benefit from a combination of object-centric and global scene reasoning [43]. Mankodiya et al. proposed an XAI system in VANETs (Vehicular Ad-Hoc Networks) to enhance trust management in AVs [44]. Figure 3.5 illustrates the system model employed for training and predicting malicious AVs. The system uses a decision tree-based random forest to solve a problem with 98.44% accuracy and an F1 score on the VeRiMi dataset. The authors evaluated the proposed model using performance measures and metrics, making it interpretable and serving the purpose of XAI. Overall, the paper aims to increase transparency and trust in AI models used in AVs.

Cultrera *et al.* presented an attention-based model for AD in a simulated environment [45]. The model uses visual attention to improve driving performance and provide explainable predictions. The model achieves state-of-the-art results on the CARLA driving benchmark. The architecture includes a multi-head design, with each head specialized for different driving commands. The attention layer assigns weights to image regions based on their relevance to the driving task. The model adopts a fixed grid to obtain an attention map of the image. Nowak et al. discussed the importance of explainable AI in law and the challenges faced in training neural networks for intelligent vehicles [46]. It highlights the need for interpretability in deep learning systems and the use of attention heat maps to improve training and eliminate misdetections. The system's interpretation helps eliminate misdetections by explaining which parts of the images triggered the decision, enhancing the reliability of vehicle autonomy.

The document also emphasizes the importance of data adequacy and the limitations of acquiring more data in real-life conditions. Dong et al. [47]

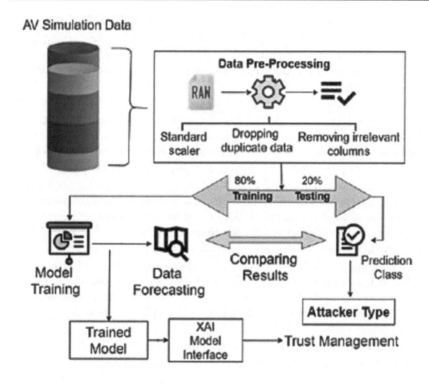

Figure 3.5 Model for XAI-AV system.

proposed a state-of-the-art (SOTA) self-attention-based model used in an explainable end-to-end autonomous driving system. This model uses deep learning computer vision (DLCV) based AV systems to guide potential driving actions and explanations. The model outperforms the benchmark model in terms of action and explanation prediction, demonstrating the efficacy of deep learning in computer vision applications.

Saravanarajan *et al.* proposed a method for improving semantic segmentation of AVs in hazy weather conditions [48]. The approach combines XAI and Adaptive Dehazing (AD) techniques. The authors trained a deep learning network using a dataset augmented with synthesized haze images. The results show improved performance in semantic segmentation compared to the network trained without haze augmentation. XAI was used to visualize network behavior and provide insights into the segmentation process. The proposed method has the potential to enhance the perception capabilities of AVs in hazy weather conditions. This article discussed the concept of Federated Learning (FL) of XAI models, known as FED-XAI [49]. The authors highlight the need for trustworthiness and explainability in AI systems, especially in the upcoming 6G era. They proposed FED-XAI as a framework that combines FL for privacy preservation and collaborative training of AI models with the goal of ensuring adequate explainability of the models. The article also discusses the challenges and potential applications of FED-XAI in various domains, including AD and V2X systems.

Deep neural networks are crucial for AD, particularly in visual perception [50]. They are essential for the explainability and inspectability of vehicle algorithms, which are crucial for legal, insurance, and engineering issues. The authors proposed a tiered approach based on semantic segmentation for an autonomous driving system. This approach provides meaningful explanations for decisions, addresses computational limitations in production vehicles, and allows input for interpretable autonomous driving systems [50]. Wang et al. [51] presented a method called IVMP (Intelligent Vehicle Motion Planning) that combines a semantic map forecasting module and a motion planning module for AVs. The semantic map forecasting module predicts future egocentric semantic maps in bird's-eye-view (BEV) space, while the motion planning module generates trajectories for self-driving vehicles (SDVs). The proposed method uses knowledge distillation techniques to enhance the student network based on the teacher network's dark knowledge. The results show improved performance in semantic map forecasting and motion planning tasks.

Scalas and Giacinto [52] discussed the importance of explainability in smart vehicles, particularly in machine learning algorithms. The authors highlight the need for explanations in both safety-critical and non-safety-critical ML-based algorithms. They explore the role of explanations in gaining trust in the decisions made by the system and discuss the different goals, stakeholders, and techniques involved in generating explanations. The paper also emphasizes the impact of explainability on the security of modern vehicles and concludes by discussing key points and concerns related to interpretability [52].

RL is a powerful tool for training artificial intelligence agents in uncertain environments, including aerospace. However, challenges in characterizing performance boundaries, explaining decision-making logic, and quantifying uncertainties hinder its adoption in real-time systems. This paper presented a three-part test and evaluation framework for RL, incorporating robustness testing, Explainable AI techniques like Shapley Additive Explanations, and validation of outputs with known solutions [53]. The framework is applied to a high-speed aerospace vehicle emergency descent problem, revealing significant features affecting RL selection. Omeiza et al. proposed an interpretable and user-centric approach to explaining autonomous driving behaviors [27]. It examines different explanation types and their impact on scenarios, focusing on emergency and collision driving conditions. The study finds that providing intelligible explanations with causal attributions can improve accountability in AD, and the proposed interpretable approach can help achieve this.

3.3 CHALLENGES AND LIMITATIONS OF XAI
IN AUTONOMOUS VEHICLES

Despite the intensive application of XAI in AD, there are still challenges that researchers need to look at. Starting from the terminology used in XAI, the research community needs to agree on the terms and the definitions sufficiently. Although such challenges are not limited to the applications of XAI in AD, it would still help a lot to come up with a unified terminology around XAI. For example, as explained by Arrieta *et al.* [54], there is a lack of consensus on the definition of XAI by D. Gunning [55], where XAI is defined by bringing understanding and trust concepts and missing other concepts such as causality, transferability, informativeness, fairness and confidence [56–58]. Other examples are the synonyms of terminology, such as *feature importance, feature relevance*, and subjectivity in explanation [59, 60]. Keeping in mind that an explainable system always considers reasoning without human post-processing as a final step of the generative process [56] or combining reasoning with human-understandable features [61]. Another challenge is related to the accessibility of the explanations to society and policymakers. The explanation of decisions was approved in 2016 by the European Union General Data Protection Regulation (GDPR), which was viewed as a promising way to conduct accountability and transparency. However, there are some uncertainties regarding their transparency and accountability [62].

The trade-off between accuracy, interpretability, and explainability poses a great challenge in XAI. For instance, making a black box model explainable does not mean having good performance. In fact, explaining black box models sometimes results in other problems. Instead, one should also add some degree of interpretability. Rudin *et al.* [63] stated that "higher complexity does not inherently mean higher accuracy, and this has been very true for such DL models." Figure 3.6 shows why there is an urgent effort to focus on improving both the performance and explainability of the model. As can be seen, models with good performance tend to have lower explainability. Hence, a reasonable trade-off is required.

The use of XAI raises several concerns regarding the lack of explanation and discrimination due to unfair bias and predictive parity [64, 65]. Data sets with private and sensitive data may disproportionately affect underrepresented groups [66]. Using these data sets leads to discriminatory, unethical, and unfair issues [67]. To solve bias issues, several studies were proposed. Kamiran *et al.* [68] proposed removing the discrimination before a classifier is learned by reweighting the data sets. Others presented a technique to optimize the representation of the data [69]. Moreover, other techniques were presented, including bias detection, adversarial debiasing during data processing, and equalized odds for post-processing [70–73].

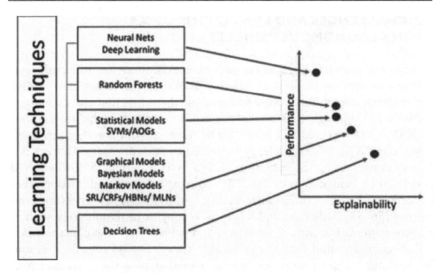

Figure 3.6 Comparison of different ML techniques, explainability, and performance (as presented by DARPA) [64].

One important goal of XAI is *transferability*, in which explainability helps to elucidate the model boundaries. The transferability of post hoc explanation methods is considered a major challenge in XAI. Post hoc explainability is required for improving the interpretability of a black box model. Figure 3.7 shows an example of a post hoc explanation, where an example is provided as evidence for why a specific prediction is given. As these post hoc methods are designed to explain specific models, they may fail for other models. Thus, generalized methods that are explainable with different post hoc methods present an open challenge.

Other challenges related to the application of XAI in AD are related to both scientific and social aspects. Hussain *et al.* [75] discussed the challenges of XAI in AV from an "engineering" perspective. In an autonomous car, XAI is highly environment and domain-dependent, especially with the existence of GDPR. One of the reasons behind this challenge is the variation in stakeholders, as different stakeholders mean different requirements. Therefore, it is expected to take a long time to achieve XAI generalization and adaptation.

An obvious challenge regarding the application of XAI in AD is its security. Although security concerns were raised in the context of AD [76, 77], the adversarial learning [78, 79] for XAI remains relatively unexplored. Moreover, the transparency and explainable nature of XAI makes it more susceptible to cybersecurity attention. Vigano *et al.* [80] proposed the Explainable Security (XSec), where they discussed the "Six Ws" of XSec (Who? What? Where? When? Why? and How?) as shown in Figure 3.8, where each "W"

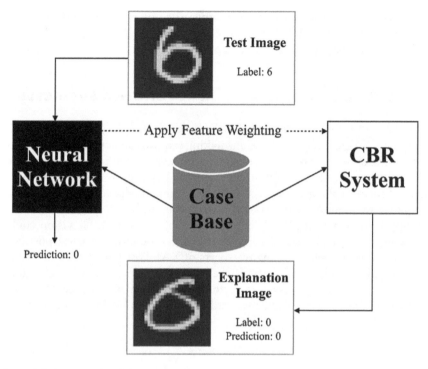

Figure 3.7 An example of post hoc explanation [74].

Figure 3.8 The Six Ws of explainable security [80].

helps to elevate the security of XAI. Other attempts to enhance the security of XAI are providing a taxonomy for XAI methods [81], Structured adversarial attacks [82], and explaining explanations [83].

3.4 FUTURE TRENDS IN XAI FOR AUTONOMOUS VEHICLES

The study of future trends of the XAI relies on current knowledge and challenges. In XAI for AD, any decision-making requires an explanation from its intelligent driving system. These explanations are in the form of visual and textual forms or feature importance scores [16]. Figure 3.9 explains how textual form explanation is used in an autonomous driving task. A natural language text summarizes a visual observation and is then used to predict an appropriate action [32]. The importance of an explainable vision could be achieved through post hoc explanations. As mentioned earlier, post hoc explanations are helpful in many aspects of XAI. Post hoc explanations can be a simple yet effective method when making a decision when a regulatory investigation is required, as in the "Molly Problem," where "A young girl called Molly is crossing the road alone and is hit by an unoccupied

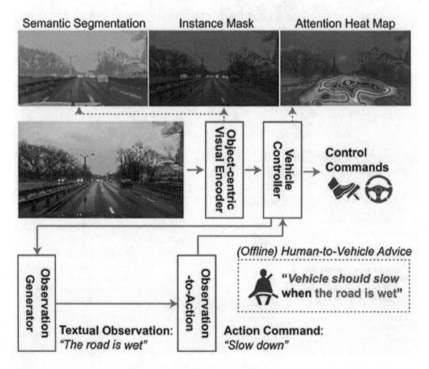

Figure 3.9 An example of textual explanation in AD [32].

self-driving vehicle. There are no eyewitnesses. What should happen next?".
Post hoc explanations provided a rationale for how the vehicle continued to
drive and caused the accident. This strategy helps investigations in a regulatory compliance environment. Therefore, future research is expected to continue in fields related to the reliability of post hoc explanations, especially
for critical traffic scenarios.

Recently, RL was viewed as a promising method in the autonomous driving
field. Unlike supervised learning, RL is effectively able to learn through trial
and error without supervision [84]. Complex AD tasks can be tackled by merging RL and DL techniques. For example, training agents with DL was found
to reach a high-performance level in robotics [85, 86] and gaming [87, 88].
RL can handle AD through the Markov Decision Process (MDP), since the
decision-making during driving can be considered a sequential problem. In
model-based RL, the learning can be explainable since the agent first learns
the model of the environment and then adjusts the policy according to its
dynamics [89, 90]. Learning a model in RL facilitates the explainability of
the model. For example, Sutton *et al.* [91–93] introduced Dyna, which learns
a world model while learning the optimal policy through interacting with
the world. This way, the model is considered explainable due to the fact that
the agent is able to choose an optimal action at a particular time step. These
results promote RL as vital for XAI in future research work, as it becomes
possible for an agent to provide intuitive explanations.

3.5 CONCLUSION

Explainable artificial intelligence (XAI) generally emerged to address the
ambiguity inside AI algorithms while preserving high-level performances.
The chapter presents the application of XAI in autonomous driving (AD).
The focus of XAI is to provide explanations, aiding end-users in comprehending and effectively managing AI systems related to AD. The explainability
involves providing insights to a targeted audience, such as domain experts,
end-users, and modeling experts, to fulfill their needs and ensure they make
sense of their domain knowledge. Several examples of XAI in AD are shown
to give a clear understanding of how XAI affects AD. Currently, XAI in
autonomous AD faces many challenges and limitations in order to fulfill its
expectations. In this chapter, we divided these challenges into two types, i.e.,
challenges related to the terminology and definition of XAI and challenges
related to the application of XAI in AVs. Unified terminology, explainability,
transferability, interpretability, and security of XAI are examples of general
challenges that the research community faces. Moreover, society and policymakers play a crucial role in conducting XAI. These challenges are extended
to AD by including the nature of AD as an application of XAI. For example,

integrating XAI in AD is expected to help investigations in a regulatory compliance environment. In the near future, XAI is expected to continue growing to overcome the current challenges. Reinforcement learning is expected to gain more attention due to the ability to get intuitive explanations, which helps to improve the performance of ML in AD.

REFERENCES

[1] S. Surdonja, T. Giuffr'e, and A. Deluka-Tibljaš, "Smart mobility solutions–necessary pre-condition for a well-functioning smart city," *Transportation Research Procedia*, vol. 45, pp. 604–611, 2020.

[2] S. Kuutti, S. Fallah, K. Katsaros, M. Dianati, F. Mccullough, and A. Mouzakitis, "A survey of the state-of-the-art localization techniques and their potentials for autonomous vehicle applications," *IEEE Internet of Things Journal*, vol. 5, no. 2, pp. 829–846, 2018.

[3] I. Yaqoob, L. U. Khan, S. A. Kazmi, M. Imran, N. Guizani, and C. S. Hong, "Autonomous driving cars in smart cities: Recent advances, requirements, and challenges," *IEEE Network*, vol. 34, no. 1, pp. 174–181, 2019.

[4] J. Harding, G. Powell, R. Yoon, J. Fikentscher, C. Doyle, D. Sade, M. Lukuc, J. Simons, J. Wang, *et al.*, *Vehicle-to-vehicle Communications: Readiness of v2v Technology for Application* (tech. rep., United States). National Highway Traffic Safety Administration, 2014.

[5] L. Liang, H. Peng, G. Y. Li, and X. Shen, "Vehicular communications: A physical layer perspective," *IEEE Transactions on Vehicular Technology*, vol. 66, no. 12, pp. 10647–10659, 2017.

[6] H. Peng, L. Liang, X. Shen, and G. Y. Li, "Vehicular communications: A network layer perspective," *IEEE Transactions on Vehicular Technology*, vol. 68, no. 2, pp. 1064–1078, 2018.

[7] H. Ye, L. Liang, G. Y. Li, J. Kim, L. Lu, and M. Wu, "Machine learning for vehicular networks: Recent advances and application examples," *IEEE Vehicular Technology Magazine*, vol. 13, no. 2, pp. 94–101, 2018.

[8] K. C. Dey, A. Rayamajhi, M. Chowdhury, P. Bhavsar, and J. Martin, "Vehicle-tovehicle (v2v) and vehicle-to-infrastructure (v2i) communication in a heterogeneous wireless network–performance evaluation," *Transportation Research Part C: Emerging Technologies*, vol. 68, pp. 168–184, 2016.

[9] F. Zhou, Y. Li, and Y. Ding, "Practical v2i secure communication schemes for heterogeneous VANETS," *Applied Sciences*, vol. 9, no. 15, p. 3131, 2019.

[10] M. Placek, *Connected Cars Worldwide—Statistics and Facts*. www.statista.com/topics/1918/connected-cars/. Accessed: 2023–08–21.

[11] S. Grigorescu, B. Trasnea, T. Cocias, and G. Macesanu, "A survey of deep learning techniques for autonomous driving," *Journal of Field Robotics*, vol. 37, no. 3, pp. 362–386, 2020.

[12] Y. Ma, Z. Wang, H. Yang, and L. Yang, "Artificial intelligence applications in the development of autonomous vehicles: A survey," *IEEE/CAA Journal of Automatica Sinica*, vol. 7, no. 2, pp. 315–329, 2020.

[13] A. Adadi and M. Berrada, "Peeking inside the black-box: A survey on explainable artificial intelligence (XAI)," *IEEE Access*, vol. 6, pp. 52138–52160, 2018.

[14] S. Atakishiyev, M. Salameh, H. Yao, and R. Goebel, "Towards safe, explainable, and regulated autonomous driving," *arXiv preprint arXiv:2111.10518*, 2021.

[15] D. Omeiza, H. Webb, M. Jirotka, and L. Kunze, "Explanations in autonomous driving: A survey," *IEEE Transactions on Intelligent Transportation Systems*, vol. 23, no. 8, pp. 10142–10162, 2021.

[16] S. Atakishiyev, M. Salameh, H. Yao, and R. Goebel, "Explainable artificial intelligence for autonomous driving: A comprehensive overview and field guide for future research directions," *arXiv preprint arXiv:2112.11561*, 2021.

[17] M. N. Ahangar, Q. Z. Ahmed, F. A. Khan, and M. Hafeez, "A survey of autonomous vehicles: Enabling communication technologies and challenges," *Sensors*, vol. 21, no. 3, p. 706, 2021.

[18] A. Biswas and H.-C. Wang, "Autonomous vehicles enabled by the integration of IoT, edge intelligence, 5g, and blockchain," *Sensors*, vol. 23, no. 4, p. 1963, 2023.

[19] P. P. Angelov, E. A. Soares, R. Jiang, N. I. Arnold, and P. M. Atkinson, "Explainable artificial intelligence: an analytical review," *Wiley Interdisciplinary Reviews: Data Mining and Knowledge Discovery*, vol. 11, no. 5, p. e1424, 2021.

[20] A. Chaddad, J. Peng, J. Xu, and A. Bouridane, "Survey of explainable AI techniques in healthcare," *Sensors*, vol. 23, no. 2, p. 634, 2023.

[21] V. Chamola, V. Hassija, A. R. Sulthana, D. Ghosh, D. Dhingra, and B. Sikdar, "A review of trustworthy and explainable artificial intelligence (XAI)," *IEEE Access*, p. 1, 2023. https://doi.org/10.1109/ACCESS.2023.3294569

[22] W. Saeed and C. Omlin, "Explainable Ai (XAI): A systematic meta-survey of current challenges and future opportunities," *Knowledge-Based Systems*, vol. 263, p. 110273, 2023.

[23] M. Nagahisarchoghaei, N. Nur, L. Cummins, N. Nur, M. M. Karimi, S. Nandanwar, S. Bhattacharyya, and S. Rahimi, "An empirical survey on explainable AI technologies: Recent trends, use-cases, and categories from technical and application perspectives," *Electronics*, vol. 12, no. 5, p. 1092, 2023.

[24] R. Deshpande and P. Ambatkar, "Interpretable deep learning models: Enhancing transparency and trustworthiness in explainable AI," *Proceeding International Conference on Science and Engineering*, vol. 11, p. 1352–1363, 2023.

[25] G. P. Reddy and Y. V. P. Kumar, "Explainable AI (XAI): Explained," in *2023 IEEE Open Conference of Electrical, Electronic and Information Sciences (eStream)*, pp. 1–6, IEEE, 2023. https://doi.org/10.1109/eStream59056.2023.10134984

[26] S. Ali, T. Abuhmed, S. El-Sappagh, K. Muhammad, J. M. Alonso-Moral, R. Confalonieri, R. Guidotti, J. Del Ser, N. Díaz-Rodríguez, and F. Herrera, "Explainable artificial intelligence (XAI): What we know and what is left to attain trustworthy artificial intelligence," *Information Fusion*, vol. 99, p. 101805, 2023.

[27] D. Omeiza, H. Web, M. Jirotka, and L. Kunze, "Towards accountability: Providing intelligible explanations in autonomous driving," in *2021 IEEE Intelligent Vehicles Symposium (IV)*, pp. 231–237, IEEE, 2021.

[28] Y. Li, H. Wang, L. M. Dang, T. N. Nguyen, D. Han, A. Lee, I. Jang, and H. Moon, "A deep learning-based hybrid framework for object detection and recognition in autonomous driving," *IEEE Access*, vol. 8, pp. 194228–194239, 2020.

[29] R. Yahyaabadi and S. Nikan, "An explainable attention zone estimation for level 3 autonomous driving," *IEEE Access*, vol. 11, pp. 93098–93110, 2023. https://doi.org/10.1109/ACCESS.2023.3309810

[30] J. Kim, A. Rohrbach, Z. Akata, S. Moon, T. Misu, Y.-T. Chen, T. Darrell, and J. Canny, "Toward explainable and advisable model for self-driving cars," *Applied AI Letters*, vol. 2, no. 4, p. e56, 2021.

[31] J. Kim and J. Canny, "Interpretable learning for self-driving cars by visualizing causal attention," in *Proceedings of the IEEE International Conference on Computer Vision*, pp. 2942–2950, IEEE, 2017. https://doi.org/10.1109/ICCV.2017.320

[32] J. Kim, S. Moon, A. Rohrbach, T. Darrell, and J. Canny, "Advisable learning for self-driving vehicles by internalizing observation-to-action rules," in *Proceedings of the IEEE/CVF Conference on Computer Vision and Pattern Recognition*, pp. 9661–9670, IEEE, 2020. https://doi.org/10.1109/CVPR42600.2020.00968

[33] G. Bendiab, A. Hameurlaine, G. Germanos, N. Kolokotronis, and S. Shiaeles, "Autonomous vehicles security: Challenges and solutions using blockchain and artificial intelligence," *IEEE Transactions on Intelligent Transportation Systems*, vol. 24, no. 4, pp. 3614–3637, 2023. https://doi.org/10.1109/TITS.2023.3236274

[34] R. Cupek, J. C.-W. Lin, and J. Syu, "Automated guided vehicles challenges for artificial intelligence," in *2022 IEEE International Conference on Big Data (Big Data)*, pp. 6281–6289, IEEE, 2022.

[35] A. S. Madhav and A. K. Tyagi, "Explainable artificial intelligence (XAI): connecting artificial decision-making and human trust in autonomous vehicles," in *Proceedings of Third International Conference on Computing, Communications, and Cyber-Security: IC4S 2021*, pp. 123–136, Springer, 2022.

[36] W. Li, V. John, and S. Mita, "Enhancing depth quality of stereo vision using deep learning-based prior information of the driving environment," in *2020 25th International Conference on Pattern Recognition (ICPR)*, pp. 7281–7286, IEEE, 2021.

[37] B. M. Keneni, D. Kaur, A. Al Bataineh, V. K. Devabhaktuni, A. Y. Javaid, J. D. Zaientz, and R. P. Marinier, "Evolving rule-based explainable artificial intelligence for unmanned aerial vehicles," *IEEE Access*, vol. 7, pp. 17001–17016, 2019.

[38] G. Rjoub, J. Bentahar, and O. A. Wahab, "Explainable ai-based federated deep reinforcement learning for trusted autonomous driving," in *2022 International Wireless Communications and Mobile Computing (IWCMC)*, pp. 318–323, IEEE, 2022.

[39] H. Mankodiya, D. Jadav, R. Gupta, S. Tanwar, W.-C. Hong, and R. Sharma, "OD-XAI: Explainable AI-based semantic object detection for autonomous vehicles," *Applied Sciences*, vol. 12, no. 11, p. 5310, 2022.

[40] E. Soares, P. Angelov, D. Filev, B. Costa, M. Castro, and S. Nageshrao, "Explainable density-based approach for self-driving actions classification," in *2019 18th IEEE International Conference On Machine Learning And Applications (ICMLA)*, pp. 469–474, IEEE, 2019.

[41] G. Rjoub, J. Bentahar, and O. A. Wahab, "Explainable trust-aware selection of autonomous vehicles using lime for one-shot federated learning," in *2023 International Wireless Communications and Mobile Computing (IWCMC)*, pp. 524–529, IEEE, 2023.

[42] F. Bellotti, L. Lazzaroni, A. Capello, M. Cossu, A. De Gloria, and R. Berta, "Explaining a deep reinforcement learning (drl)-based automated driving agent in highway simulations," *IEEE Access*, vol. 11, pp. 28522–28550, 2023.

[43] Y. Xu, X. Yang, L. Gong, H.-C. Lin, T.-Y. Wu, Y. Li, and N. Vasconcelos, "Explainable object-induced action decision for autonomous vehicles," in *Proceedings of the IEEE/CVF Conference on Computer Vision and Pattern Recognition*, pp. 9523–9532, IEEE, 2020.

[44] H. Mankodiya, M. S. Obaidat, R. Gupta, and S. Tanwar, "XAI-AV: Explainable artificial intelligence for trust management in autonomous vehicles," in *2021 International Conference on Communications, Computing, Cybersecurity, and Informatics (CCCI)*, pp. 1–5, IEEE, 2021.

[45] L. Cultrera, L. Seidenari, F. Becattini, P. Pala, and A. Del Bimbo, "Explaining autonomous driving by learning end-to-end visual attention," in *Proceedings of the IEEE/CVF Conference on Computer Vision and Pattern Recognition Workshops*, pp. 340–341, IEEE, 2020.

[46] T. Nowak, M. R. Nowicki, K. Cwian, and P. Skrzypczyn´ski, "How to improve object detection in a driver assistance system applying explainable deep learning," in *2019 IEEE Intelligent Vehicles Symposium (IV)*, pp. 226–231, IEEE, 2019.

[47] J. Dong, S. Chen, S. Zong, T. Chen, and S. Labi, "Image transformer for explainable autonomous driving system," in *2021 IEEE International Intelligent Transportation Systems Conference (ITSC)*, pp. 2732–2737, IEEE, 2021.

[48] V. S. Saravanarajan, R.-C. Chen, C.-H. Hsieh, and L.-S. Chen, "Improving semantic segmentation under hazy weather for autonomous vehicles using explainable artificial intelligence and adaptive dehazing approach," *IEEE Access*, vol. 11, pp. 38194–38207, 2023.

[49] A. Renda, P. Ducange, F. Marcelloni, D. Sabella, M. C. Filippou, G. Nardini, G. Stea, A. Virdis, D. Micheli, D. Rapone, et al., "Federated learning of explainable AI models in 6g systems: Towards secure and automated vehicle networking," *Information*, vol. 13, no. 8, p. 395, 2022.

[50] M. Hofmarcher, T. Unterthiner, J. Arjona-Medina, G. Klambauer, S. Hochreiter, and B. Nessler, "Visual scene understanding for autonomous driving using semantic segmentation," in W. Samek, G. Montavon, A. Vedaldi, L.

Hansen, and K. R. Müller (eds.), *Explainable AI: Interpreting, Explaining and Visualizing Deep Learning*, vol. 11700, pp. 285–296, Springer, 2019. https://doi.org/10.1007/978-3-030-28954-6_15

[51] H. Wang, P. Cai, Y. Sun, L. Wang, and M. Liu, "Learning interpretable end-to-end vision-based motion planning for autonomous driving with optical flow distillation," in *2021 IEEE International Conference on Robotics and Automation (ICRA)*, pp. 13731–13737, IEEE, 2021.

[52] M. Scalas and G. Giacinto, "On the role of explainable machine learning for secure smart vehicles," in *2020 AEIT International Conference of Electrical and Electronic Technologies for Automotive (AEIT AUTOMOTIVE)*, pp. 1–6, IEEE, 2020.

[53] A. K. Raz, S. M. Nolan, W. Levin, K. Mall, A. Mia, L. Mockus, K. Ezra, and K. Williams, "Test and evaluation of reinforcement learning via robustness testing and explainable AI for high-speed aerospace vehicles," in *2022 IEEE Aerospace Conference (AERO)*, pp. 1–14, IEEE, 2022.

[54] A. B. Arrieta, N. Díaz-Rodríguez, J. Del Ser, A. Bennetot, S. Tabik, A. Barbado, S. García, S. Gil-López, D. Molina, R. Benjamins, et al., "Explainable artificial intelligence (XAI): Concepts, taxonomies, opportunities and challenges toward responsible ai," *Information Fusion*, vol. 58, pp. 82–115, 2020.

[55] D. Gunning, "Explainable artificial intelligence (XAI)," *Defense Advanced Research Projects Agency (DARPA), and Web*, vol. 2, no. 2, p. 1, 2017.

[56] D. Doran, S. Schulz, and T. R. Besold, "What does explainable AI really mean? A new conceptualization of perspectives," *arXiv preprint arXiv:1710.00794*, 2017.

[57] Z. C. Lipton, "The mythos of model interpretability: In machine learning, the concept of interpretability is both important and slippery," *Queue*, vol. 16, no. 3, pp. 31–57, 2018.

[58] A. Vellido, J. D. Martín-Guerrero, and P. J. Lisboa, "Making machine learning models interpretable." in *ESANN*, vol. 12, pp. 163–172, Citeseer, 2012.

[59] A. Preece, D. Harborne, D. Braines, R. Tomsett, and S. Chakraborty, "Stakeholders in explainable ai," *arXiv preprint arXiv:1810.00184*, 2018.

[60] T. Miller, "Explanation in artificial intelligence: Insights from the social sciences," *Artificial Intelligence*, vol. 267, pp. 1–38, 2019.

[61] A. Bennetot, J.-L. Laurent, R. Chatila, and N. Díaz-Rodríguez, "Towards explainable neural-symbolic visual reasoning," *arXiv preprint arXiv:1909.09065*, 2019.

[62] S. Wachter, B. Mittelstadt, and L. Floridi, "Why a right to explanation of automated decision-making does not exist in the general data protection regulation," *International Data Privacy Law*, vol. 7, no. 2, pp. 76–99, 2017.

[63] C. Rudin, "Stop explaining black box machine learning models for high stakes decisions and use interpretable models instead," *Nature Machine Intelligence*, vol. 1, no. 5, pp. 206–215, 2019.

[64] C. O'Neil, *Weapons of Math Destruction: How Big Data Increases Inequality and Threatens Democracy*. Crown, 2017.

[65] R. Benjamins, A. Barbado, and D. Sierra, "Responsible AI by design in practice," *arXiv preprint arXiv:1909.12838*, 2019.

[66] A. Rawal, J. McCoy, D. B. Rawat, B. M. Sadler, and R. S. Amant, "Recent advances in trustworthy explainable artificial intelligence: Status, challenges,

and perspectives," *IEEE Transactions on Artificial Intelligence*, vol. 3, no. 6, pp. 852–866, 2022.

[67] B. d'Alessandro, C. O'Neil, and T. LaGatta, "Conscientious classification: A data scientist's guide to discrimination-aware classification," *Big Data*, vol. 5, no. 2, pp. 120–134, 2017. PMID: 28632437.

[68] F. Kamiran and T. Calders, "Data preprocessing techniques for classification without discrimination," *Knowledge and Information Systems*, vol. 33, no. 1, pp. 1–33, 2012.

[69] R. Zemel, Y. Wu, K. Swersky, T. Pitassi, and C. Dwork, "Learning fair representations," in *International Conference on Machine Learning*, pp. 325–333, PMLR, 2013.

[70] M. Hardt, E. Price, and N. Srebro, "Equality of opportunity in supervised learning," *Advances in Neural Information Processing Systems*, vol. 29, 2016.

[71] B. H. Zhang, B. Lemoine, and M. Mitchell, "Mitigating unwanted biases with adversarial learning," in *Proceedings of the 2018 AAAI/ACM Conference on AI, Ethics, and Society (AIES '18)*, pp. 335–340, Association for Computing Machinery, 2018. https://doi.org/10.1145/3278721.3278779

[72] Y. Ahn and Y.-R. Lin, "Fairsight: Visual analytics for fairness in decision making," *IEEE transactions on Visualization and Computer Graphics*, vol. 26, no. 1, pp. 1086–1095, 2019.

[73] E. Soares and P. Angelov, "Fair-by-design explainable models for prediction of recidivism," *arXiv preprint arXiv:1910.02043*, 2019.

[74] E. M. Kenny, C. Ford, M. Quinn, and M. T. Keane, "Explaining black-box classifiers using post-hoc explanations-by-example: The effect of explanations and error-rates in XAI user studies," *Artificial Intelligence*, vol. 294, p. 103459, 2021.

[75] F. Hussain, R. Hussain, and E. Hossain, "Explainable artificial intelligence (XAI): An engineering perspective," *arXiv preprint arXiv:2101.03613*, 2021.

[76] A. Nanda, D. Puthal, J. J. Rodrigues, and S. A. Kozlov, "Internet of autonomous vehicles communications security: overview, issues, and directions," *IEEE Wireless Communications*, vol. 26, no. 4, pp. 60–65, 2019.

[77] M. Koschuch, W. Sebron, Z. Szalay, A. Török, H. Tschiürtz, and I. Wahl, "Safety & security in the context of autonomous driving," in *2019 IEEE International Conference on Connected Vehicles and Expo (ICCVE)*, pp. 1–7, IEEE, 2019.

[78] N. Akhtar and A. Mian, "Threat of adversarial attacks on deep learning in computer vision: A survey," *IEEE Access*, vol. 6, pp. 14410–14430, 2018.

[79] K. Ren, T. Zheng, Z. Qin, and X. Liu, "Adversarial attacks and defenses in deep learning," *Engineering*, vol. 6, no. 3, pp. 346–360, 2020.

[80] L. Vigano and D. Magazzeni, "Explainable security," in *2020 IEEE European Symposium on Security and Privacy Workshops (EuroS&PW)*, pp. 293–300, IEEE, 2020.

[81] A. Kuppa and N.-A. Le-Khac, "Black box attacks on explainable artificial intelligence (XAI) methods in cyber security," in *2020 International Joint Conference on Neural Networks (IJCNN)*, pp. 1–8, IEEE, 2020.

[82] K. Xu, S. Liu, P. Zhao, P.-Y. Chen, H. Zhang, Q. Fan, D. Erdogmus, Y. Wang, and X. Lin, "Structured adversarial attack: Towards general implementation and better interpretability," *arXiv preprint arXiv:1808.01664*, 2018.

[83] B. Mittelstadt, C. Russell, and S. Wachter, "Explaining explanations in ai," in *Proceedings of the Conference on Fairness, Accountability, and Transparency (FAT* '19)*, pp. 279–288, Association for Computing Machinery, 2019. https://doi.org/10.1145/3287560.3287574

[84] K. Arulkumaran, M. P. Deisenroth, M. Brundage, and A. A. Bharath, "A brief survey of deep reinforcement learning," *arXiv preprint arXiv:1708.05866*, 2017.

[85] S. Levine, C. Finn, T. Darrell, and P. Abbeel, "End-to-end training of deep visuomotor policies," *The Journal of Machine Learning Research*, vol. 17, no. 1, pp. 1334–1373, 2016.

[86] D. Kalashnikov, A. Irpan, P. Pastor, J. Ibarz, A. Herzog, E. Jang, D. Quillen, E. Holly, M. Kalakrishnan, V. Vanhoucke, et al., "Scalable deep reinforcement learning for vision-based robotic manipulation," in *Conference on Robot Learning*, pp. 651–673, PMLR, 2018.

[87] V. Mnih, K. Kavukcuoglu, D. Silver, A. Graves, I. Antonoglou, D. Wierstra, and M. Riedmiller, "Playing atari with deep reinforcement learning," *arXiv preprint arXiv:1312.5602*, 2013.

[88] V. Mnih, K. Kavukcuoglu, D. Silver, A. A. Rusu, J. Veness, M. G. Bellemare, A. Graves, M. Riedmiller, A. K. Fidjeland, G. Ostrovski, et al., "Human-level control through deep reinforcement learning," *Nature*, vol. 518, no. 7540, pp. 529–533, 2015.

[89] H. Yao and C. Szepesvári, "Approximate policy iteration with linear action models," in *Proceedings of the AAAI Conference on Artificial Intelligence*, vol. 26, pp. 1212–1218, IEEE, 2012.

[90] T. M. Moerland, J. Broekens, A. Plaat, C. M. Jonker, *et al.*, "Model-based reinforcement learning: A survey," *Foundations and Trends® in Machine Learning*, vol. 16, no. 1, pp. 1–118, 2023.

[91] R. S. Sutton, "Dyna, an integrated architecture for learning, planning, and reacting," *ACM Sigart Bulletin*, vol. 2, no. 4, pp. 160–163, 1991.

[92] R. S. Sutton, C. Szepesvári, A. Geramifard, and M. P. Bowling, "Dyna-style planning with linear function approximation and prioritized sweeping," *arXiv preprint arXiv:1206.3285*, 2012.

[93] H. Yao, S. Bhatnagar, D. Diao, R. S. Sutton, and C. Szepesvári, "Multi-step dyna planning for policy evaluation and control," *Advances in Neural Information Processing Systems*, vol. 22, 2009.

Chapter 4

XAI applications in autonomous vehicles

Lina E. Alatabani and Rashid A. Saeed

4.1 INTRODUCTION

XAI became evident recently as it discusses different techniques and approaches to break the complexity of machine learning (ML) models and construct human-level clarifications and explanations. These explanations would provide a simplified outcome, which results in a clearer view of the overall model.

XAI is mostly useful in models that produce decisions; such models are used to improve the performance of autonomous vehicles. What makes XAI important is that it provides trust; in other words, it is vital to explain these decisions in order to trust them. Furthermore, XAI detects and comprehends the bias in these decisions, enabling the system to eliminate bias [1]. It uses a set of techniques to produce explainability to a complex ML model.

Artificial Intelligence AI provides data-driven decision-making systems with a number of algorithms ranging from primitive to simple, such as linear regression, logistic regression, and decision tree (DT). These models are not as precise as they should be; however, more complex ML models would naturally serve the quality of real-world data more accurately and efficiently as real data are highly non-linear and complex in nature, which makes the processing of this huge amount of data challenging. Deep Nural Network (DNN) was introduced to overcome the non-linearity and complexity of real-world data as it extracts useful information from these huge datasets [2]. Following the use of DNNs, researchers have concluded that deeper networks are better in producing decisions than shallow networks [3]. Extracting patterns from complex datasets needs a DNN to be trained using large datasets. DNN uses a set of convolutional filters/kernels to highlight all the variations resulting from the non-linearity of the real data, and this provides highly performed AI models. Nevertheless, the addition of filters adds more pressure to the next layer; therefore, even shallow networks might have several layers with a number of filters and neurons. As a result, DNN for complex applications might have a huge number of parameters counting to millions and even billions; the primary representations and flows with

DOI: 10.1201/9781003502432-4

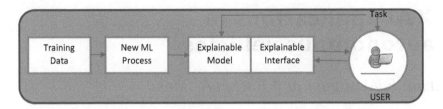

Figure 4.1 XAI positioning within a model.

network layers are hard to examine as the network complexity becomes higher [4].

Many factors influence both the structural design of DNN models and learning techniques, which creates the black-box dilemma, which represents ML models that are very complex and cannot be easily interpreted [5].

The main objective of XAI is to get human interpretable models that are useful in applications that require a high level of security, such as military, banking, healthcare, and intelligent transport systems. The explainability provided by XAI helps in justification, control, improvement, and discovery.

It is extremely beneficial to explore these black-box models to help individuals detect any negative results coming from the process of automated decision-making, perform more informed options, detect and protect against security loopholes, and combine algorithms with human values [6].

Surveys have shown that 94% of accidents arise from human-induced factors, such as distractions, violations of traffic rules, lack of attention, and jaywalking pedestrians [7, 8]. As a result, the need for XAI in autonomous vehicles can be summed up into these areas: (1) traffic accident and safety issues, and (2) the design, development, and implementation of autonomous vehicles should consider human views as humans are the users of this technology, i.e., taking the user's views and opinions into consideration when attempting to design an autonomous vehicle system. Explaining decisions provided by ML models provides expressive information about the cause of the action taken in critical situations [9,10]. Considering these diverse factors, XAI can provide benefits to autonomous vehicles represented in human-centered design, trust, transparency, and accountability in the overall system [11].

4.2 BACKGROUND AND REVIEW OF RELATED WORK

4.2.1 XAI method for convolutional neural networks in self-driving cars

Hong-Sik Kim and Inwhee JoeID [14] proposed an XAI method that consists of multiple stages to the learning process in convolutional neural networks, which is represented by multiple layers to the neural networks aiming at learning a certain behavior in autonomous vehicles. The methodology consists of two preparatory stages and four stages in the proposed XAI algorithm that starts with a gray-scaling phase of the images, which turns the images into gray images in order to simplify the learning process, then it moves to a pre-learning phase, of which the main job is to clean the learning dataset and remove any redundancy. Next, the main XAI algorithm operates first with the modifying image stage, the main purpose of which is to explain the changes that were made to an image, which is done to all parts of the image. The second stage is finding the vector, which is a comparative stage that compares the original images to the modified images by inputting both images into the network and generating the output vectors of the last hidden layer for all images. The third stage is the computing difference stage, which purposely compares the original output vectors for the original images and modified output vectors for the modified images and produces the difference using Euclidean distance. The last stage in the XAI methodology is making explanations, which aims at filling all parts of the copied original images with relative amounts to the resulting difference between the original output vector and modified output vector computed in the previous stage [12].

The main XAI algorithm describes each element of the methodology with a given representation to support the mathematical implementation of the algorithm, including such elements as the original image, the width and height of the image, the sub-image, and the number of sub-images divided from the original image, the width and height of the sub-images, the vector of the last hidden layer in the CNN, and the number of elements. This is to calculate the difference between the original output vectors for the original images and modified output vectors for the modified images; this is represented by:

$$dif(V_0, V_{n,m}) = \sum (V_0^K, V_{n.m}^K)^2, k = 0, 1, ..., K - 1 \qquad (1)$$

Where V_0 is the vector of the last hidden layer, $V_{n,m}$ is the vector of the last hidden layer when inputting sub-images n,m, and K is the number of elements in the vector [13].

The algorithm functions by adding a gray-scaling function and then generating an explanation image where a dataset of four images was used from a dataset containing two categories of images: "vehicle and non-vehicle". A test image was input to the pre-trained CNN to get preliminary results. In calculating the difference stage, the larger the difference, the better the result of the explanation. As a result, the methodology helped in analyzing the prediction capabilities of the CNN model to ensure its credibility in addition to analyzing the reasons why CNN models might fail in detecting autonomous vehicle accidents [14].

4.2.2 The internet of vehicles structure and need for XAI-IDS

The necessity of Explainable Artificial Intelligence (XAI) in developing an intrusion detection system within an Internet of Vehicles (IoV) framework arises due to the extensive data exchange among vehicles, communication towers, and roadside units in such networks. According to Huang [15] and Contreras-Castillo et al. [16], an IoV network consists of three layers: an application layer (service platform), a network layer (channel for V2X communication), and a perception layer (ensuring the incorporation of intelligent devices into the connected vehicles). IoV is often faced with a challenging issue when it comes to effective communications between thousands of connected vehicles, onboard unit data processing, big data combination with IoV, and intrusion detection and prevention [48]. In combination with ML, AI has improved the performance of IoV network efficiency in addition to other issues such as the rapidly changing nature of IoV, communication channel modeling, and energy efficiency. Several authors have been discussing the application of XAI to resolve the security aspect of the network. This is to overcome the issues not efficiently covered by the traditional AI/ML algorithms [17].

4.2.3 XAI frameworks

Sarhan et al. [18] and Das et al. [19] discussed the introduction of XAI in IoV models for its ability to explain and interpret classification model decisions. The aim of XAI is to manage progressive threats and attack techniques efficiently and to develop ML algorithms that create more explainable techniques while maintaining effective learning performance. XAI manifests the human perspective of understanding the model's decisions. As a quickly spreading area, it helps with the extraction of information and anticipation of the generated results with the utmost transparency [20].

The National Institute of Standards (NIST) stated types of explanations for AI as follows: (1) inform the subject of an algorithm by explaining how the model ensures the security of the system, (2) comply with regulations, for example, AI algorithms should give details on how they follow applicable traffic laws in an IoV system, (3) build community trust in AI systems by developing explanations that support the model and methodology [21], and (4) help with coming system development.

4.2.4 Practical implementation of XAI-based models

Slijepcevic, Horst, Lapuschkin, Raberger, Zeppelzauer, Samek, Breiteneder, Schöllhorn, and Horsak used layer-wise relevance propagation (LRP) incorporating Convolutional Neural Networks (CNNs) to decompose the input significance ratings; LRP is a technique used for generating explanations for ML models predictions operating in the input space [22, 23].

Another study showed the employment of deep neural networks with SHapley Additive exPlanations (SHAP), also called "DeepSHAP", which is able to interpret the effectiveness of ML for spoofing identification. The study's results showed that SHAP analysis calls attention to the consideration accommodated by a given classifier at decreased Spectro-temporal ranges, which showed increased trustworthiness of the entire system when experimented with by detecting attacks [24–26].

4.3 INTERNET OF VEHICLES (IOV) NETWORK ARCHITECTURE

The IoV is a technology that allows vehicles to communicate with their surroundings in a connected manner using a certain network topology. The minimal IoV network architecture consists of three major elements: (1) cloud, (2) connection, and (3) clients. The main target of IoV is to process the collected data within the network securely to improve the quality of autonomous behavior and road safety [27]. This is all incorporated with new and emerging technologies, such as fifth generation (5G), to make use of the features provided by them, such as Vehicular Cloud Computing (VCC), advanced signal processing, and Software Defined Network (SDN), allow maximum use of Intelligent Transport System (ITS) requirements.

The cloud is responsible for the storage and commuting of all data distributed on the network. The communications element is the backbone of the architecture that encompasses wireless communication technology such as 5G. The client elements are the end users using the IoV system [28].

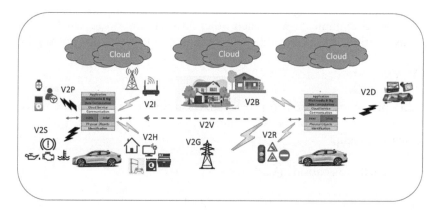

Figure 4.2 Autonomous vehicle components and their functions and the levels of autonomy.

A universal architecture was introduced in research that states that a vehicle has multiple communication channels with its surroundings, suggesting two interaction models: Intra-Vehicle, where the communications interactions take place within the vehicle itself (examples of this model are V2S, V2D, and D2D), and Inter-Vehicle, where the interactions take place between vehicles and between the vehicle and its surroundings (examples of this model are V2V, V2I, V2P, V2H, V2R, V2B, V2X, and V2G). A summary of these interactions is as follows.

I. Vehicle-to-Sensors (V2S)

Sensors and actuators are required for communication with other devices and infrastructure using different technologies.

II. Vehicle-to-Driver (V2D)

Vehicles within the IoV infrastructure send alerts and important messages to drivers of vehicles and motorcycles. Interaction of vehicles with the environment and motorcycles uses Bluetooth to send alerts to the motorcycle driver's audio helmet.

III. Device-to-Device (D2D)

This interaction model states that a number of devices connect and communicate with one another through the use of IP networks or the Internet. They use protocols such as Bluetooth, ZigBee, or Z-Wave to develop direct D2D communication.

IV. Vehicle-to-Vehicle (V2V)

Vehicles communicate with each other to share important information, such as location, using GPS and vision systems to allow accurate positioning.

V. Vehicle-to-Pedestrian (V2P)

LED projection is used to project image information on road surfaces, allowing communication between humans and cars to decrease pedestrian accidents at night.

VI. Vehicle-to-roadside (V2R)

Interaction between vehicles and roadside units aims to broadcast and collect information regarding vehicle behavior and road safety reports. V2R communication provides instant response to safety concerns, detects incoming crashes, and alerts the driver to take the necessary safety measures.

VII. Vehicle-to-infrastructure (V2I)

In this communication, data is exchanged between vehicles and road infrastructure. This is enabled by a combination of hardware, software, and firmware. Communication has been established with road infrastructure such as lane markings, road signs, and traffic lights, which broadcast information wirelessly to vehicles and vice versa.

VIII. Vehicle-to-Barrier (V2B)

V2B ensures the minimization of passenger vehicle crashes caused by (ROR) Run-off-Road crashes. This is feasible through the development of communication systems along the road.

IX. Vehicle-to-Home (V2H)

V2H provides backup to power outages by using bidirectional charging to transfer the energy stored in the battery of parked electric vehicles.

X. Vehicle-to-Everything (V2X)

V2X stands for the ability to communicate between the vehicle and other elements within an IoV system, such as sensors and other sources of information, to collect data through high-bandwidth, low-latency, and highly reliable links to reach a fully autonomous driving experience.

XI. Vehicle-to-Grid (V2G)

With the introduction of electric vehicles (EVs), the V2G system has introduced benefits to power systems by stabilizing the fluctuations and instability of energy demands using Plug-in electric vehicles to reduce energy costs [29].

4.3.1 Autonomous vehicle components and design

AI techniques and methods are used in most self-driving vehicle components, as autonomous vehicles are complex systems in need of careful design and deployment to overcome security challenges. Introducing explainability to autonomous vehicle systems will provide AI models with a human-like understanding of driver behavior, view of road conditions, and the overall environment [30].

An autonomous vehicle has a set of components working together to serve the autonomy of vehicles. These components are a minimum requirement that must be available at any AV, as stated in what follows [31].

I. Global Positioning System (GPS)

GPS allows the vehicle to navigate freely in an area without needing human intervention.

II. Radar and Ultrasonic Sensors

These sensors measure the distance between a car and any surrounding obstacles, deriving car speed, road conditions, and overall vehicle behavior.

III. Light Detection and Ranging LiDAR

LiDAR optimizes laser lights to calculate the distance between still and moving objects.

IV. Central Computing Unit (CCU)

The CCU processes and analyzes the data collected from sensors and maps them to read conditions. AI mechanisms and methods are continuously applied to the CCU to improve the autonomy experience.

V. Video Cameras

Video cameras detect traffic lights and moving objects and help in parking and detecting road conditions. Modern cars have 360° camera view [32].

The autonomy of vehicles is characterized by five levels, ranging from Level 0 up to Level 5. Level 0 means no automation, and Level 5 aims at full automation of the driving experience to eliminate driver-related errors, i.e., the human factor.

Autonomous car developers use modern design techniques, such as simulation and virtual modeling techniques, for better optimization and integration of components used in vehicle development achieved by using hardware and software used by the automotive concept design discipline [32].

4.3.1.1 AV technologies

Emerging technologies in autonomous vehicles aim to reduce the rate at which accidents occur; consequently, vehicle weight reduces as AV technologies are integrated into the majority of vehicles. Emerging technologies such as Lane Change Assistant (LCA) will help achieve the objective of AV [33].

I. Lane Change Assistant (LCA)

Monitors a surrounding area of 50 meters and then sends a warning to the driver should any dangerous situation occur. It is mounted on the sides of the vehicle and the front and back.

II. Park Distance Control (PDC)

Informs the driver through the display, audio, or optical signals when the driver is attempting to park the vehicle. It helps the driver to maneuver in tight spaces.

III. Lane Departure Warning (LDW)

Sends vibrations in the vehicle's seat or the steering wheel when the driver is about to leave the lane accidentally.

IV. Forward Collision Warning (FCW)

Using radar sensors mounted on the front of the vehicle, FCW acts as a warning when the distance between the vehicle and the one in front of it is short.

V. Adaptive Cruise Control (ACC)

With the use of a distance sensor and adjacent lever, the ACC component measures the distance and speed with relevance to the vehicles ahead.

VI. Stop-and-Go Control (SAGC)

Automatic distance control with a range set between 0 to 250 Km/h in addition to detecting vehicles ahead with the same system limits.

VII. Lane Keeping Assist (LKA)

Detects lane markings and performs corrective action to adjust and keep the vehicle in the lane and prevent it from deviating to other lanes.

VIII. Park Assist (PA)

Provides automatic guidance for a vehicle to park without intervention from the driver. It also calculates parking space.

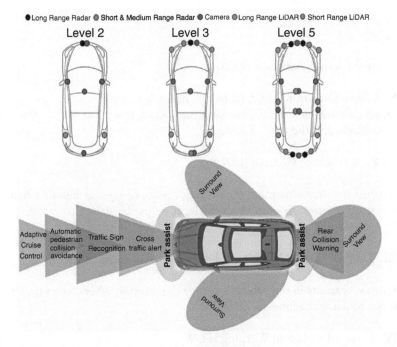

Figure 4.3 Autonomous vehicle components and their function and the levels of autonomy.

4.3.1.2 AV components communication mechanism

Communication between the components occurs through the use of the Controller Area Network (CAN bus), which connects with the Electronic Control Units (ECUs) to share the information collected by the ECUs. AV technologies move the vehicle by the information collected from various sensors that detect important data, such as speed, distance, environmental conditions, lane, LiDAR, and radar.

The CAN bus mechanism works by having two basic wires: one to transmit and the other to receive from the ACC. This means that each ECU coming to the CAN system transmits a size 0 to 8 bytes message in the message header. As multiple messages are received, their priority should be determined by the message header, which sends the message with the highest priority. Multiple systems are connected to the CAN bus line, working in harmony to direct a vehicle in a smart system setting [34].

I. Engine Control Module (ECU)

The ECU is responsible for adjusting the travel speed by managing the digital throttle of the vehicle's power engine,

II. Brake Control Module (BCU)

The BCU controls the counterforce of the system and sets on the digital brake system when it is called by the ACC module.

III. The use of sensors (such as the Brake Pedal Sensor, Radar, Accelerator Pedal Sensor, etc.) and actuators (such as the Brake Actuator [BA] and Throttle Actuator [TA], etc.) are increasing rapidly with additional functions in autonomous vehicles. The main functionality of Brake Assist Controller is to control vehicle speed by sending signals to the vehicle throttle actuator (TAC), whose main function is to manage the throttle value based on the needs of the ACC system.
IV. The radar system contains a set of multiple radars installed in the front, rear, and sides of the vehicle to detect surrounding objects. This provides the ability to detect vehicles and objects at a distance up to 120 meters away because the radar system uses three overlapping radar beams at 76–77 Khz frequency.

An autonomous vehicle's function is to decrease the rate of accidents and increase driver satisfaction with the autonomous driving experience by traveling at safe speed limits with routes set up by the driver.

Four control processes manage the speed and suitable distance between vehicles. These processes are the Lane Keeping System (LKAS), Electric Power Assisted Steering System (EPAS), CCD Camera, and ACC system [35, 36].

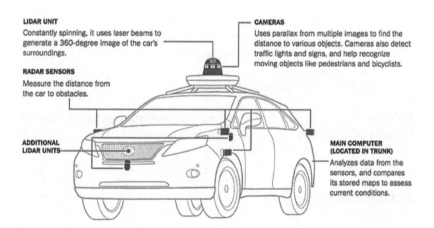

LIDAR UNIT
Constantly spinning, it uses laser beams to generate a 360-degree image of the car's surroundings.

RADAR SENSORS
Measure the distance from the car to obstacles.

ADDITIONAL LIDAR UNITS

CAMERAS
Uses parallax from multiple images to find the distance to various objects. Cameras also detect traffic lights and signs, and help recognize moving objects like pedestrians and bicyclists.

MAIN COMPUTER (LOCATED IN TRUNK)
Analyzes data from the sensors, and compares its stored maps to assess current conditions.

Figure 4.4 Autonomous vehicle technology components.

4.3.2 Applications and services

Autonomous vehicles are a rapidly growing concept with the technological advancement of today's smart applications in smart cities and the IoT. There is a need for driverless vehicles to work within the idea of smart cities in many applications, such as Intelligent Transportation Systems with driverless buses, trains, taxis, etc., spreading to reach other applications, such as autonomous robots and drones. The applications and services provided by AV are discussed in the following list.

I. Public Transportation

AV was first discussed in the application of public transportation systems in response to the need for an increased safety system in crowded and cluttered areas.

II. Autonomous Underground Vehicle

Used in many applications, such as transportation and underground mining, a fully automated underground vehicle was introduced in Denmark with high performance that encouraged the public to optimize it fully in the transportation system.

III. Autonomous Electric Tram

Developed in 2018 using smart technologies such as intelligent sensors, smart cameras, and intelligent LiDAR systems, autonomous electric trams travel through crowded areas without obstacles. Trams will operate safely due to the use of intelligent algorithms and intelligent controlling and monitoring systems with a prompt response to crossing objects, such as humans, animals, other vehicles, or any other obstacles.

IV. Autonomous Microbus

With the aim of decreasing the public transportation load and the utilization of available resources, the first autonomous microbus was tested in Finland during the year 2018. It is mostly suitable for transporting people short distances and for transporting employees.

V. Automated Robotics Bus

A Japan–Finland effort led to the introduction of an automated shuttle that operates in any weather condition with accurate obstacle detection and navigation. It moves at a speed of 45 Km/h and carries 18 passengers.

VI. Autonomous Electric Helicopter

Introduced in 2020 by Airbus, VSR700 is a prototype of the first electric autonomous helicopter. It was developed to help naval assets by enhancing information collection capabilities to maximize the benefits of surveillance since it is equipped with smart technologies, such as sensors and cameras.

VII. Autonomous Underwater Vehicle (AUV)

Different types of autonomous robots serve functions and have applications in marine and underwater services. AUVs include marine robots, hybrid automated underwater vehicles, bluefin hovering AUVs, hybrid dolphins, and solar-powered autonomous vehicles (SAUVs). The main purpose of this type of system is to collect enhanced images of the seafloor and high-resolution imagery for the vessels on the surface.

Other applications and services start from surveillance and remote sensing through autonomous drones, construction through autonomous trucks, and agriculture and mining through autonomous vehicles of agriculture and mining. These services and applications aim for better utilization of technology to serve humanity by improving quality of life through the use of technology and artificial intelligence [37].

4.3.3 Current issues

Although rapid technological development is present when considering the development of autonomous vehicles, they are faced with issues and challenges that modern research continuously addresses.

One of the commonly known issues concerning the development of self-driving cars is that it is provided a perfect environment to learn and act upon, which resembles the uncertain Markov Decision Process (uMDP) in which the agent has full observation state about the environment to make the optimal decision. But, this is not the case in real-world applications where the information fed to vehicles can be missing, or environmental conditions can affect vision. Here, the problem equals the uncertain Partially Observable Markov Decision Process (uPOMDP), which means that the state and the probability of the transition function are uncertain. Unlike the computational representation of the probabilities and transition functions, which are easily modeled, the real-world application of this representation is complex.

Additionally, in real-world applications, the vehicle is not the only agent in an environment; rather, it is one among many other agents, and it needs to act and interact with these agents, which maximizes the complexity of the issue to resemble uncertain Partially Observable Stochastic Game (uPOSG), which is one of the most difficult classes of computational problems to solve.

Another problem is that, just like humans, learning is an endless journey. Therefore, intelligent agents need to be learning continuously to improve the system. It is almost impossible to learn and predict every possible scenario in a rapidly changing environment. This could be addressed through the suggestion of transferred learning, where a vehicle learns from a previously learned model to transfer the knowledge acquired previously by adding new environment changes [38].

Another challenge is the insufficient implementation of the proposed algorithms in real-world scenarios due to a lack of data in this area of research. No real-world experiments are done in the area of pedestrian detection to clarify the ability of the proposed method to classify objects in real time rather than in a learning environment. Also, studies of the prediction of pedestrian behavior lack sufficient experimentation and testing.

These issues could be addressed and possibly solved by the introduction of XIA, which are autonomous vehicles where a human overview is needed in the decision-making process of self-driving vehicles [39].

4.4 XAI METHODS AND ALGORITHMS

4.4.1 XAI methods can be sub-divided into four categories

I. Complexity-Related

This can be categorized into two types: post hoc, which is presented in addition to the black-box model, and by design, which is presented within the model training phase. The complexity of ML models is related to their interpretability, i.e., an extremely complex model provides less interpretability [40–42].

II. Model-Related

This is classified into model-specific, which can only be used with specified types of algorithms, while model-agnostic is the opposite; it can be applied to any algorithm. Model-specific makes the selection of models closed to certain types of models, which decreases the model's representation and degrades the accuracy. On the other hand, the opposite is applied in model-agnostic interpretation [43].

III. Scope-Related

This has two classifications: global and local. Global means that the overall system should be understood along with the relationship between the input and output variables to allow every decision to be understandable. It is useful but difficult to implement. Local allows only one decision to be explained. This type is easy to implement and widely used [44, 45].

IV. Input Data Types

There is a huge amount of data available to be used in models, which allows the determination of the type of exploitability to use depending on the available data type, which varies between tabular, image, text, or graphical. More than one type of data can be used in multiple settings [46, 47].

There are five types of XAI methods: explanation by influence, visual explanations, explanation by simplification, example-based explanation, and text explanations.

I. Explanation by Influence

Explanation by influence methods aims to analyze the relevance of model features for prediction performance. This type has three characteristics: sensitivity analysis, layer-wise relevance propagation (LRP), and feature importance. Sensitivity analysis aims to discover the influence of the input or weight disturbance on the output. LRP includes multiple layers, such as input, hidden, and output layers of artificial neural networks (ANN), where a relevance value can be calculated backward, starting from the output layer and calculating the value at each neuron in each layer with respect to the weights, activation, and relevance value of the neuron on a deeper layer. Feature extraction methods can generate either local or global explanations by using SHapley Additive exPlanations (SHAP) and random trees, respectively, by which the contribution of each feature to the prediction is calculated.

II. Visual Explanation

Visual explanation aims to make illustrations of AI model's behavior by interaction analysis of input parameters. It is used with other techniques to increase the understanding of models. Partial Dependence Plot (PDP), Individual Conditional Expectation (ICE), and Feature Relevance Visualization are techniques used in visualization. PDP maps the partial relationships between input variables and the predicted outcome of post hoc interpretable AI algorithms. ICE is a model-agnostic way that activates local interpretability. Feature importance collects more than one method to visualize specific features relevant to an AI algorithm [48].

III. Explanation by Simplification

Explanation by simplification develops new explainable models based on the trained AI model. This leads to decreased complexity while maintaining prediction accuracy within the same level. Three approaches are used to reach explanation by simplification: rule extraction, model distillation, and surrogate models. The objective of rule extraction is achieved through extracting rules for the decision-making path of ANN using input and output data. Model distillation is a type of model compression applied to Deep Neural Networks (DNN), while a deep network is referred to as teacher-trained with large datasets, which produces a less complicated model referred to as "student". The teacher transferred the trained model as knowledge to the student with the goal of mimicking the teacher. This leads to a less complex model while maintaining prediction accuracy. The surrogate model is model-agnostic with local or global interpretability. Its aim is reducing model complexity. These models are approximations of the actual AI algorithms through the use of linear regression to train on the prediction of the black-box model [49].

IV. Example-Based Explanation

Example-based explanation models are often used if the distribution of the training datasets is complicated and difficult to comprehend. This model uses approaches like prototypes, criticisms, and counterfactual explanations. A prototype is a sample of the bigger original dataset, "a representative data from the original dataset", criticism is "an instance of data that is not well represented by the set of prototypes", and counterfactual explanations aim to fetch the slightest change in the feature value so it can alter the decision to the needed outcome [50].

V. Text Explanation

Text explanation supplies a natural language resulting from a learning process that provides an explanation of the AI model's results. Therefore, it cannot be considered a stand-alone explanation method; as a result, it is used with other methods and techniques that provide visual inputs to the text explanation model, and a natural language is generated as an output [51].

4.4.2 XAI algorithms in autonomous vehicles

Explainability defines the ability to understand and clarify the internal processes of Deep Learning and ML that are to be presented in human terms. On the other hand, interpretability refers to the prediction of what will come next based on the explained models. It observes the causes and effects of an operated model.

I. Explainability

In this context, explainability refers to the active properties of a learning model based on succeeding knowledge targeted at clearing its functionality. Explainability is subjective; it depends on the end-user's insight into the provided explanation and whether it sounds believable or not.

II. Interpretability

Defined as having passive property of an ML model based on previous knowledge, its aim is to make sure that a learning model is logically comprehensible to a human observer using proper tools, such as visual or textual, to boost transparency. Interpretability is defined by two characteristics: transparency and completeness. There are dimensions defining transparency which are simulatability, decomposability, and algorithmic.

- Simulatability

This is viewed at the model level, where transparency is defined by the ability of a person to understand the entire model. A user should be able to take input data, place it side by side with parameters, and produce predictions accordingly.

- Decomposability

With individual components in view, a model is sub-divided into parts (inputs, parameters, and computations) and then explained depending on the decomposition of the given model.

- Algorithmic

Explaining a model is performed at the training algorithm level. This is to understand the actual process a model performs to generate outputs.

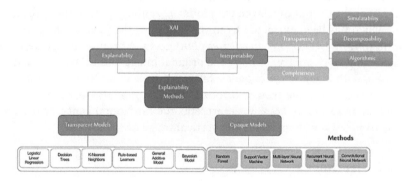

Figure 4.5 XAI chart, its divisions, and methods.

Completeness is aiming at precisely assessing the functionality of a model; therefore, we can say that an explanation is complete if it anticipates or predicts the behavior of a system within different conditions. It is challenging for XAI to provide explanations that are both interpretable and complete [52].

4.4.2.1 Algorithm 1

Following equation one in the related work section, a proposed algorithm based on CNN first inputs an image with its original size I_O into the CNN and then generates the vector of the last hidden layer V_O, in the next stem of the algorithm, the original sized image is sub-divided into $n \times m$ sub-images, and then the new sub-images $I_{0,0}, \ldots, I_{(N-1),(M-1)}$ are input into the CNN and generate the vector of the last hidden layer once again. Finally, the difference $dif(V_O, V_{n,m})$ between V_O and $V_{n,m}$ is calculated using Euclidean distance. All of these steps are made to prepare for the making an explanation step, where a copy of the original image I_O is made then denoted by I_C, then the area of I_C corresponding to $I_{n,m}$, $n = 0, \ldots, N-1$, $m = 0, M-1$ is filled with purple color, where the cloudiness is in the amount of the value $dif(V_O, V_{n,m})$ the larger this value, the more clear the color purple in the filled area. With these given insights, we can use the copied image I_C to approximate the part of the image that impacted the final prediction of the model, as the last hidden layer output is used instead of the final prediction because the last hidden layer contains more parameters and the output value of the last hidden layer is impacted by the difference between the input.

The proposed algorithm has three main functions: function grayscale (*img*), function predict (*img, model, i*), and function fill (*img, y_0, y_1, x_0, x_1, opacity, explan*). Function grayscale (*img*) takes an input image (*img*) and executes gray-scaling to *img* and then returns the gray-scaled image. Function predict (*img, model, i*) is a set of parameters, an input image *img*, convolutional neural network model *model*, and layer index $i = 0, \ldots, layers-1$ for *layers* equals the number of layers in the *model*. It is true that $i_{out} < i_{in}$ where i_{out} is the output of a layer, with index i_{out} and i_{in} is the input of the next layer, which has been extracted from the output of the previous layer. Function fill (*img, y_0, y_1, x_0, x_1, opacity, explan*) gets the original image *img* and integer values y_0, y_1, x_0, x_1 to copy the original image and fill the area within the image with black when *explan* = false or purple when *explan* = true with *opacity* variation range from 0.0 to 0.1 when *explan* = false or 0.75 when *explan* = true, x_0 to x_1 ($x_0 < x_1$) represents the horizontal range of the area and y_0 to y_1 ($y_0 < y_1$) represents the vertical range of the area [14].

4.4.2.2 Algorithm 2

Yolo V4 algorithm was proposed for use in traffic sign recognition with the use of a proper dataset. It is constructed with a three element structure consisting of (1) backbone, (2) neck, and (3) head. The backbone uses a neural activation function named mish, which can be represented by:

$$f(x) = x \tanh(\ln(1+e^x))$$ (2)

Where $\ln(1+e^x)$ represents the soft plus activation function.

Bag of Freebies (BoF) is a technique that lets the object detector extract more reliable accuracy without adding any load to the inference cost by replacing the training strategy or updating the training expense. On the other hand, the Bag of Special (BoS) presents enhancements in the receptive field, introduction of features, postprocessing, and use of attention. All these previous techniques are specifications of the Yolo V4 algorithm.

With the introduction of Yolo V4-tiny, more enhancements have been added to the model, such as faster training, detection, and recognition processes in addition to its efficient performance when we have limited computing resources. The difference between Yolo V4 and Yolo V4-tiny is that the network size decreases significantly, and the convolutional layer is compressed.

Yolo algorithm is an end-to-end network construction; it adopts one-stage dense prediction in the head element. It also divides the input images into grids; clusters are used to determine boundary lines.

The K-means technique is used to demonstrate dimensional clusters with an aimed boxes dataset and receives nine boxes of varied sizes. Moreover, the algorithm permits bounding box anchors for all ground-truth objects, enabling the grid to identify an object. The algorithm starts with given k cluster center points with a known width and height anchor box $(W_i, H_i), i \in \{1,2,3,4,...k\}$, the next step is to approximate the distance between ground truth and all cluster cored *(box,centroid) = 1 − IoU (box,centroid)*, once this step is done, the cluster center is recalculated using $W_i = \frac{1}{N_i}\sum W_i, H_i = \frac{1}{N_i}\sum H_i$ where N_i is the number of clusters. Re-execute the previous steps until groups are gathered.

Yolo V4 architecture consists of five phases as follows:

I. Separates the image into $(S \times S)$ grids, then it constructs K bounding boxes for each grid along with an approximate of anchor boxes.
II. The CNN draws out all the object features from images, then it predicts the bounding boxes *b* according to:

$$b_x = \sigma(t_x) + c_x$$ (3)

$$b_y = \sigma(t_y) + c_y$$ (4)

$$b_w = p_w e^{t_w}$$ (5)

$$b_h = p_h e^{t_h}$$ (6)

Where x,y are the core coordinates, w, h are the width and height of the estimates, t is the network output, c_x and c_y are the top left coordinates, and p_w and p_h are the anchor dimensions of the box.

CNN also estimates the class for $class = [P1, P2, P3, P4]^T$

III. A review of the excellent confidence IOU^{truth}_{pred} of the K bounding boxes, with the condition IOU_{thres}; if $IOU^{truth}_{pred} > IOU_{thres}$, then the bounding box contains the object; otherwise, it doesn't include the object.

IV. The category with the largest probability value as the target type is chosen.

V. To execute the full local search to opt out of the duplicated boxes and output, Non-Maximum Suppression (NMS) is used.

A dataset containing traffic signs is used to train the model [53].

4.5 XAI MODELS TO IMPROVE OVERALL SYSTEM PERFORMANCE

For XAI, three more steps are to be added to the detection model, including mask generation, model inquiry, and saliency estimation.

I. Mask Generation

For an input image I and a bounding box $b = (x_1, y_1, x_2, y_2)$ detected by a detection function f a set of local masks LM is generated by masking various parts of b and its closest pixels $LM = \{lm_1, lm_2, \ldots, lm_N\}$. The local masking area MA is calculated by considering coordinates of b and five surrounding pixels $MA = \{x_{1-5}, y_{1-5}, x_2 + 5, y_2 + 5\}$. The masking process is initiated by individually sub-dividing the masking area by two in horizontal and vertical directions, and then the sub-divided areas are once again divided into two, which continues until it reaches smaller sub-areas with up to 20 pixels. Each sub-area is masked by replacing the value of pixels with the average of pixel values. Local masks aim at "estimating the importance of pixels within a detected object and its surroundings".

Global Masking is a process that aims to detect outliers or data irrelevant to the detected object. It works by investigating parts of the input image and determining if these outliers have an effect on the output of the model. Global masks usually come in two sizes of pixels: 20 × 20 and 50 × 50.

The process of global mask generation is initiated by masking a square with the size 20 × 20 or 50 × 50 at the upper left side of the image. Afterward, the square moves in vertical and horizontal directions, and the process proceeds until the masking reaches the lower right side of the image; then the pixel value is replaced the same way in the local masking process.

II. Model Inquiry

Model inquiry acts as a mediator between the object detection model and the explanation model. This model receives the masked images, submits them back into the object detection model in order to generate new bounding boxes to be detected by the object detector, and then sends them to the saliency estimation module. The inquiry model is a model-agnostic method that has no data about the AI technique used, whether the neural network, activation function, loss function, or the hyperparameters used in the ML model; i.e., it's a stand-alone method that can be used to explain any object detection model, despite which ML model is used.

III. Saliency Estimation

This module collects the original estimation generated by the object detection in addition to the estimations generated by the local and global masks. It aims to calculate the difference between the original and new predictions, and, finally, it develops a heat map to visualize the importance of the difference between the original and new images for a particular detected object within an image.

This process can be represented mathematically by the given inputs: input image I with a size of $w \times h$, an original bounding box generated by object detection $b = (x_1, y_1, x_2, y_2)$ with a detection function f, local masks $LM = \{lm_1, lm_2, \ldots, lm_N\}$, Global masks $GM = \{gm_1, gm_2, \ldots, gm_j\}$, a combination of new bounding boxes $B' = \{b'_1, b'_2, \ldots, b'_k\}$ which are detected by a detection function f for all the globally and locally masked copies of the input image I where $b'_k = \{x'_1, y'_1, x'_2, y'_2\}$. The goal is to calculate a saliency map in the form of a matrix with the size of $w \times h$.

The mathematical procedure is as follows:

$$similarity\,(b, B') = \max_{b'_k \in B'} IOU\,(b, b'_k) \tag{7}$$

In this equation, the similarity between the original and new bounding boxes is calculated using the maximum Intersection Over Unit between b and every $b'_k \in B'$. This is done for all local masks $lm_n \in LM$.

The similarity value falls in a range between 0 and 1, calculated as the IOU threshold.

$$IOU_{thres}\,; if\,IOU_{pred}^{truth} > IOU_{thres} \tag{8}$$

If the value is larger than the IOU threshold, then an object that has been detected within the new masked image that has a large amount of shared area with the object in the original image, i.e., the original detected box b resembles the new bounding box of the masked images $b'_k \in B'$

However, if the similarity is smaller than the IOU threshold, it means the difference between the original and new masked images is huge. This difference can be calculated using the minimum distance between b and $b'_k \in B'$.

$$difference(b, B') = \min_{b'_k \in B'} Distance(b, b'_k) \tag{9}$$

Where $Distance(b, b'_k) = \dfrac{1}{IOU(b, b'_k)}$ for the distance between two bounding boxes is measured by the inverse of IOU between the boxes. With the addition of the distance between b and B' the saliency map can be calculated as:

$$SM[lm_n] = SM[lm_n] + difference(b, B') \tag{10}$$

The same saliency process for local masks is done to the global mask for $gm_j \in GM$.

For the last stage in the explanation method, the heatmap is visualized by mapping the saliency map SM on the input image with different colors that specify the levels of importance [54].

4.6 DISCUSSION

The performance of models is often affected by the training dataset used; thus, there are reliable datasets used such as "vehicle vs. non-vehicle", "Taiwan Traffic Sign Dataset", and "Common Objects in Context Dataset (COCO)". These datasets contain thousands and hundreds of thousands of traffic images used to train models on object detection. With the introduction of XAI into models, more meaningful results are shown, which leads to elevated performance in the autonomous vehicles service. This method presents the original image with visualization explanations to see which image has influenced the final prediction. Explainability contributes to understanding the prediction patterns of CNN models to promote transparency and trustworthiness. Additionally, when autonomous cars are involved in accidents, XAI helps analyze why the CNN model failed to predict it correctly.

Yolo V4 showed highly dependable precision in the detection of objects. Its performance was tested against prediction accuracy and detection speed, and Yolo V4 obtained the highest precision accuracy compared to other algorithms. As Yolo is one-stage object detection, it divides an input image I into N grids with equal sizes; afterward, it detects and localizes objects within grids. Having one-stage detection properties, Yolo can perform much faster than other methods with two-stage properties, such as R-CNN and fast R-CNN. This makes it efficient for applications in real-time environments. The heatmap generated to visualize the explanation of the detection model represents each object with a different color, identifying Car, Truck, Bus, and Motorcycle by green-, purple-, orange-, and yellow-colored bounding boxes. Then it shows objects that are important in determining the detection, such as the lower parts of the vehicle because the hood, wheels, and lower parts are highly important to detect trucks while wheels, hood, and boot had higher importance in detecting cars, and the wheels and seat had higher value in the detection of motorcycles [14, 53, 54].

4.7 CONCLUSION

As AI advances with ML and deep learning, its services in multiple aspects of modern life, such as smart cities, automation, security, and health, will increase. More human-intensive points of view are needed to make the human vs. machine interaction outcomes more effective for the applications under review.

The introduction of explainable AI (XAI) methods has added a human perspective to AI models in order to make them more understandable, which helps in recognizing patterns within the models, how they operate, and why they sometimes fail to perform.

Through this chapter, the operations, methods, and architectures of XAI and autonomous vehicles were discussed, with examples of algorithms that are used in current research in the field of autonomous vehicles. The results of these methods were presented in the discussion section, showing that the introduction of XAI in autonomous vehicles has improved the performance of their applications. The execution of XAI within autonomous vehicles will lead to embracing the fact that fully autonomous vehicles can be more beneficial in applications such as ITS. The human perspective added to ML and DL models used in autonomous vehicles will eventually lead to the introduction of fully autonomous vehicles due to the trustworthiness introduced by XAI.

It is highly recommended that XAI be applied to other tasks served by ML models, such as classification, segmentation, lane recognition, and path planning. This will result in fewer traffic collisions, less traffic, and a more eco-friendly world.

REFERENCES

[1] Z. B. Arikan, "An introduction to Explainable Artificial Intelligence (XAI)", Mobiquity, 27 July 2022.
[2] A. Saxe, S. Nelli, C. Summerfield, "If deep learning is the answer, what is the question?" Nat. Rev. Neurosci. 22 (2021) 55–67.

[3] F. Piccialli, V. Di Somma, F. Giampaolo, S. Cuomo, G. Fortino, "A survey on deep learning in medicine: Why, how and when?" Inf. Fusion. 66 (2021) 111–137.

[4] Z. Li, F. Liu, W. Yang, S. Peng, J. Zhou, "A survey of convolutional neural networks: Analysis, applications, and prospects", IEEE Trans. Neural Netw. Learn. Syst. 33 (12) (Dec. 2021) 6999–7019. https://doi.org/10.1109/TNNLS.2021.3084827

[5] L. Edwards, M. Veale, "Slave to the algorithm: Why a right to an explanation is probably not the remedy you are looking for", Duke L. Tech. Rev. 16 (2017) 18.

[6] S. Ali, T. Abuhmed, S. El-Sappagh, K. Muhammad, J. M. Alonso-Moral, R. Confalonieri, R Guidotti, J. Del Ser, N. Díaz-Rodríguez, F. Herrera, "Explainable Artificial Intelligence (XAI): What we know and what is left to attain trustworthy artificial intelligence", (2023), https://doi.org/10.1016/j.inffus.2023.101805

[7] S. Singh, "Critical reasons for crashes investigated in the national motor vehicle crash causation survey", Art and Design Rev. 10 (4) (2022).

[8] K. Bucsuházy, E. Matuchová, R. Zúvala, P. Moravcová, M. Kostíková, R. Mikulec, "Human factors contributing to the road traffic accident occurrence", Trans. Res. Pro. 45 (2020) 555–561.

[9] U. Ehsan, M. O. Riedl, "Human-centered explainable ai: towards a reflective sociotechnical approach", In International Conference on Human-Computer Interaction, Springer, 2020, pp. 449–466.

[10] S. Dhanorkar, C. T. Wolf, K. Qian, A. Xu, L. Popa, Y. Li, "Who needs to know what, when? Broadening the explainable AI (XAI) design space by looking at explanations across the AI lifecycle", In Proceedings of the 2021 ACM Designing Interactive Systems Conference (DIS '21), Association for Computing Machinery, 2021, pp. 1591–1602. https://doi.org/10.1145/3461778.3462131

[11] S. Atakishiyev, M. Salameh, H. Yao, R. Goebel," Explainable Artificial Intelligence for autonomous driving: A comprehensive overview and field guide for future research directions", arXiv:2112.11561v3 [cs.AI] (2023).

[12] C. Ching-Ju, C. Ling-Wei, et al., "Improving CNN-based pest recognition with a PostHoc explanation of XAI", Res. Sqa. (2021), https://doi.org/10.21203/rs.3.rs-782408/v1.

[13] H. S. P. Mandeep, A. Malhi, Deep Learning-Based Explainable Target Classification for Synthetic Aperture Radar Images, IEEE, 2022, https://doi.org/10.1109/HSI49210.2020.9142658.

[14] K. Hong-Sik, I. Joe, An XAI Method for Convolutional Neural Networks in Self-Driving Cars, 2022, https://doi.org/10.1371/journal.pone.0267282.

[15] J. M. Huang, "Research on internet of vehicles and its application in intelligent transportation", In Mechatronics and Industrial Informatics; Applied Mechanics and Materials, Trans Tech Publications Ltd., 2013; Volume 321, pp. 2818–2821.

[16] J. Contreras-Castillo, S. Zeadally, J. A. Guerrero-Ibañez, "Internet of vehicles: Architecture, protocols, and security", IEEE Internet Things J. 5 (2018) 3701–3709 (Appl. Sci. 2023, 13, 1252 26 of 29).

[17] C. Xu, H. Wu, H. Liu, W. Gu, Y. Li, D. Cao, "Blockchain-Oriented Privacy Protection of Sensitive Data in the Internet of Vehicles", IEEE Trans. Intell. Veh. 8 (2) (2022) 1057–1067. https://doi.org/10.1109/TIV

[18] M. Sarhan, S. Layeghy, M. Portmann, "An explainable machine learning-based network intrusion detection system for enabling generalisability in securing IoT networks", arXiv. (2021).

[19] S. Das, N. Agarwal, S. Shiva, "DDoS explainer using interpretable machine learning", In Proceedings of the 2021 IEEE 12th Annual Information Technology, Electronics and Mobile Communication Conference (IEMCON), Vancouver, BC, Canada, 27–30 October 2021, pp. 0001–0007.

[20] G. Srivastava, R. H. Jhaveri, S. Bhattacharya, S. Pandya, P. K. R. Maddikunta, G. Yenduri, J. G. Hall, M. Alazab, T. R. Gadekallu, "XAI for cybersecurity: State of the art, challenges, open issues and future directions", arXiv 2022, arXiv:2206.03585.

[21] A. B. Arrieta, N. Díaz-Rodríguez, J. D. Ser, J. A. Bennetot, S. Tabik, A. Barbado, S. Garcia, S. Gil-Lopez, D. Molina, R. Benjamins, et al., "Explainable Artificial Intelligence (XAI): Concepts, taxonomies, opportunities and challenges toward responsible AI", Inf. Fusion. 58 (2020) 82–115.

[22] D. Slijepcevic, F. Horst, S. Lapuschkin, A. M. Raberger, M. Zeppelzauer, W. Samek, C. Breiteneder, W. I. Schöllhorn, B. Horsak, "On the explanation of machine learning predictions in clinical gait analysis", arXiv 2019, arXiv:1912.07737.

[23] S. M. Lundberg, S. I. Lee, "A unified approach to interpreting model predictions", arXiv 2017, arXiv:1705.07874.

[24] W. Ge, J. Patino, M. Todisco, N. Evans, "Explaining deep learning models for spoofing and deepfake detection with Shapley additive explanations", In Proceedings of the ICASSP 2022–2022 IEEE International Conference on Acoustics, Speech and Signal Processing (ICASSP), Singapore, 23–27 May 2022, pp. 6387–6391.

[25] B. Gulmezoglu, "XAI-based microarchitectural side-channel analysis for website fingerprinting attacks and defenses", IEEE Trans. Dependable Secur. Comput. 19 (6) (2021) 4039–4051. https://doi.org/10.1109/TDSC.2021.3117145

[26] C. Ifeanyi Nwakanma, L. A. Chijioke Ahakonye, J. Nkechinyere Njoku, J. Chioma Odirichukwu, S. Adiele Okolie, C. Uzondu, C. C. Ndubuisi Nweke and D.-S. Kim, "Explainable artificial intelligence (XAI) for intrusion detection and mitigation in intelligent connected vehicles: A review", Appl. Sci. 13 (2023) 1252. https://doi.org/10.3390/app13031252

[27] J. Contreras, S. Zeadally, J. A. Guerrero-Ibanez, "Internet of Vehicles: Architecture, Protocols, and Security," IEEE Internet Things J. 4662, no. c, pp. 1–1, 2017.

[28] T. Mohammed Saad, H. Burairah, H. Aslinda Hassan, "Converging VANET with vehicular cloud networks to reduce the traffic congestions: A review", International Journal of Appl. Eng. Res. 12 (21) (2017).

[29] A. LI-Minn, S. Kah Phooi, G. K. Ijemaru, A. Murtala Zungeru, Deployment of IoV for Smart Cities: Applications, Architecture, and Challenges, IEEE, 2018.

[30] S. Grigorescu, B. Trasnea, T. Cocias, G. Macesanu, "Asurvey of deep learning techniques for autonomous driving", J. Field Robot. 37 (3) (2020) 362–386.

[31] A. J. London, D. Danks, "Regulating autonomous vehicles", In Proceedings of the 2018 AAAI/ACM Conference onAI, Ethics, and Society, New York, NY, December 2018, pp. 216–221.

[32] G. Bathla, K. Bhadane, S. Rahul Kumar, R. Kumar, R. Aluvalu, R. Krishnamurthi, A. Kumar, R. N. Thakur, S. Basheer, "Autonomous vehicles and intelligent automation: Applications, challenges, and opportunities", Hindawi Mob. Inf. Sys. 2022, Article ID 7632892.

[33] M. Teti, W.E. Hahn, S. Martin, C. Teti, E. Barenholtz, "A systematic comparison of deep learning architectures in an autonomous vehicle", arXiv 2018, arXiv:abs/1803.09386.

[34] L. C. Davis, "Dynamic origin-to-destination routing of wirelessly connected, autonomous vehicles on a congested network", Phys. A: Stat. Mech. Appl. 478 (2017) 93–102. https://doi.org/10.1016/j.physa.2017.02.030

[35] T. Surakka, F. Härri, T. Haahtela, A. Horila, T. Michl, "Regulation and governance supporting systemic MAAS innovations", RTBM. 27 (2018) 56–66. https://doi.org/10.1016/j.rtbm.2018.12.001

[36] P. Shakouri, J. Czeczot, A. Ordys, "Adaptive cruise control system using balance-based adaptive control technique", In 2012 17th International Conference on Methods & Models in Automation & Robotics (MMAR), Miedzyzdroje, 2012, 27–30 August 2012, 510–515. https://doi.org/10.1109/MMAR.2012.6347866

[37] F. Ali Paker, New Autonomous Vehicle Technologies Effect on Automotive Concept Design Stages, Scientific Research Publishing Inc., 2022

[38] P. Srinivas, "Literature survey on autonomous rover", TURCOMAT. 12 (13) (2021) 82–88.

[39] S. Mahmoud, E. Billing, H. Svensson, S. Thill, "Where to from here? On the future development of autonomous vehicles from a cognitive systems perspective", (2022), https://doi.org/10.1016/j.cogsys.2022.09.005.

[40] D. Parekh, N. Poddar, A. Rajpurkar, M. Chahal, N. Kumar, G. Prasad Joshi, W. Cho, "A review on autonomous vehicles: Progress, methods and challenges", Electronics 11 (14) (2022) 2162. https://doi.org/10.3390/electronics11142162

[41] A. Adadi, M. Berrada, "Peeking inside the black-box: A survey on explainable artificial intelligence (XAI)", IEEE Access. 6 (2018) 52138–52160. https://doi.org/10.1109/ACCESS.2018.2870052

[42] R. Alamri, B. Alharbi, "Explainable student performance prediction models: A systematic review", IEEE Access. 9 (2021) 33132–33143. https://doi.org/10.1109/ACCESS.2021.3061368

[43] S. Mohseni, N. Zarei, E. D. Ragan, "A multidisciplinary survey and framework for design and evaluation of explainable AI systems", ACM Trans. Interact. Intell. Syst. 11 (3–4) (2021) 1–45. https://doi.org/10.1145/3387166

[44] A. F. Markus, J. A. Kors, P. R. Rijnbeek, "The role of explainability in creating trustworthy artificial intelligence for health care: A comprehensive survey of the terminology, design-choices, and evaluation strategies", J. Biomed. Inform. 113 (2021) 1–11. https://doi.org/10. 1016/j.jbi.2020.103655

[45] P. Ivaturi, M. Gadaleta, A. C. Pandey, M. Pazzani, S. R. Steinhubl, G. Quer, "A comprehensive explanation framework for biomedical time series classification", IEEE J. Biomed. Health Inform. 25 (7) (2021) 2398–2408. https://doi.org/10.1109/JBHI.2021.3060997

[46] M. Setzu, R. Guidotti, A. Monreale, F. Turini, D. Pedreschi, F. Giannotti, "GLocalX—from local to global explanations of black box AI models", AI. 294 (2021) #103457. https://doi.org/10.1016/j.artint.2021.103457

[47] X. -H. Li, C. C. Cao, Y. Shi, W. Bai, H. Gao, L. Qiu, C. Wang, Y. Gao, S. Zhang, X. Xue, L. Chen, "A survey of data-driven and knowledge-aware explainable AI", IEEE Trans. Knowl. Data Eng. 34 (1) (2020) 29–49. https://doi.org/10.1109/TKDE.2020.29839 30

[48] P. Linardatos, V. Papastefanopoulos, S. Kotsiantis, "Explainable AI: A review of machine learning interpretability methods", Entropy. 23 (1) (2021) 1–45. https://doi.org/10.3390/e23010018

[49] H. Hakkoum, A. Idri, I. Abnane, "Assessing and comparing interpretability techniques for artificial neural networks breast Cancer classification", Comput. Methods Biomech. Biomed. 9 (6) (2021) 587–599. https://doi.org/10.10 80/21681163.2021.1901784

[50] A. Bennetot, J.-L. Laurent, R. Chatila, N. Díaz-Rodríguez, "Towards explainable neural-symbolic visual reasoning", In Proceedings of the 28th International Joint Conference on Artificial Intelligence, Macao, China, 2019. https://doi.org/10.48550/arXiv.1909.09065

[51] J. Gerlach, P. Hoppe, S. Jagels, Licker, M. H. Breitner, "Decision support for efficient XAI services - A morphological analysis, business model archetypes, and a decision tree", Electron. Mark. https://doi.org/10.1007/s12525-022-00603-6, 2022.

[52] P. E. D. Love, W. Fang, J. Matthews, S. Porter, H. Luo, L. Ding, "Explainable Artificial Intelligence (XAI): Precepts, methods, and opportunities for research in construction", https://doi.org/10.48550/arXiv.2211.06579, 2023

[53] C. Dewi, C. Rung-Ching, X. Jiang, H. Yu, "Deep convolutional neural network for enhancing traffic sign recognition developed on Yolo V4", Multimedia Tools Appl. 81 (26) (Nov. 2022) 37821–37845. https://doi.org/10.1007/s11042-022-12962-5.

[54] M. Moradi, K. Yan, D. Colwell, M. Samwald, R. Asgari, "Model-agnostic explainable artificial intelligence for object detection in image data", arXiv:2303.17249 (2023).

Chapter 5

Emerging applications and future scope of internet of vehicles for smart cities

A Survey

Jyoti Sharma, Manish Bhardwaj, and Neelam Chantola

5.1 INTRODUCTION

In the era of the internet, transportation systems can be seen as a mix of traditional and technological systems where traditional consists of autonomous
vehicles and technological consists of connected vehicles [1–3]. Autonomous
vehicles focus on intravehicle communication, whereas connected vehicles
focus on intervehicle communication. The motivation behind developing a
transportation system always remains safety by overcoming several issues
and challenges in existing systems. The evolution of IoV started with the
invention of wheels and continues through self-driving cars ranging from
light to heavy vehicles [4]. In the initial years of the invention of automobiles,
evolution has been very slow, but in the last two decades, it has grown exponentially after merging Information and Communication Technologies (ICT)
and the transportation sector. ICT has significantly reduced some issues like
congestion, safety, security and infotainment on the road to avoiding any
casualties happening on the roads. It is leading to smart transportation and
advanced traffic management systems aimed at smart cities [5–8]. When ICT
is merged into the transportation system, it is called Intelligent Transportation System (ITS). This new term evolved in the 19th century. In the 20th
century, a significant innovation was observed in ITS, and an infrastructure-
less network of vehicles was invented, termed the CITS, where C stands for
cooperative. Later, it was termed the Vehicular Ad hoc Network, which was
a form of a Mobile Ad hoc Network. It created the concept of intervehicle
communication. Then, in 2010, with the invention of IoT, a third layer of the
internet cloud of vehicles was added on top of the vehicular cloud, starting
a new technology in transportation system called the Internet of Vehicles
(IoV). Figure 5.1 shows the changes in and years of technological inventions
in the transportation system. The invention of the internet cloud in intervehicle communication is the basis of IoV and the future of IoV, i.e., cloud-
based IoV (CIoV) [9]. At the same time, the internet cloud is the platform
of the frameworks IoV and CIoV. In CIoV, all transportation solutions are
based upon machine learning and Artificial Intelligence [10].

DOI: 10.1201/9781003502432-5

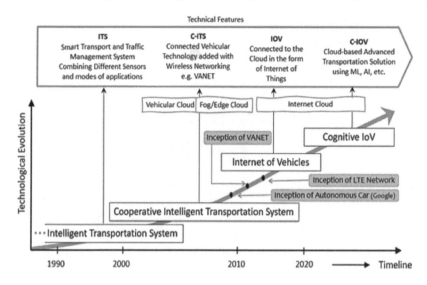

Figure 5.1 Evolution of IoV.

Due to the advancement of Information and Communication Technologies (ICT) and using lots of sensors in modern vehicles, the Intelligent Transport Systems (ITS) have evolved and become key to the development of smart cities [11]. Its sole purpose is to gather, detect and disseminate the vehicles' data to improve safety, security, efficiency and privacy while providing other services like infotainment [12–14].

Safety of the road can be ensured by providing prior information about traffic on the road, pedestrians walking on the road and exact information about the weather. Security is to protect the vehicle's information from any suspicious attack. Privacy is to keep the vehicle's authenticity secure. Privacy can be a subset of security. When we discuss the Internet of Vehicles, we first start with the Internet of Things because vehicles can be considered things. The Internet of Vehicles can be considered a vehicular version of IoT where things are replaced by vehicles. Furthermore, vehicles are a mobile entity, and vehicles on roads do not follow any infrastructure, which is the same as the infrastructure-less network of mobile phones. So we can say it is a vehicular version of Mobile Ad hoc Networks (MANET), termed VANET [15–17]. So, it can be concluded that VANET takes the attributes of the Internet of Things and Mobile Ad hoc Network. ITS is to provide intelligent services and innovative technologies to an infrastructure-less, dynamic and self-organized network of vehicles. In this chapter, we review the architecture, issues, challenges, applications and scope of IoV.

The interrelationship between IoT, MANET, VANET and IoV is shown in Figure 5.2.

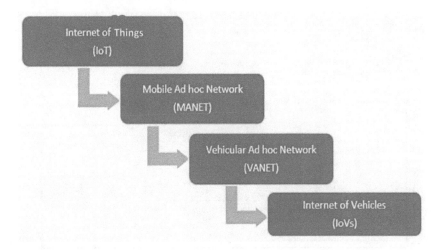

Figure 5.2 Hierarchy of different technologies.

IoT is the global communication network of different entities like mobile phones, home appliances, sensors, cameras, industrial instruments, vehicles (road, air and marine) and all living things incorporated in making smart homes, smart devices, smart offices, smart cities, smart healthcare industry, etc., as shown in Figure 5.3.

MANET is a subgroup of IoT where things are replaced with mobile entities like mobile phones. These mobile entities in MANET are connected together wirelessly and without the pre-establishment of a physical infrastructure network. So MANET comes under the category of an infrastructure-less network [18]. These mobile entities work as nodes in the network, and all nodes communicate using sensors or cameras embedded in phones with the help of multi-hopping routing protocols [19]. These routing protocols are specially designed for dynamic and frequently changing scenarios. Routing protocols designed for wired networks are not capable of coping with the issues and challenges of infrastructure-less wireless networks [20–24]. These are:

- No static topology.
- Limitation on bandwidth (it is very low).
- Distributed control.
- No stable communication channel.
- Security threats.
- Limited storage and power.
- Shared communication channel causing information loss.

The requirements of such infrastructure-less networks have been increasing rapidly in recent years, so researchers are constantly working on the

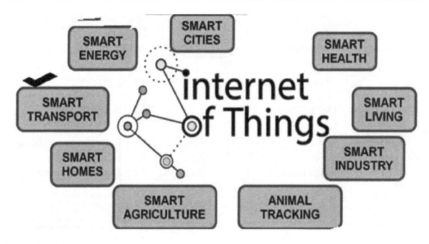

Figure 5.3 IoT areas focusing on smart transport.

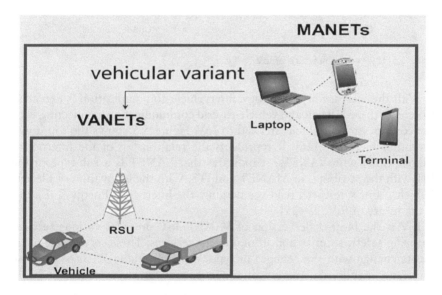

Figure 5.4 VANET as a subgroup of MANET.

issues and challenges existing in MANET, like energy consumption, utilization of bandwidth, efficient routing and security protocols, and a significant improvement can be seen in comparison to the initial phase of MANET. As we have already seen, VANET is a variant of MANET where mobile nodes are vehicles, so challenges present in MANET are more or less present in VANET (see Figure 5.4). As compared to MANET, changes in the topology and the mobility of nodes in VANET are higher. VANET allows units with the aim of an efficient, congestion-free, safe transportation system [25].

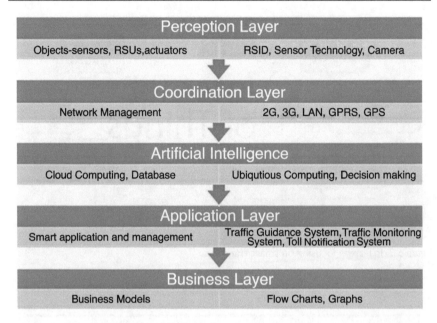

Figure 5.5 Layered architecture of IoV.

With the increase in technology, intervehicle communication is extended to vehicle-to-pedestrian and vehicle-to-grid communication, connecting with the concept of IoT, which later led to IoV. Figure 5.5 shows the top-down invention hierarchy [26]. It represents the relationship of the Internet of Things (IoT) with VANETs. It indicates that VANET is a sub-type of the IoT with the attributes of MANET and ITS. With the innovation of Electric Vehicles, a new research field is emerging: the Internet of Energy (IoE). IoE is the future of IoV [27–29].

IoV is the large-scale version of VANET. IoV provides various services ensuring safety, security and infotainment services. These services' requirements change with the changes in types of roads. Table 5.1 lists all those services and entities' communication. These services are as follows:

While moving on the highways or expressways:

- Speed monitoring of vehicles and self-adjustment (intravehicle and V2V).
- Climate sensing during driving (V2I).
- Estimated arrival time with updated route information.
- Seamless internet connectivity is of utmost importance to ensure the smooth functioning of all applications while traveling on expressways and highways.

Table 5.1 Services Required Depending upon the Road Type

S. No.	Services	Highways or Expressways	Intracity Roads	Communication
1	Speed monitoring	Highly required and ensured	Not required highly	Intravehicle communication (V2D)
2	Self-adjustment	Highly required in case of high speeds	Not much required	V2V
3	Climate sensing	Highly required during long travel	Not required	V2I
4	Toll notification	Required	Not required	V2R
5	Estimated time updates	Highly required	Not much required; sometimes required if a deadline is necessary	V2I
6	Route updating in case of bad road conditions	Not required	Highly required	V2R, V2D
7	Vehicle adjustment in case of bad road condition	Not required	Highly required	V2R
8	Traffic rule violations	Not required	Highly required	V2V, V2P, V2I
9	Driver health status	Required	Required	V2P

- Notification of arrival at toll booths.
- Current status of location.
- Current vehicle loads indicator on highways.
- Best and alternate route suggestions in case of road blockage ahead.

While moving on city roads:

- Triggering alert to violate traffic rules.
- Vehicle self-monitoring.
- Moderate connectivity is enough if moving on city roads.
- Auto-adjusting the vehicle to road conditions.
- Connectivity problems.
- Driver health status.

5.2 LAYERED ARCHITECTURE OF IOV

Kaiwartya et al. proposed a five-layer architecture: perception, coordination, artificial intelligence (AI), application and business. Figure 5.5 depicts the layered architecture.

1. **The perception layer** gathers data from the various actuators in the area, such as sensors inside the car (for example, speed, direction and position of the car, as well as driver attitudes) and outside the car (for example, traffic environments and weather conditions), and securely transmits the information to the coordination layer [30–33]. This layer consists of numerous gadgets, smartphones, roadside units (RSUs), roadside actuators (RAs) and other components of the intelligent infrastructure.

2. **The coordination layer** ensures information gathered from the perception layer is transferred for processing in artificial intelligence securely and in a unified structure (5G). The network layer is crucial to the Internet of Vehicles [34]. It is comprised of a module to manage the disparate networks connecting the various components of the intelligent infrastructure and guarantees the ability for autonomous data exchanges. WAVE, 4G and 5G, Wi-Fi, WLAN, Bluetooth and satellite networks are among the networks that smart automobiles employ for communication. These networks transfer data from the artificial intelligence layer to the perception layer.

3. **The IoV ecosystem's AI layer**, represented by the virtualized cloud substructure, is its brain. It is in charge of managing the data from the coordinating layer and uses algorithms to make decisions to examine this aggregating data. In the cloud environment, it oversees a variety of services based on a careful examination of the information obtained. In order to assess the collected data and determine what action is necessary at any given time, it uses ML, AI and cloud computing. It consists of specialized equipment, big data analysis tools and cloud computing components like self-driven vehicles that use image processing to detect objects on the road.

4. **The application layer** creates intelligent applications that inform end users of what the AI layer has learned. The IoV technology is commercialized by the application layer. The AI layer's outputs are used to give end users applications like remote car control, multimedia watching services, driving aids and safe driving apps, among others. This layer disseminates user data and sends it to the business layer for further processing [35].

5. **The business layer** employs a business model that assesses the budget planning for operating the applications by analyzing the statistics

of the applications using various techniques like use case diagrams, graphs, differentiation tables, flowcharts, etc. The architecture's last layer is in charge of communicating consumer experience insights to the development organization [36, 37]. It comes with a selection of tools to help the firm make decisions about resource use and investment, forecast future business trends and advise future initiatives.

5.3 LITERATURE SURVEY

Habib et al. [38] reviewed the popular and developing IoV frameworks and network layered structures. A novel, modern design of the Internet of Vehicles (IoV) model has been proposed to assess the efficiency of the IoV ecosystem as a network structure, encompassing the processes of detecting, collecting, storing, processing acquired data, and ultimately utilizing the services. The client layer, communication layer, cloud layer and cater service layer are the four levels that make up CIoV. The primary features of the IoT application ecosystems, which can be implemented for various and diverse communication models, are taken into consideration when approaching CIoV. The CIoV protocol suite was presented for each layer in the design as a case study, taking operational and security dimensions.

Sharma et al. [39] presented an IoV communication system that consists of three zones: the car zone, the collaboration zone and the smart city zone. In order to achieve this, we predetermined an in-car gateway design that permits communication and information sharing across these three zones. This in-car gateway's hardware and software architecture were presented. Our novel architecture might support a number of cutting-edge services, including driverless driving. As a result, in the preceding section, key information flow and functions for autonomous driving services were emphasized. To support our proposal, we also suggested an autonomous lane-changing method. We want to use our gateway in the targeted network to verify its effectiveness in future work.

Bhardwaj [40] presented a seven-layered architecture for IoV. This paper first identified the key components of the IoV ecosystem, outlining their functions and proposing a model for how they interact. It also introduced a network paradigm made up of the environmental model and the intra-vehicular model. This study developed a protocol stack that meets the standards needed for interoperability across all parties and incorporates current protocols into the IoV ecosystem. It concluded by presenting a situational analysis and a sequence diagram that illustrate how the suggested seven-layered architecture might be used in a practical IoV situation. It made the case that the suggested architecture will help readers understand the interaction model, network model and layered architecture. IoV will encourage the fusion of the automotive and IT industries.

In Kumar et al. [41], it was suggested that vehicles having IoV capabilities might scan the passengers for any potential health hazards, such as a driver who is intoxicated or patients who require medical attention, and then notify the appropriate health care services or authorities. Ensuring that the driver is in a state that is safe for driving will significantly reduce the rate of careless driving and traffic accidents. Pressure sensors can adjust the wheels to the appropriate working situations, good reflex frameworks can be integrated and special actuators can improve the cabin's interior environment. Additionally, it is possible to link the driver's identity to the car so that only the driver may operate it. If the car is stolen, all available information will be relayed to the driver, including whether the car is in motion or parked. IoV may also implement a smart template matching system that makes it simple for traffic police to identify the vehicle, ensuring theft protection.

A machine learning-based Delimited Anti-Jamming approach was put forth by Sunil Kumar et al. (2019) and was useful in scenarios involving vehicular traffic. The discriminating signal of the jamming car is found and filtered to determine the specific location of the affected vehicles. The research in question specifically developed a model for a vehicular interference system emphasizing the geolocation of cars in the defined jamming circumstances. To assess the performance, the existing methods and the suggested anti-jammer method were compared. The proposed approach proved to perform better than existing approaches based on a variety of performance factors.

Bhardwaj et al. [42] defined CIoV as a network-centric framework for intelligent cars, wherein vehicles are primarily thought of as context-aware agents under the vehicular networking notion. It is a sensory network made up of road components like cars and other related infrastructure that allows for little human engagement while receiving real-time information from the road and covering the physical world, including people and the environment. It used integrated cognitive algorithms and in-vehicle applications to observe real-time data in live broadcasts and do computations like pattern matching. This evolving architecture facilitated and maintained data for vehicle-to-vehicle and thing-to-thing communication in each cloud utilizing cutting-edge machine learning techniques like deep learning, artificial neural networks and data mining, this heterogeneous database was used for knowledge discovery.

5.3.1 Applications of IoV in smart cities

IoV is used to make transportation systems advanced and automated. After IoV, communication entities have been broadened to two or more by using different technologies like MANET technologies for mobile communication,

N geospatial technologies for fetching locations and Sensor Networking for exchanging sensed information like temperature, driver status, parking sensors, etc. [43–45]. Before IoV, only intravehicle autonomous communication was available in VANET, which was not enough to develop smart cities. IoV has given rise to Vehicle to Everything (V2X). Now, IoV has become an important application of ITS. Further, IoV has vast applications, from autonomous to automated, connected vehicles. These technologies are combined with real-time communication between all entities. IoV applications can be divided into various perspectives, including safety, efficiency, comfort and infotainment.

1. **Safety-centric IoV applications:** IoV ensures safety as one of its requirements. Safety parameters are how vehicles respond before and after detecting a threat to collision. IoV implements Cooperative Collision Avoidance Systems (CCAS) that detect collisions with the help of sensors and instructs drivers to take required actions. For instance, if there are traffic jams, accident-prone roads or accidents, a V2V communication takes place, and an emergency message is triggered to alert the drive to take certain actions. Gope and Sikdar proposed the controlled remote access cloud computer architecture system to make CCAS more effective [46].

2. **Efficiency-centric applications:** Applications that are efficiency-based seek to increase the mobility of vehicle objects inside an IoV network. The timing of traffic signals at intersections based on the volume of traffic to minimize waiting times is an example of such an application. In Churi and Pawar [47], it was suggested that a V2V-based strategy be used by grouping cars as they approached the intersection. To determine the timing cycle for traffic signals, the density of cars within the cluster is computed and the data is transmitted to the controllers. By scheduling the signalized intersection to maximize both traffic efficiency and fairness, another work in Kagalwalla et al. [48] offered a fuzzy logic technique. They employed a two-stage process. A green-phase selector was created in the first step to choose the next green phase. Another illustration of efficiency-based applications is provided for cooperative driving, which suggests modeling vehicle trajectories in advance for those close to traffic signals to decrease halting frequency and travel duration and enhance the travel volume of the road in accordance with traffic circumstances and the situation surrounding nearby vehicles.

3. **Comfort-centric IoV applications:** Comfort-based IoV applications are designed to provide drivers with information to make their journeys more joyful and comfortable. This could include information on the weather, route navigation, parking lots and the locations of tourist information kiosks, restaurants, gas stations and other facilities.

Applications based on information and entertainment are intended to provide drivers and passengers with information about amusement. Access to the internet and other file-sharing services fall under this category. Due to the dynamic and evolving nature of the vehicle objects in the IoV network, it is currently difficult to provide vehicles with access to the global internet and maintain the information. In order to provide QoS-enabled internet access in vehicle networks, Vidhi et al. [49] suggested a VANET to internet protocol. Their strategy made use of the IEEE 802.11p EDCA protocol and the Prediction-based Routing (PBR) algorithm.

4. **Infotainment-centric IoV applications:** Information and entertainment are combined under the term "infotainment". In-vehicle infotainment (IVI) refers to all available information and entertainment systems for use in automobiles. Social networking sites, navigation and other entertainment-related technologies are all connected to mobile devices. As voice recognition, the IoT and automobiles come together, IVI has been expanding in recent years. When a driver issues a voice command to check the weather, music or timetable, the route guide can be consulted. Anyone with access to the internet can operate a home appliance while on the go using IoT networks.

For large-scale data gathering, transfer and processing from smart items within the smart city environment, the IoV can be employed as a practical solution to meet the needs of smart cities. The vehicle nodes inside the IoV do not experience the resource limitations of limited battery power and information processing as do traditional wireless sensor networks (WSNs). Vehicles serve as mobile smart nodes or objects inside the sensing network within the IoV.

5.4 ISSUES AND CHALLENGES OF IOV

There are lots of challenges and issues with existing IoV technology. The rapid evolution of the Internet of Vehicles is breaking down many barriers on the path to building smart cities, but several significant challenges still remain.

1. **Security:** According to our expertise, the most important and challenging step in developing an IoT system is assuring security. The key obstacles the sector faces in terms of security for connected vehicles continue to be new difficulties. Since IoV networks are self-configuring and connected to the internet directly, they confront a number of security-related difficulties. Due to the movable nature of the deployed devices, the topology of these networks is likewise dynamic. Due to internet connectivity, nodes are extremely vulnerable to outside threats. Based on the data provided by the nodes, unauthorized users are capable of

engaging in malicious conduct. As a result, interruptions by the malicious can lead to catastrophic outcomes like accidents.

2. **Protracted product lifetime:** The time it takes to develop and release a linked car is a major barrier for manufacturers among all the issues with connected vehicles. It will still take months to release each new smart car onto the market, even though this time will shorten as IoV technology develops.

   The extended connected car production cycle may make it difficult for manufacturers to monitor market developments constantly and provide timely upgrades.

3. **Stability:** Having a stable connection is crucial for the Internet of Things with autonomous vehicles because network bottlenecks, DoS attacks and communications issues can all seriously impair the infrastructure's functionality. Manufacturers must address the issue of mobility and ensure that all nodes can send and receive data regardless of the speeds and locations of all cars.

   If any piece of hardware is compromised or uncooperative, stability may also suffer.

4. **Processing enormous volumes of information:** Big data is a benefit of IoV technology, but managing the continuous influx of data presents serious difficulties for providers. Cloud computing can be hampered, and the system can be damaged by insufficient storage or slow network speeds.

5. **Integrity:** Across disciplines, integrity can mean many various things, but in networking, it refers to a trustworthy multiparty interaction. It describes the position in which a network node or other entity acknowledges the reliance of others. Any network party must, therefore, offer information regarding the situation, such as the accuracy of the data given the circumstances. This idea or signature is complicated in a vehicle network and is dependent on precision, timeliness, accessibility and interoperability. Additionally, integrity is varied as a result of the C-introduction the IoV's massive amounts of data. Integrity is more crucial than ever because of the multifaceted and expanding connectivity within and outside the transportation system of the smart city.

5.5 FUTURE SCOPE OF IOV

Traditional Internet of Vehicles (IoV) is limited to the concept of intra- and inter-connecting vehicles and the infrastructure of roads to share information about the vehicles and roadside units and their observation globally and provide internet-based services to the users, such as infotainment. However, it is generally recognized that the concept of a single internet connection and its limited service is insufficient to meet demand and expectations. Furthermore, by applying cutting-edge technology, the internet cloud can be used to give users the ability to feel, comprehend, learn and think independently of the physical and social worlds. This assumption gave rise to the Cloud-based Internet of Vehicles (CIoV) paradigm, which enables cognitive computing capabilities for networks using technologies like software-defined networking, artificial intelligence, machine learning and similar ones. Its primary goal is to create a link between the social environment, which includes human demand, awareness and social behavior, and the transportation system, which includes vehicles and road infrastructure. In the context of smart cities, the evolved CIoV is working to integrate the vast real physical environment with digital control by sensing, comprehending and programming it. As a result, information loss and host or device control loss are also possible outcomes. Any information security breach poses a risk to commuters' personal relationships as well as their lives on the road. Absolute security must be achieved to develop a transportation system for network nodes, peers and the cloud to share trustworthy and authentic information.

5.6 CONCLUSION

The application of machine learning, artificial intelligence and cloud computing has given new dimensions to the Internet of Vehicles. This chapter covered the technological, social, security, safety and trust issues and challenges with the traditional IoV and presented the future scope of IoV's contribution to making smart cities smarter. Also, new technology brings some new expectations and new challenges, so futuristic IoE and V2E also have some challenges due to the heterogeneous entities added to make IoV into V2X. IoV was only serving as the global network of vehicles along with RSUs, but V2X includes intravehicle communication, inter-vehicle communication and communication from vehicle to pedestrian, vehicle to infrastructure, vehicle to home and vehicle to everything. This chapter illustrated how the evolution of the Intelligent Transportation System has evolved into a connected architecture from an autonomous architecture and from VANET to IoV, then IoV to CIoV. Overall, the chapter concluded that Cloud, ML and AI-based IoV is capable of reducing human dependency and fatal crashes to a large extent. Cloud-based IoV now has much more to explore.

REFERENCES

[1] J. Wan, D. Zhang, S. Zhao, L. T. Yang, & J. Lloret, Context-aware vehicular cyber-physical systems with cloud support: Architecture, challenges, and solutions. The IEEE Communications Magazine, vol. 52, no. 8, pp. 106–113, 2014.
[2] D. K. Choi, J. H. Jung, S. J. Koh, J. I. Kim, & J. Park, In-vehicle infotainment management system in internet-of-Things networks. International

Conference on Information Networking, pp. 88–92, 2019. https://doi.
org/10.1109/ICOIN.2019.8718192

[3] S. Kumar, K. Singh, S. Kumar, O. Kaiwartya, Y. Cao, H. Zhou, Delimitated
anti jammer scheme for internet of vehicle: Machine learning based security
approach. IEEE Access, 7, 2019.

[4] A. Arooj, M. S. Farooq, T. Umer, & R. U. Shan, Cognitive internet of vehicles and disaster management: A proposed architecture and future direction. Transactions on Emerging Telecommunications Technologies, p. e3625,
2019.

[5] O. Kaiwartya et al., Internet of vehicles: Motivation, layered architecture, network model, challenges, and future aspects. IEEE Access, vol. 4, pp. 5356–5373,
2016.

[6] I. Wagner, Number of Passenger Cars and Commercial Vehicles in Use Worldwide From 2006 to 2015 in (1,000 Units). Statista, 2018.

[7] J. Voelcker, It's Official: We Now Have One Billion Vehicles on the Planet.
Green Car Reports, 2011.

[8] L. Lakkadi, A. Mishra, & M. Bhardwaj, Security in ad hoc networks. American Journal of Networks and Communications, vol. 4, no. 3–1, pp. 27–34,
2015.

[9] J. Ishita & B. Manish, A survey analysis of COVID-19 pandemic using machine
learning (July 14, 2022). In Proceedings of the Advancement in Electronics &
Communication Engineering, 2022. https://ssrn.com/abstract=4159523 or
http://dx.doi.org/10.2139/ssrn.4159523

[10] S. Al-Sultan et al., A comprehensive survey on vehicular ad hoc network.
Journal of Network and Computer Applications, vol. 37, no. 1, pp. 380–392,
2014.

[11] M. N. O. Sadiku et al., "Internet of vehicles: An introduction. International
Journal of Advanced Research in Computer Science and Software Engineering, vol. 8, no. 1, pp. 11–13, 2018.

[12] Y. Fangchun et al., An overview of internet of vehicles. China Communications, vol. 11, no. 10, pp. 1–15, 2014.

[13] M. Nitti et al., On adding the social dimension to the internet of vehicles:
Friendship and middleware. In Proceedings of IEEE International Black
Sea Conference on Communications and Networking, Odessa, Ukraine,
pp. 134–138, 2014.

[14] M. Gerla et al., Internet of vehicles: From intelligent grid to autonomous
cars and vehicular clouds. In 2014 IEEE World Forum on Internet of Things
(WF-IoT), Seoul, pp. 241–246, 2014.

[15] K. Sha et al., Adaptive privacy-preserving authentication in vehicular networks. In 2006 First International Conference on Communications and Networking in China, Beijing, pp. 1–8, 2006.

[16] Y. Sun et al., Security and privacy in the internet of vehicles. In 2015 International Conference on Identification, Information, and Knowledge in the
Internet of Things (IIKI), Beijing, pp. 116–121, 2015.

[17] E. K. Lee et al., Internet of vehicles: From intelligent grid to autonomous cars
and vehicular fogs. International Journal of Distributed Sensor Networks,
vol. 12, no. 9, pp. 1–14, 2016.

[18] A. Sharma, A. Tyagi, & M. Bhardwaj, Analysis of techniques and attacking
pattern in cyber security approach: A survey. International Journal of Health

Sciences, vol. 6, no. S2, pp. 13779–13798, 2022. https://doi.org/10.53730/ijhs.v6nS2.8625

[19] A. Tyagi, A. Sharma, & M. Bhardwaj, Future of bioinformatics in India: A survey. International Journal of Health Sciences, vol. 6, no. S2, pp. 13767–13778, 2022. https://doi.org/10.53730/ijhs.v6nS2.8624.

[20] P. Chauhan & M. Bhardwaj, Analysis the performance of interconnection network topology C2 torus based on two dimensional torus. International Journal of Emerging Research in Management &Technology, vol. 6, no. 6, pp. 169–173, 2017.

[21] J. Kang et al., Location privacy attacks and defenses in cloud-enabled internet of vehicles. IEEE Wireless Communications, vol. 23, no. 5, pp. 52–59, 2016.

[22] J. Joy & M. Gerla, Internet of vehicles and autonomous connected car—Privacy and security issues. In 2017 26th International Conference on Computer Communication and Networks (ICCCN), Vancouver, pp. 1–9, 2017.

[23] J. Ni et al., Security, privacy, and fairness in fog-based vehicular crowdsensing. IEEE Communications Magazine, vol. 55, no. 6, pp. 146–152, 2017.

[24] J. Ni et al., Privacy-preserving real-time navigation system using vehicular crowdsourcing. In Proceedings of 2016 IEEE Vehicular Technology Conference (VTC-Fall), pp. 1–5, 2016.

[25] J. Ni et al., Secure and deduplicated spatial crowdsourcing: A fog-based approach. In Proceedings of IEEE Global Communications Conference (GLOBECOM), pp. 1–6, 2016.

[26] N. S. Pourush & M. Bhardwaj, Enhanced privacy-preserving multi-keyword ranked search over encrypted cloud data. American Journal of Networks and Communications, vol. 4, no. 3, pp. 25–31, 2015.

[27] M. Bhardwaja & A. Ahlawat, Evaluation of maximum lifetime power efficient routing in ad hoc network using magnetic resonance concept. Recent Patents on Engineering, vol. 13, no. 3, pp. 256–260, 2019.

[28] C. Huang et al., Vehicular fog computing: Architecture, use case, and security and forensic challenges. IEEE Communications Magazine, vol. 55, no. 11, pp. 105–111, 2017.

[29] Q. Kong et al., A privacy-preserving sensory data sharing scheme in internet of vehicles. Future Generation Computer Systems, vol. 92, pp. 644–655, 2019.

[30] J. Joy et al., Internet of vehicles: Enabling safe, secure, and private vehicular crowdsourcing. Internet Technology Letters, vol. 1, no. 1, pp. 1–6, 2017.

[31] L. Wang et al., NOTSA: Novel OBU with three-level security architecture for internet of vehicles. IEEE Internet of Things Journal, vol. 5, no. 5, pp. 3548–3558, 2018.

[32] Y. Qian et al., Secure enforcement in cognitive internet of vehicles. IEEE Internet of Things Journal, vol. 5, no. 2, pp. 1242–1250, 2018.

[33] L. Zhu et al., PRIF: A privacy-preserving interest-based forwarding scheme for social internet of vehicles. IEEE Internet of Things Journal, vol. 5, no. 4, pp. 2457–2466, 2018.

[34] M. Bhardwaj & A. Ahalawat, Improvement of lifespan of Ad hoc network with congestion control and magnetic resonance concept. In International Conference on Innovative Computing and Communications, Springer, Singapore, pp. 123–133, 2019.

[35] J. C. Castillo et al., "Internet of vehicles: Architecture, protocols, and security. Internet of Things Journal, vol. 5, no. 5, pp. 3701–3709, 2018.

[36] J. Kang et al., Privacy-preserved pseudonym scheme for fog computing supported internet of vehicles. IEEE Transactions on Intelligent Transportation Systems, vol. 19, no. 8, pp. 2627–2637, 2018.

[37] C. Chen et al., A secure authentication protocol for internet of vehicles. IEEE Access, vol. 7, pp. 12047–12057, 2019.

[38] M. A. Habib et al., Security and privacy based access control model for internet of connected vehicles. Future Generation Computer Systems, vol. 97, pp. 687–696, 2019.

[39] M. Sharma, S. Rohilla, & M. Bhardwaj, Efficient routing with reduced routing overhead and retransmission of manet. American Journal of Networks and Communications (Special Issue: Ad Hoc Networks), vol. 4, nos. 3–1, pp. 22–26, 2015. https://do.org/10.11648/j.ajnc.s.2015040301.15

[40] M. Bhardwaj, 7 Research on IoT governance, security, and privacy issues of internet of things. Privacy Vulnerabilities and Data Security Challenges in the IoT, vol. 115, 2020.

[41] A. Kumar, S. Rohilla, & M. Bhardwaj, Analysis of cloud computing load balancing algorithms. International Journal of Computer Sciences and Engineering, vol. 7, pp. 359–362, 2019.

[42] M. Bhardwaj, A. Ahlawat, & N. Bansal, Maximization of lifetime of wireless sensor network with sensitive power dynamic protocol. International Journal of Engineering & Technology, vol. 7, no. 3.12, pp. 380–383, 2018.

[43] M. Bhardwaj & A. Ahlawat, Wireless power transmission with short and long range using inductive coil. Wireless Engineering and Technology, vol. 9, pp. 1–9, 2018. https://do.org/10.4236/wet.2018.91001.

[44] G. Sun et al., Security and privacy preservation in fog-based crowd sensing on the internet of vehicles. Journal of Network and Computer Applications, vol. 134, pp. 89–99.

[45] M. Poddar et al., Privacy in the internet of vehicles: Models, algorithms, and applications. In 2019 International Conference on Information Networking (ICOIN), Kuala Lumpur, Malaysia, pp. 78–83, 2019.

[46] P. Gope & B. Sikdar, An efficient privacy-preserving authentication scheme for energy internet-based vehicle-to-grid communication. IEEE Transactions on Smart Grid, vol. 10, no. 6, pp. 6607–6618, 2019.

[47] P. P. Churi & A. V. Pawar, A systematic review on privacy preserving data publishing techniques. Journal of Engineering Science & Technology Review, vol. 12, no. 6, pp. 17–25, 2019.

[48] N. Kagalwalla, T. Garg, P. Churi, & A. Pawar, a survey on implementing privacy in healthcare: An Indian perspective. International Journal of Advanced Trends in Computer Science and Engineering Available, vol. 8, no. 3, pp. 963–982, 2019.

[49] K. Vidhi, R. Singh, R. Reddy, & P. Churi, Privacy Issues in Wearable Technology: An Intrinsic Review. In Proceedings of the International Conference on Innovative Computing & Communications (ICICC), p. 3566918, 2020 http://dx.doi.org/10.2139/ssrn.3566918

Chapter 6

Future issues and challenges of internet of vehicles

A Survey

Manish Bhardwaj, Sumit Kumar Sharma, Nitin Kumar, and Shweta Roy

6.1 INTRODUCTION

The Internet of Vehicles (IoV) is an offshoot of the Internet of Things (IoT) that resulted from the rising prevalence of cellular networks in vehicles, their subsequent reconstruction, and their connectivity to the IoT [1]. Through the IoV, intelligent transportation systems, pedestrians, and autonomous objects near the road are able to communicate with one another and share data in real time by linking physical devices, network transmission media, and cloud platforms. This data is used to reduce the financial burden of operating and maintaining transportation systems, improve public safety, enhance traveler convenience, and provide solutions to the problems posed by increasing urbanization [2]. The Internet of Vehicles (IoV) was developed from the concept of Vehicular Ad Hoc Networks (VANETs), which allowed for the emergence of wireless connections between vehicles on their own. Smart and connected vehicles require a stable network to function in the IoV.

The IoV interacts with the groundwork, other cars, and pedestrians in the area. A smart city ecosystem is made possible by the large amounts of data generated by this communication and saved in the cloud for easy access and analytics [3]. There is a pressing need to realize the full interoperability of all entities within the IoV ecosystem so that it can gain the advantages of a completely integrated environment. IEEE defines interoperability as "the capacity of two or more systems or components to share information and use the information that has been exchanged" [3] in their glossary of software engineering vocabulary. Data sharing and transfer between IoV entities are assumed to be trustworthy based on this definition. Data exchanged between these parties also needs to be useable to underpin IoV services and applications [4]. In spite of this, seamless integration of components in the IoV is difficult due to the variety and complexity of applications and end nodes using varying data formats and internal architecture. With its inherent heterogeneous connections of cyber and physical components operating in highly dynamic contexts, IoV is a large-scale, decentralized network [5].

DOI: 10.1201/9781003502432-6

Previous studies have looked into issues with vehicle communication with everything else (V2X). Vehicle-to-vehicle (V2V), vehicle-to-infrastructure (V2I), vehicle-to-roadside units (V2R), vehicle-to-pedestrian (V2P), vehicle-to-grid (V2G), vehicle-to-building (V2B), device (V2D), and cloud (V2C) communications are all part of V2X, as indicated in Figure 6.1. Efficient implementation of IoV applications will be possible after the obstacles of integrating these heterogeneous entities have been overcome. Vehicular networks are also defined by their inherent volatility and their inherent variability [6]. Since this changeability impacts data transmission in the network, maintaining consistent communication is challenging. Moreover, the growth of communication networks and Artificial Intelligence (AI) will lead to enhanced capabilities in traffic management systems. With this development comes the need for IoV-connected organizations to meet varying QoS criteria for things like real-time traffic monitoring, low-latency communication, and a few missed packets.

A counterintuitive interaction framework is presented by the interaction of IoV entities, which does not ensure frictionless interactions and real-time information sharing. Services, such as collision avoidance systems and

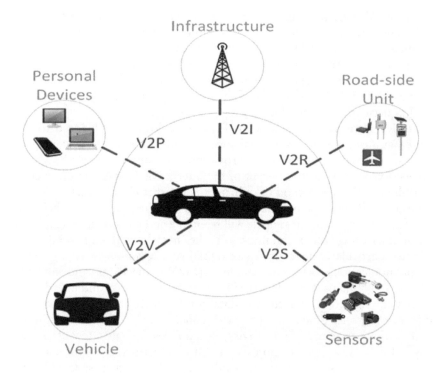

Figure 6.1 Basic architecture of the Internet of Vehicles.

emergency services, are made possible by IoV thanks to the involvement of application domains with varying needs and information models. Vehicles in the Internet of Things (IoT) interact with a wide variety of other devices that have varying technological specifications and adhere to a variety of protocols. In this case, coordinating vehicle movement and ensuring the safety of road users requires flawless application interactions and information exchange across the network [7]. A technological hurdle in the IoV ecosystem is reaching a consensus among the various entities involved in this interaction. A completely connected ecosystem that enables real-time applications is now unattainable due to the fragmented nature of the device market and the fact that different entities within it use incompatible interaction standards and protocols.

Vehicle use has increased as the population rises. The result would be more congestion and the potential for more accidents. This is a huge difficulty that people face on a regular basis. Within the past decade, mobile ad hoc networks have been differentiated into what are known as vehicular ad hoc networks (VANETs) (MANET). V2V and V2R communications are utilized in VANET to transmit data from vehicle to vehicle and vehicle to roadside. The Internet of Vehicles (IoV) has emerged from the IoT as a means to improve VANET functionality and cut down on traffic and road accidents (IoT). The Internet of Vehicles (IoV) is an upgraded version of the Internet of Things (IoT) designed to address complex problems in the modern urban transportation system. Travel itineraries and access to networks are two more services that drivers, passengers, and those in traffic management can get, thanks to IoV. IoV refers to the linking of different road networks via wireless networking technology.

Intelligent transportation system (ITS) technology has advanced to the point that it can now be used to enhance the traffic monitoring system, provide more accident protection, and provide a more convenient dashboard for drivers. Expanding on the concept of the Internet of Things, the Internet of Everything (IoE) is a method of utilizing the internet to link together actual hardware and end-user products. To accomplish these tasks, it is believed that, in the near future, all gadgets will be online and will communicate with one another using D2D technology. IoE relies heavily on the following technologies, particularly direct-to-device (D2D) connections.

Communications between machines (M2M), machines and humans (M2H), and humans themselves (P2P) depict the many links and interdependencies among people, objects, and data. IoE is widely utilized now because of its fast response time and high performance. Smart traffic monitoring, a smart parking system, and self-driving automobiles are only a few of the key uses of IoE in the transportation sector and road networks [8]. IoE has also been put to use in several areas of healthcare, such as patient-specific health monitoring, intelligent drug recommendation systems, and smart clinical care systems. Smartwatches, belts, and bands allow people to track their health data remotely. Doctors and clinical care systems receive the data gathered from a variety of smart healthcare devices and use it to take appropriate action. These days, you can buy a wide variety of intelligent wearable devices that measure everything from blood pressure and glucose levels to heart rate and temperature to how much you walk around throughout the day. In addition, IoE is utilized in numerous smart home applications, including window/door/room temperature/light/security alarm management. All the aforementioned programs need to have a fast response time in order to send the signal to the user or server. Efficient high-wireless networks are required to perceive and collect varied data from IoT devices [9]. These days, wireless network technologies like 4G and 5G have undergone tremendous improvements and advancements. Thanks to recent developments in wireless networking technology, physical devices may now detect signals and send them to the client and server in a timely fashion. In addition, the 5G network is utilized to fix problems with wireless connections and delays in data transmission between the various Internet of Things devices and the user or server. The 5G network is essential in advancing IoT to IoE technology. Everyday life is being revolutionized by the implementation of cutting-edge technologies like the Internet of Things (IoT), the Internet of Everything (IoE), and the Fifth Generation Mobile Network (5G cellular).

In this study, we contribute the following:

- Discuss all the parts of the IoV environment that are important for achieving interoperable and smooth integration.
- Based on a scan of existing literature, we provide the interoperability criteria for IoV and evaluate potential research avenues moving forward.
- Propose five groups of interoperability issues in IoV that prevent us from achieving the goals of a unified IoV ecosystem.
- Provide a summary of the literature's interoperability approaches and the difficulties that still exist in putting them into practice.
- Discuss the unresolved issues and highlight upcoming research directions in IoV cooperation.

6.2 LITERATURE SURVEY

Here, we first survey the prior literature on interconnection between various platforms, the Internet of Things (IoT) domain, and IoT applications. Before talking about the IoV interoperability work, various literature reviews will be discussed in what follows:

In various works, authors investigated potential applications and platform-specific interoperability solutions. Perumal et al. [10] present a solution based on simple object access protocol technology (SOAP) for interoperability issues in the smart home environment. Moon et al. [11] suggest building a service called ubiquitous middleware connection, and Park et al. [12] propose a method called video production room bridge adapter. Difficulties about incompatibility between in- and out-of-house gadgets are addressed by Park et al. using a paradigm that uses virtual network systems in the omnipresent home. In the context of smart manufacturing, Zeid et al. [13] zero in on the difficulties of interoperability. The authors investigate the semantic and semantic interconnection of factories and the cloud in production, along with the architectural model solutions provided by prominent platforms, as Industries 4.0 and the Industrial Internet Consortium (IIC). Relationship (network connectivity), interaction (data syntax), semantic (data understanding), dynamic (context changes), cognitive (action matching), and conceptual are the five layers of interoperability that make up the adaptation framework presented by Pantsar-Syva Niemi et al. [14] for situation-based and self-adaptive applications in a connected world (modeling and abstraction). However, the aforementioned projects are likely to only apply to smart homes, smart factories, and smart environments rather than the IoV as a whole.

Noura et al. [15] provide a comprehensive overview of the difficulties inherent in interconnecting heterogeneous devices and the solutions available across the various IoT platforms. Tools supplied by adapters/gateways can be used, such as mediators; virtual networks can be formed on top of the physical layer; networking technologies, open APIs, and service-oriented architectures can all be found at the network layer [16]. According to Lee et al. [17], worldwide standards that have been created and adopted by official bodies are necessary for achieving interoperability and security in the IoT.

As a result, Jain and Bhardwaj investigate and synthesize the worldwide norms for IoT interoperability and security [18].

In order to tackle the issue of semantic interoperability in the Internet of Things, Rahman et al. [19] categorize current solutions into ontology, middleware, and the Semantic Web. Additionally, outstanding research issues are highlighted, and frameworks and tools for assessing and evaluating IoT interoperability are described by Bhardwaj and Ahalawat [20].

Lack of resources, using proprietary technology, network complexity, different security requirements, and heterogeneous devices are all mentioned as potential obstacles to tackling IoT interoperability by Konduru and Bharamagoudray [21]. Google Weave, IoTivity, Alljoyn, and Apple Home Kit are just a few of the open-source technologies, frameworks, and APIs that the authors highlight as having been developed with the intention of resolving interoperability difficulties in the IoT. However, proposed IoT solutions are insufficient to meet interoperability concerns in IoV because of the unique difficulties associated with device-to-device communication in this domain.

Issues and responses to IoV interoperability have been explored and implemented before, and this work refines the application of IoT interoperability to the surface transportation field. The cross-domain, cross-syntactic, and cross-semantic interoperability are presented by Hussain et al. [22]. Increased execution time, latency, and a lack of mobility support are some of the drawbacks the authors highlight when discussing interoperability techniques. By underlining the absence of standards that may enable smooth interconnection of IoV components, Hussain et al. [23] investigate the elements that make interoperability problematic. They offer a seven-tiered taxonomy of IoV interoperability, with the lowest level being non-interoperability and the highest level being complete interoperability at the technical, syntactic, semantic, pragmatic, dynamic, and conceptual levels. As an additional step toward interoperability in IoV, they recommend looking into IoT middleware solutions. However, the authors did not explain the middleware solution or how it can fix the problem of IoV incompatibility. In their definition of "smart cities," Datta et al. [24] characterize vehicles as "connected resources" that provide services like traffic management and pollution detection. According to the authors, a fully linked IoV that connects customers, autos, and computing platforms were unable to be developed due to a lack of universal architecture and standards, as well as the presence of data silos. To deal with these issues, they suggest an IoT architecture that employs open standards for interoperability in the IoV, such as SenML, oneM2M, and semantic web technologies [25]. They also detailed the phases of operation for the proposed framework and how it may be utilized as a guide for creating IoV apps.

However, the heterogeneity of devices and data conveyed in the IoV ecosystem and the changing architecture of the IoV were not taken into account by the offered solutions [26]. Different from prior efforts, our study seeks to unify the assumptions, challenges, methods, and research difficulties in the field of IoV interoperability.

The authors of this chapter provide a thorough analysis of the needs of interworking heterogeneous entities in the IoV and propose a comprehensive taxonomy of interoperability in IoV, taking into account the heterogeneity and dynamic topology of vehicular networks. Additionally, we provide a review of outstanding issues in the pursuit of a fully functional IoV ecosystem.

6.3 IOV ECOSYSTEM

The ecology of the Internet of Vehicles and the various nodes involved in its communication is covered in this section. The authors also detail the IoV ecosystem, including its users, apps, and platform. Figure 6.2 shows the Internet of Vehicles layered architecture with a security layer and provides a

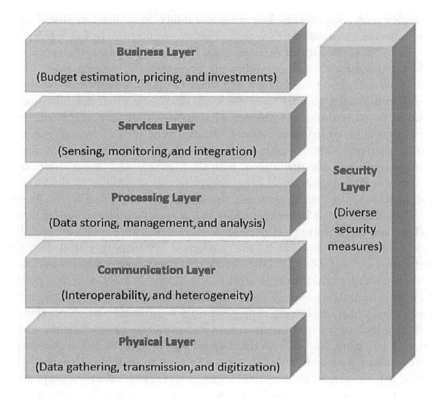

Figure 6.2 Internet of Vehicles layered architecture with a security layer.

more nuanced look at how the framework's layers can be used to structure the IoV ecosystem.

Because it provides a framework for integrating "things," intelligent vehicles, humans, and the encompassing infrastructure via channels such as the internet and the Internet, IoV makes it possible for vehicles to connect with other entities in their operational environment. Interactions between cars (V2V), the grid (V2G), buildings (V2B), roadside units (V2R), and the cloud (V2C) are all made possible by the IoV, which enables the development of highly interconnected, heterogeneous systems capable of running a wide range of applications and services [27]. Because of this, the various components of the ecosystem are able to share knowledge and collaborate to build an advanced infrastructure suitable for smart city services. To reduce traffic and pollution, ease traffic congestion, free up parking spots, and cut costs, IoV is expected to increase ride-sharing services. When compared to ITS, IoV is distinguished by its capacity to turn every car on the road into a self-contained computing, storage, and networking node that can exchange data with other cars, pedestrians, and roadside infrastructure.

Several architectural levels for IoV have been proposed based on the interaction of communication nodes. Layers of the architecture include perception, the network, and the application. To enable communication and interoperability, each layer requires collaboration from multiple levels. At the perception layer of IoV, there is a plethora of flawless data sources (heterogeneous devices). At the application layer, there is a suite of programs and tools for analyzing the information gleaned from these devices [28]. Connectivity, data extraction, transmission, and security between the two higher-level layers are all made possible by the network layer, making it a crucial component of IoV operations. Effective V2X communication is enabled by the network layer's central location, which allows it to cater to the needs of all the other levels and devices [29].

The edge devices, such as sensors, actuators, and the related computational resources, are hosted by the perception layer, the biggest drop. This layer is responsible for perceiving and collecting data by way of the vehicles' in-built sensors, which can record data about the surrounding environment, such as highway and traffic conditions, obstacles, and driving habits. Due to the volume and variety of information collected by the perception layer's sensors, collaboration amongst IoV entities is essential for making the most of available resources. In addition, the layer facilitates the digitization of analog data for subsequent processing, storage, and dissemination. Using wireless and wired connections, smart objects process the gathered data locally, typically in real-time, and disseminate the results to other devices in the same layer or network [30]. Wi-Fi, Bluetooth, ZigBee, and radio-frequency are all utilized for wireless connectivity at this layer, while standard serial interfaces like I2C, SPI, and Ethernet are used for cable connectivity. Because devices in the perception layer employ a wide variety of communication technologies and protocols, achieving interoperability is essential to ensuring that sensed data is transmitted quickly and effectively throughout the network. Sensors and other IoV devices should be able to reliably interact with one another and join the automotive network on the fly if there is commonality at the perception layer [31]. Adopting standards would also guarantee that equipment can be managed and connected regardless of their core platform, specifications, or models.

This layer utilizes network technology to determine the paths sensor data must take to reach the various services that make up the IoV. Communication is facilitated at this level via portals, switches, hubs, and routing devices [32]. Technologies such as 4G/LTE, 5G/6G, Bluetooth, and Wi-Fi are used to send information to programs in heterogeneous networks. Other technologies include wireless access in vehicle environment (WAVE) and international standardization for microwave access (WiMAX). There are benefits and drawbacks to each of these technological options. Examples include WAVE's ability to connect devices via dedicated short-range communications (DSRC), which necessitates a mobility layer that can handle things like handoffs and ensures that traffic is managed in a way that doesn't degrade network quality of service.

6.4 INTERNET OF VEHICLES APPLICATIONS

There are two main categories for IoV applications: (1) ITS applications and (2) smart city apps. In this article, we'll go over the various uses for IoV and how they're categorized. The uses of ITS encompass a wide range of technologies that can be applied to the transportation system to improve its dependability, efficiency, safety, and sustainability without disrupting the existing infrastructure. There are five broad types of ITS-related IoV applications:

1. **Safety Applications:** These applications focus on enhancing road safety by utilizing vehicle-to-vehicle (V2V) and vehicle-to-infrastructure (V2I) communication to exchange information about potential hazards, such as accidents, road obstacles, or adverse weather conditions. Examples include collision warning systems, emergency brake assistance, and lane departure warning systems.
2. **Traffic Efficiency and Management:** These applications aim to improve traffic flow, reduce congestion, and enhance transportation efficiency. They often involve real-time data collection, analysis, and dissemination to optimize traffic signal timing, manage traffic flow, and provide dynamic route guidance to drivers. Examples include adaptive traffic signal control, congestion prediction systems, and dynamic route guidance applications.
3. **Environmental Sustainability:** These applications focus on reducing the environmental impact of transportation by promoting eco-friendly driving behaviors, optimizing vehicle routes to minimize fuel consumption and emissions, and supporting the adoption of alternative fuel vehicles. Examples include eco-driving assistance systems, electric vehicle charging station locators, and emission monitoring applications.
4. **Driver Assistance and Comfort:** These applications aim to enhance driver comfort, convenience, and overall driving experience. They may include features such as advanced driver assistance systems (ADAS), infotainment services, remote vehicle diagnostics, and maintenance reminders. Examples include adaptive cruise control, parking assistance systems, and in-car entertainment services.
5. **Commercial and Logistics Applications:** These applications target the commercial and logistics sectors, focusing on optimizing freight transportation, fleet management, and supply chain operations. They may involve real-time tracking of vehicles and shipments, route optimization,

load balancing, and delivery scheduling. Examples include fleet tracking and management systems, cargo tracking solutions, and logistics optimization platforms.

Applications of IoV that prioritize safety aid in increasing the likelihood of avoiding mishaps by vehicles. Common automotive safety features are often referred to as "collision avoidance" systems [33]. Past efforts look at IoV apps that prioritize user safety, such as forward vehicle identification and collision warning systems techniques like active learning and symmetry utilizing computer-aided learning or night vision. The safe integration of these technologies has been because the IoV ecosystem of mission-critical applications is not negotiable. Vehicles can talk internally and externally with other vehicles and road users, alerting them to the possibility of or actuality of a collision for the sake of safety.

The importance of a timely and accurate diagnosis cannot be overstated. Data from vehicle diagnostic systems is crucial for identifying and fixing any potential points of failure of the machinery within a car [34]. Fault alerts can be sent to users and other forms of artificial intelligence, such as their smartphones and the screens installed in cars. Remote diagnosis must be successfully implemented. End nodes must be connected invisibly. Networked and diagnostics software needs to be tightly integrated into the system as a whole. Transmission means must be dependable to run smoothly to check and identify problems in real time.

Autonomous vehicle security is a common concern, including assaults on both availability and integrity, denial Sybil attacks, denial-of-service assaults, and spoofing effects on entity and safety application quality of service, meaning "the IoVs." Protection applications for IoV guarantee that by meeting these requirements, communications are safe and secure. Standards ensuring privacy, verifiability, accessibility, and incorruptibility are essential in various domains, particularly in technologies involving data handling, communication, and verification [35]. To help the productive security in IoV implementation, including ISO/IEC 27001:2013 Telecommunications Standards in Europe and WAVE Institute elucidates risk profiles, information architectures, secure ITS communication, and certificate formats. Additionally, security-focused solutions to problems with IoVs have included the introduction of encryption, intrusion detection systems, and digital signature methods to ensure privacy, identity, and traffic data integrity and an internal catastrophe recovery environment.

Information and entertainment (infotainment) apps offer vehicle users the latest news, entertainment, etc., giving them the possibility to stay productive or enjoy in-flight entertainment, which could make the trip more enjoyable [36]. Applications that provide these services are crucial, and in light of media streaming and IoV entities that function together, seamlessly personalized and geo-targeted services are possible, providing content to people in a moving car.

IoV's quick data sharing between nodes makes it a desirable tool for use in smart cities. In order for smart cities to gather, transport, and evaluate massive amounts of intelligence data from embedded sensors, IoV can be used. In addition, unlike conventional wireless sensor networks, the cars in IoV are not limited by issues like battery life or information processing capabilities. Each IoV communication object is thought to serve four functions [37].

Each node in an IoV network is linked to others in the same topology to facilitate resource sharing among them. Connectivity in the IoV relies on the peer-to-peer relationships between vehicles [38].

Vehicle objects make service requests to IoV and operate as consumers of those services.

Data collector devices gather information produced by smart nodes and send it to servers. Since each smart object in IoV has limited access to resources like computing, memory, and power, the communicating nodes employ a distributed computing model to pool their resources and perform more complex computations.

6.5 SUMMARIZED CHALLENGES AND FUTURE RESEARCH DIRECTIONS

Although a lot of work has gone into solving interoperability problems in IoV, researchers are always looking for new ways to make it easier to connect devices and solve the key problems that arise in real-time. Emerging technologies that will aid in the implementation of a fully integrated, secure, and interoperable IoV ecosystem are still in the early stages of development because IoV is still in its infancy, and the whole spectrum of unique technologies involved is evolving. In this part, we detail some of the outstanding research questions that have yet to be answered and propose potential avenues for answering those questions.

- Security

Due to the increasing number of technological gadgets installed in cars, it is no longer sufficient to simply lock the doors and windows. When it comes to creating a fully linked IoV ecosystem, security is a big worry for automakers and tech enthusiasts alike. Cybercriminals love cars because they can do all sorts of bad things with the information they steal from them [39]. The IoV relies on wireless media for information sharing and computationally heavy operations, leaving the ecosystem vulnerable to attack.

Additionally, a variety of entities linked to the standard comms infrastructure may pose potential threats. While the interoperability of IoV platforms

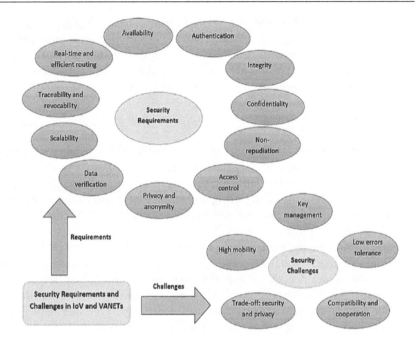

Figure 6.3 Security challenges and requirements of IoV.

makes it easier to handle data in IoV infrastructure, it also makes the system more susceptible to cyber threats. Secured packet delivery in the network requires security methods such as cryptography for application data transfer and other approaches that do not affect the quality of service of IoV infrastructure. Figure 6.3 shows the security requirements of the Internet of Vehicles.

- Scalability

Solutions for IoV must be easily scalable; otherwise, the argument for their adoption would collapse under the weight of the resources needed to construct or modify them. High scalability in design technology, i.e., architectures that can switch between centralized and decentralized control modes depending on network demands, is also required because the network contains a wide variety of vehicular nodes and deployment environments to process data and ensure sustainable service. There needs to be a standardization of services to intelligently manage, distribute, and secure data from connected devices, all while keeping operational costs low so that solutions can adapt to the unpredictable nature of the IoV's traffic [40]. Flexible and optimized search engine designs are necessary for managing requests and retrieving data needed by linked nodes, in addition to developing a standardized scheme for storing vehicle data, like the cloud platform. Furthermore, effective admission methods need to be created for dynamic networks where nodes can join and leave the network at any time in order to decrease the latency of joining a network and accept node requests.

- Trust Management

Trust between the communicating entities in the IoV is necessary for them to cooperate based on mutually understood context data. The storage and computation of trust-related information creates overhead that causes latencies in nodes with limited computing and storage capabilities due to the need for regular updates by trust evaluation algorithms aiming to reduce the risk of untrusted nodes in the network.

Algorithms for trust management for information credibility that are scalable and efficient, formalizing and optimizing entity reputation and available resources, are needed to meet this problem. Solutions that leverage the decentralized capabilities of blockchain are interesting techniques that can provide a safe framework for efficient and scalable trust management. Moreover, the design of trust management models should take semantic interoperability into account.

- Artificial Intelligence

Improving the cognitive performance of IoV applications and tackling complicated challenges like routing, resource management, and task offloading are made possible using AI methodologies like deep and reinforcement learning. To increase network security and efficiency, IoV nodes can learn to make rational decisions using AI.

However, the use of AI techniques in IoV is far from simple, as they rely significantly on sensor data, which can be influenced by factors such as complex traffic situations, poor network topology stability, and electromagnetic interference from natural or manmade sources. For instance, snow might influence the performance of light detection and ranging systems, leading to incorrect input for object categorization from the AI subsystem. To back IoV applications, we need to develop AI algorithms that are resilient in uncertain operating situations and robust in urban settings. Additionally, AI algorithms are computationally intensive, necessitating high-powered, high-energy-consumption computing resources like graphics processing units.

The creation of high-performance hardware resources with low energy utilization is necessary for IoV for large-scale commercial AI applications, despite the fact that hardware innovations like field-programmable gate arrays boost the performance of GPUs.

- Semantics and Syntax of Data

The solutions we looked at take different tacks when it comes to managing data. However, the syntax, semantics, or absence of data is often inconsistent with these approaches. Addressing this difficulty requires a defined schema to guarantee a common, formal data syntax throughout the IoV ecosystem. Context extraction that works well requires a standard schema to handle variations in data syntax. In order to support IoV applications, it is helpful to combine data normalization and data fusion techniques with the creation of distributed data analytic modules that efficiently manage noise reduction and error correction. Additionally, ontologies that can provide consistent data formats for multimodal IoV data require technologies like web semantics. Cross-platform data interchange between IoV applications might also benefit from open APIs that permit devices operating in different domains to interact.

- Cross-Domain Integration

The availability of services to ecosystem users can be further improved by integrating other areas, such as smart homes, ITS, and health.

Existing vertical domains' applications and services need to be supported by others using a variety of communication protocols and Quality of Service (QoS) criteria. However, because solutions in these areas are typically created independently, interoperability is often difficult to establish. A standardized foundation for intelligent device production is essential for cross-platform and cross-domain integration. Also, similar to the BIG IoT API for general IoT platforms, a uniform interface for accessing data should be provided via application programming interfaces and resource discovery tools.

In order to foster collaborations between disparate domains and improve cross-platform access to data, it is necessary to adopt vertical silos for IoV platforms and provide users with domain-specific interfaces.

- Emerging Technology Adaptation

Low-latency networks like the IoV, 5G, 6G, and mmWave offer superior connection with increased data transmission rate, decreased communication delay, powerful detection capabilities, and greater security. Integration of these technologies to serve vehicle applications requires an understanding of channel measurements in dynamic situations, impacts of signal obstructions, and dynamics of antenna directionality. If these technologies were integrated with preexisting vehicular networks such as Cellular V2X, WiMax, and DSRC, as well as architectures like NDN, SDN, and SIoV, the IoV's quality of service would be greatly enhanced. Data for channel measurement is increased due to the interaction of these technologies with current ones, which complicates data processing and the knowledge of the nature of communication channels. Wireless channel modeling and data management can both benefit from the use of deep learning methods like generative adversarial networks.

6.6 CONCLUSION

Integrating heterogeneous entities that may support these services and applications and addressing interoperability difficulties in IoV are essential for ensuring sustainable services. In this study, we go into the difficulties of interoperability in IoV and provide a comprehensive taxonomy of these obstacles. To gain a competitive edge in the smart city ecosystem, we give a detailed overview of the various approaches that have been presented to handle IoV interoperability. We argue that IoV interoperability, advanced intelligence methods, flexible network architecture, and an appropriate harmony between security and privacy are essential. In order to realize the exciting potential of IoV, it is necessary to overcome these obstacles and create an ecosystem that improves the smooth, real-time communication of network components.

REFERENCES

[1] Y. Ma, Z. Wang, H. Yang, and L. Yang, "Artificial intelligence applications in the development of autonomous vehicles: A survey," IEEE/CAA Journal of Automatica Sinica, vol. 7, no. 2, pp. 315–329, 2020.

[2] R. Iqbal, T. A. Butt, M. Afzaal, and K. Salah, "Trust management in social internet of vehicles: factors, challenges, blockchain, and fog solutions," International Journal of Distributed Sensor Networks, vol. 15, no. 1, p. 1550147719825820, 2019.

[3] U. Javaid, M. N. Aman, and B. Sikdar, "A scalable protocol for driving trust management in internet of vehicles with blockchain," IEEE Internet of Things Journal, vol. 7, no. 12, pp. 11 815–11 829, 2020.

[4] C.-X. Wang, J. Huang, H. Wang, X. Gao, X. You, and Y. Hao, "6g wireless channel measurements and models: Trends and challenges," IEEE Vehicular Technology Magazine, vol. 15, no. 4, pp. 22–32, 2020.

[5] A. Sharma, A. Tyagi, and M. Bhardwaj, "Analysis of techniques and attacking pattern in cyber security approach: A survey," International Journal of Health Sciences, vol. 6, no. S2, pp. 13779–13798, 2022. https://doi.org/10.53730/ijhs.v6nS2.8625

[6] A. Tyagi, A. Sharma, and M. Bhardwaj, "Future of bioinformatics in India: A survey," International Journal of Health Sciences, vol. 6, no. S2, pp. 13767–13778, 2022. https://doi.org/10.53730/ijhs.v6nS2.8624.

[7] N. S. Pourush and M. Bhardwaj, "Enhanced privacy-preserving multi-keyword ranked search over encrypted cloud data," American Journal of Networks and Communications, vol. 4, no. 3, pp. 25–31, 2015.

[8] M. Bhardwaja and A. Ahlawat, "Evaluation of maximum lifetime power efficient routing in Ad hoc network using magnetic resonance concept," Recent Patents on Engineering, vol. 13, no. 3, pp. 256–260, 2019.

[9] C. R. Storck and F. Duarte-Figueiredo, "A survey of 5g technology evolution, standards, and infrastructure associated with vehicle-to-everything communications by internet of vehicles," IEEE Access, vol. 8, pp. 117 593–117 614, 2020.

[10] T. Perumal, C. Y. Leong, K. Samsudin, S. Mansor, et al., "Interoperability among heterogeneous systems in smart home environment," in Web-Based Information Technologies and Distributed Systems, Springer, 2010, pp. 141–157.

[11] K.-D. Moon, Y.-H. Lee, C.-E. Lee, and Y.-S. Son, "Design of a universal middleware bridge for device interoperability in heterogeneous home network middleware," IEEE Transactions on Consumer Electronics, vol. 51, no. 1, pp. 314–318, 2005.

[12] H. Park, J.-H. Park, and N. Kim, "A framework for interoperability of heterogeneous devices in ubiquitous home," in 2010 Second International Conference on Advances in Future Internet, IEEE, 2010.

[13] A. Zeid, S. Sundaram, M. Moghaddam, S. Kamarthi, and T. Marion, "Interoperability in smart manufacturing: Research challenges," Machines, vol. 7, no. 2, p. 21, 2019.

[14] S. Pantsar-Syvaniemi, A. Purhonen, E. Ovaska, J. Kuusijarvi, and A. Evesti, "Situation-based and self-adaptive applications for the smart environment," Journal of Ambient Intelligence and Smart Environments, vol. 4, no. 6, pp. 491–516, 2012.

[15] M. Noura, M. Atiquzzaman, and M. Gaedke, "Interoperability in internet of things: Taxonomies and open challenges," Mobile Networks and Applications, vol. 24, no. 3, pp. 796–809, 2019.

[16] S. Lakkadi, A. Mishra, and M. Bhardwaj, "Security in ad hoc networks," American Journal of Networks and Communications, vol. 4, nos. 3–1, pp. 27–34, 2015.

[17] E. Lee, Y.-D. Seo, S.-R. Oh, and Y.-G. Kim, "A survey on standards for interoperability and security in the internet of things," IEEE Communications Surveys & Tutorials, vol. 23, no. 2, 2021.

[18] I. Jain and M. Bhardwaj, "A survey analysis of COVID-19 pandemic using machine learning (July 14, 2022)," Proceedings of the Advancement in Electronics & Communication Engineering, 2022. https://ssrn.com/abstract=4159523 or http://dx.doi.org/10.2139/ssrn.4159523

[19] H. Rahman and M. I. Hussain, "A comprehensive survey on semantic interoperability for internet of things: State-of-the-art and research challenges," Transactions on Emerging Telecommunications Technologies, vol. 31, no. 12, p. e3902, 2020.

[20] M. Bhardwaj and A. Ahalawat, "Improvement of lifespan of Ad hoc network with congestion control and magnetic resonance concept," in International

Conference on Innovative Computing and Communications, Springer, pp. 123–133, 2019.

[21] V. R. Konduru and M. R. Bharamagoudra, "Challenges and solutions of interoperability on iot: How far have we come in resolving the iot interoperability issues," in 2017 International Conference On Smart Technologies For Smart Nation (SmartTechCon), IEEE, 2017.

[22] S. M. Hussain, K. M. Yusof, and S. A. Hussain, "Interoperability in connected vehicles–a review," International Journal of Wireless and Microwave Technologies, vol. 9, no. 5, pp. 1–11, 2019. https://doi.org/10.5815/ijwmt.2019.05.01

[23] S. M. Hussain, K. M. Yosof, and S. A. Hussain, "Interoperability issues in internet of vehicles-a survey," in 2018 3rd International Conference on Contemporary Computing and Informatics (IC3I), IEEE, 2018, pp. 257–262.

[24] S. K. Datta, J. Haerri, C. Bonnet, and R. F. Da Costa, "Vehicles as connected resources: Opportunities and challenges for the future," IEEE Vehicular Technology Magazine, vol. 12, no. 2, pp. 26–35, 2017.

[25] M. Sharma, S. Rohilla, and M. Bhardwaj, "Efficient routing with reduced routing overhead and retransmission of manet," American Journal of Networks and Communications. Special Issue: Ad Hoc Networks, vol. 4, nos. 3–1, pp. 22–26, 2015. https://doi.org/10.11648/j.ajnc.s.2015040301.15

[26] J. Cheng, G. Yuan, M. Zhou, S. Gao, C. Liu, H. Duan, and Q. Zeng, "Accessibility analysis and modeling for IOV in an urban scene," IEEE Transactions on Vehicular Technology, vol. 69, no. 4, pp. 4246–4256, 2020.

[27] J. Zhang and K. B. Letaief, "Mobile edge intelligence and computing for the internet of vehicles," Proceedings of the IEEE, vol. 108, no. 2, pp. 246–261, 2019.

[28] S. Sun, J. Bi, M. Guillen, and A. M. Perez-Marín, "Assessing driving risk using internet of vehicles data: An analysis based on generalized linear models," Sensors, vol. 20, no. 9, p. 2712, 2020.

[29] L. Atzori, A. Floris, R. Girau, M. Nitti, and G. Pau, "Towards the implementation of the social internet of vehicles," Computer Networks, vol. 147, pp. 132–145, 2018.

[30] D. Furelos Blanco, A. Bucchiarone, and A. Jonsson, "Carpool: collective adaptation using concurrent planning," in Proceedings of the 17th International Conference on Autonomous Agents and Multiagent Systems (AAMAS '18), AAMAS, 2018, pp. 1815–1817.

[31] M. Bhardwaj, "7 Research on IoT governance, security, and privacy issues of internet of things," Privacy Vulnerabilities and Data Security Challenges in the IoT, vol. 115, 2020.

[32] A. Kumar, S. Rohilla, and M. Bhardwaj, "Analysis of cloud computing load balancing algorithms," International Journal of Computer Sciences and Engineering, vol. 7, pp. 359–362, 2019.

[33] M. Bhardwaj, A. Ahlawat, and N. Bansal, "Maximization of lifetime of wireless sensor network with sensitive power dynamic protocol," International Journal of Engineering & Technology, vol. 7, no. 3.12, pp. 380–383, 2018.

[34] M. Bhardwaj and A. Ahlawat, "Wireless power transmission with short and long range using inductive coil," Wireless Engineering and Technology, vol. 9, pp. 1–9, 2018. https://doi.org/10.4236/wet.2018.91001.

[35] P. Chauhan and M. Bhardwaj, "Analysis the performance of interconnection network topology C2 torus based on two dimensional torus," International Journal of Emerging Research in Management &Technology, vol. 6, no. 6, pp. 169–173, 2017.

[36] S. K. Datta, C. Bonnet, and J. Haerri, "Fog computing architecture to enable consumer centric internet of things services," in 2015 International Symposium on Consumer Electronics (ISCE), IEEE, 2015, pp. 1–2.

[37] T. Zugno, M. Drago, M. Giordani, M. Polese, and M. Zorzi, "Toward standardization of millimeter-wave vehicle-to-vehicle networks: Open challenges and performance evaluation," IEEE Communications Magazine, vol. 58, no. 9, pp. 79–85, 2020.

[38] A. Bazzi, B. M. Masini, A. Zanella, and I. Thibault, "On the performance of IEEE 802.11 p and lte-v2v for the cooperative awareness of connected vehicles," IEEE Transactions on Vehicular Technology, vol. 66, no. 11, pp. 10 419–10 432, 2017.

[39] S. Zeadally, M. A. Javed, and E. B. Hamida, "Vehicular communications for its: Standardization and challenges," IEEE Communications Standards Magazine, vol. 4, no. 1, pp. 11–17, 2020.

[40] A. Ahamed and H. Vakilzadian, "Issues and challenges in VANET routing protocols," in 2018 IEEE international conference on electro/information technology (EIT), IEEE, 2018, pp. 0723–0728.

Chapter 7

Feature designing and security considerations in electrical vehicles utilizing explainable AI

Mandeep Kaur and Vinayak Goel

7.1 FEATURE DESIGNING FOR SMART ELECTRICAL VEHICLES

i. User Interface Design for Smart Cars (*A historical perspective of explainable Artificial Intelligence—Confalonieri—2021 — WIREs Data Mining and Knowledge Discovery—Wiley Online Library*, 2021)

User interface design plays a crucial role in the successful implementation of smart cars. As these vehicles become more advanced and incorporate artificial intelligence (AI) technologies, it is essential to design user interfaces that are intuitive, informative, and promote trust and transparency. In this section, we will explore the key considerations and best practices for user interface design in smart cars. The importance of user interface design is quite critical in smart cars as it directly impacts the user experience and safety of the vehicle. A well-designed user interface can enhance the driver's ability to interact with the car's features and functions effectively. It should provide clear and concise information, allowing the driver to make informed decisions while minimizing distractions.

ii. Design Principles for Smart Car Interfaces (Phillips et al., 2020)

When designing user interfaces for smart cars, several principles should be considered to ensure usability and effectiveness. These principles include:

a. Simplicity and Clarity

Smart car interfaces should be simple and easy to understand. The information presented should be clear and concise, avoiding unnecessary complexity. The use of intuitive icons, symbols, and visual cues can help drivers quickly grasp the meaning of different controls and indicators.

DOI: 10.1201/9781003502432-7

b. Consistency

Consistency in design is crucial to ensure that drivers can easily navigate and interact with the interface. The placement of controls, the use of colors and fonts, and the overall layout should follow established design patterns and conventions. This consistency helps drivers develop mental models of how the interface works, reducing cognitive load and improving usability.

c. Contextual Awareness

Smart car interfaces should be contextually aware, providing relevant information based on current driving conditions. For example, the interface can display real-time traffic updates, weather conditions, or nearby points of interest. By tailoring the information to the driver's context, the interface can enhance situational awareness and assist in decision-making.

d. Feedback and Confirmation

Providing feedback and confirmation is essential to ensure that drivers understand the actions they have taken and the system's response. Visual and auditory cues can be used to acknowledge user inputs, such as button presses or voice commands. Additionally, the interface should provide clear feedback on the status of the vehicle's systems, such as battery charge level or engine temperature.

e. Minimizing Distractions

One of the primary concerns in smart car interface design is minimizing distractions. The interface should prioritize essential information and functions, reducing the cognitive load on the driver. Unnecessary alerts, notifications, or complex menus should be avoided to prevent driver distraction and maintain focus on the road.

f. Integration of Explainable AI in User Interfaces (Clinciu and Hastie, 2019)

Explainable AI techniques can play a significant role in enhancing the user interface design of smart cars. By providing transparent and interpretable explanations of the AI algorithms and decision-making processes, drivers can better understand and trust the system's recommendations and actions. Here are some ways in which explainable AI can be integrated into smart car user interfaces:

i. Visualizing AI Outputs

One approach to incorporating explainable AI in user interfaces is by visualizing the outputs of AI algorithms. For example, if the smart car uses

AI for object detection, the interface can display the detected objects and their confidence levels. This visualization helps drivers understand how the AI system perceives the environment and makes decisions.

ii. Providing Contextual Explanations

Explainable AI can provide contextual explanations to drivers, helping them understand why certain recommendations or actions are being suggested. For instance, if the smart car suggests taking a specific route, the interface can explain that the recommendation is based on real-time traffic data or historical patterns. This contextual information helps drivers make informed decisions and builds trust in the system.

iii. Interactive Explanations

Interactive explanations allow drivers to explore the AI system's decision-making process further. The interface can provide additional information about the features or factors that influenced a particular recommendation or action. By enabling drivers to interact with the explanations, they can gain a deeper understanding of how the AI system works and its limitations.

iv. Error Handling and Recovery

Explainable AI can also assist in error handling and recovery in smart car interfaces. If the AI system encounters an error or uncertainty, the interface can provide explanations and alternative options to the driver. This transparency helps drivers understand the limitations of the AI system and enables them to take appropriate actions.

iii. Usability Testing and Iterative Design (Natarajan et al., 2020)

To ensure the effectiveness of user interfaces in smart cars, usability testing and iterative design are crucial. Usability testing involves observing and collecting feedback from drivers as they interact with the interface. This feedback helps identify usability issues, areas of confusion, and opportunities for improvement. Based on the feedback, the iterative design allows for the refinement and enhancement of the interface to meet the needs and expectations of the drivers better.

User interface design is a critical aspect of smart car development. It should prioritize simplicity, clarity, consistency, and contextual awareness while minimizing distractions. The integration of explainable AI techniques can enhance the transparency and trustworthiness of the interface. By visualizing AI outputs, providing contextual explanations, enabling interactive explanations, and assisting in error handling, smart car interfaces can empower drivers to make informed decisions and interact effectively with the vehicle's AI systems. Usability testing and iterative design further ensure that the interface meets the drivers' needs and enhances their overall experience.

7.2 EXPLAINABLE RECOMMENDATIONS AND DECISION SUPPORT

In the realm of smart cars, explainable AI plays a crucial role in providing recommendations and decision support to both drivers and passengers (Alufaisan et al., 2020). The ability to understand and explain the reasoning behind these recommendations is essential for building trust and ensuring the safety and satisfaction of users.

i. Explainable Recommendations

Explainable recommendations in smart cars involve providing users with suggestions and advice based on various factors such as traffic conditions, user preferences, and historical data. These recommendations can range from route suggestions to personalized entertainment options during the journey. However, it is not enough to simply provide recommendations; it is equally important to explain why a particular recommendation is being made.

Explainable AI techniques can be employed to provide transparent and interpretable recommendations. For example, a smart car system can explain that a specific route is being recommended because it has the least traffic congestion based on real-time data. By providing this explanation, users can understand the rationale behind the recommendation and make informed decisions.

ii. Decision Support

In addition to recommendations, smart cars can provide decision support to drivers in critical situations. For instance, when faced with a sudden obstacle on the road, the car's AI system can analyze the situation and provide guidance on the best course of action. This decision support can be particularly valuable in emergency situations where split-second decisions can make a significant difference in avoiding accidents.

Explainable AI techniques can enhance decision support by providing clear explanations for the suggested actions. For example, if the AI system advises the driver to brake suddenly, it can explain that it detected an imminent collision based on sensor data. By understanding the reasoning behind the decision, drivers can trust the system and act accordingly.

iii. Transparency and Trust

Using explainable AI in recommendations and decision support fosters transparency and builds trust between humans and machines. When users understand the logic behind the system's suggestions, they are more likely to trust and rely on the recommendations provided. This trust is crucial for the widespread adoption of smart car technologies. Moreover, transparency in recommendations and decision support can also help users identify potential biases or errors in the system. By providing explanations, users can question and challenge the system's suggestions, leading to improvements and refinements in the AI algorithms.

iv. User-Centric Design

To ensure the effectiveness of explainable recommendations and decision support, it is essential to adopt a user-centric design approach. This involves understanding the needs, preferences, and limitations of the users and tailoring the recommendations and explanations accordingly.

User feedback and iterative design processes play a vital role in refining the recommendation and decision support systems. By collecting feedback from users, developers can identify areas for improvement and make necessary adjustments to enhance the user experience. This iterative design approach ensures that the recommendations and support for decisions align with the expectations and requirements of the users.

v. Ethical Considerations

While explainable recommendations and decision support offer numerous benefits, there are also ethical considerations that need to be addressed. One of the primary concerns is the potential for overreliance on AI systems, leading to a loss of human agency and decision-making capabilities. It is crucial to strike a balance between providing support and empowering users to make their own informed choices. Additionally, privacy and data protection are significant ethical considerations in the context of smart cars. As AI systems collect and analyze vast amounts of data to provide recommendations and decision support, it is essential to ensure that user data is handled securely and in compliance with privacy regulations. Users should have control over their data and be informed about how it is being used. Explainable recommendations and decision support are integral components of smart car systems. By employing explainable AI techniques, these systems can provide transparent and interpretable suggestions, enhancing user trust and satisfaction. However, it is crucial to consider ethical considerations and adopt a user-centric design approach to ensure the responsible and effective use of these technologies. With continued advancements in explainable AI, the future of recommendations and decision support in smart cars looks promising, offering users a safer and more personalized driving experience.

vi. Trust and Transparency in Human-Machine Interaction

Trust and transparency are crucial aspects of human-machine interaction in smart cars. As these vehicles become more autonomous and rely heavily on Artificial Intelligence (AI) systems, it is essential to ensure that users have confidence in the decisions made by the AI algorithms. Explainable AI plays a vital role in building trust and providing transparency in the decision-making process of smart cars.

vii. Importance of Trust in Human-Machine Interaction

Trust is the foundation of any successful human-machine interaction. In the context of smart cars, users must trust the AI systems to make safe and reliable decisions. When users have confidence in the technology, they are more likely to embrace and adopt it. Trust is particularly crucial in situations where the AI system takes control of critical functions, such as autonomous driving.

Explainable AI helps establish trust by providing users with insights into how the AI algorithms make decisions. When users understand the reasoning behind the AI's actions, they are more likely to trust the system. This transparency allows users to assess the reliability and safety of the AI system, leading to increased trust and acceptance.

viii. Transparency in Decision-Making (Sovrano and Vitali, 2021)

Transparency is closely related to trust and refers to the ability to understand and explain the decision-making process of AI systems. In the context of smart cars, transparency is essential to ensure that users can comprehend why the AI system made a particular decision. This understanding is crucial for users to feel in control and have confidence in the technology.

Explainable AI techniques provide transparency by offering insights into the internal workings of AI algorithms. These techniques enable users to understand the factors considered by the AI system when making decisions. For example, feature importance techniques can highlight the specific features or inputs that influence a decision. This transparency allows users to validate the decisions made by the AI system and identify any potential biases or errors.

7.2.1 Building trust through explainable recommendations

In addition to decision-making transparency, explainable AI can enhance trust through explainable recommendations. Smart cars often provide recommendations to users, such as route suggestions or personalized settings. By explaining the rationale behind these recommendations, users can better understand why the AI system made a particular suggestion.

Explainable recommendations provide users with the opportunity to assess the validity and relevance of the suggestions. For example, if the AI system recommends a longer route due to traffic conditions, users can understand the reasoning behind the recommendation and make an informed decision. This transparency helps build trust by empowering users to evaluate and validate the recommendations made by the AI system.

7.3 ADDRESSING USER CONCERNS AND MISCONCEPTIONS

Trust and transparency in human-machine interaction also involve addressing user concerns and misconceptions about AI systems. Many users may have reservations about relying on AI algorithms for critical tasks, such as driving. It is essential to address these concerns and provide accurate information to alleviate any misconceptions. Explainable AI techniques can help address user concerns by providing clear explanations of how the AI system works and the safety measures in place. By highlighting the robustness of the AI algorithms and the extensive testing and validation processes, users can gain confidence in the technology. Additionally, by addressing potential biases or limitations of the AI system, users can have a more realistic understanding of its capabilities.

7.3.1 User education and training

User education and training are crucial to foster trust and transparency in human-machine interaction. Users need to be informed about the capabilities and limitations of the AI systems in smart cars. By providing comprehensive training and educational materials, users can develop a better understanding of how AI algorithms work and the benefits they offer.

User education can include explaining the underlying principles of AI, the data used for training the algorithms, and the ethical considerations involved. By empowering users with knowledge, they can make informed decisions and have realistic expectations about the AI system's performance. This education also helps users understand the importance of transparency and trust in the context of smart cars.

7.3.2 Continuous improvement and feedback

Continuous improvement and user feedback are essential to maintain trust and transparency in human-machine interaction. Smart car manufacturers should actively seek user feedback and incorporate it into the design and development process. By listening to user concerns and suggestions, manufacturers can address any issues and enhance the transparency and trustworthiness of the AI systems.

User feedback can help identify areas where the AI system may lack transparency or where users may have difficulty understanding the decisions made. By iteratively improving the explainability of the AI algorithms and incorporating user feedback, manufacturers can build trust and ensure that the technology meets user expectations.

In conclusion, trust and transparency are critical in human-machine interaction in smart cars. Explainable AI techniques play a vital role in establishing trust by providing transparency in the decision-making process. By explaining the reasoning behind AI decisions and recommendations, users can better understand and trust the technology. User education, continuous improvement, and feedback are also essential to maintain trust and enhance transparency in the evolving field of smart cars.

7.3.3 User feedback and iterative design

User feedback and iterative design play a crucial role in the development and improvement of smart cars. As smart cars become more advanced and complex, it is essential to gather feedback from users to understand their needs, preferences, and concerns. This feedback can then be used to iterate and enhance the design of smart cars, making them more user-friendly, efficient, and safe.

7.3.4 Importance of user feedback

User feedback is invaluable in the development of smart cars. It provides insights into how users interact with the technology, what features they find useful, and what areas need improvement. By collecting feedback from a diverse range of users, including drivers, passengers, and other stakeholders, developers can gain a comprehensive understanding of the user experience and identify areas for enhancement.

One of the primary benefits of user feedback is that it helps identify usability issues. Users can provide valuable insights into the ease of use, intuitiveness, and overall user experience of smart car interfaces and features. By understanding the pain points and challenges users face, developers can make informed design decisions to improve the user interface and enhance the overall user experience.

User feedback also helps identify potential safety concerns. Users may encounter situations where the smart car's behavior or response is unexpected or unsafe. By collecting feedback on these incidents, developers can identify and address potential safety risks, ensuring that smart cars operate reliably and securely.

Furthermore, user feedback can shed light on the effectiveness of explainable AI techniques implemented in smart cars. Users can provide insights into the clarity and comprehensibility of the explanations provided by the AI system. This feedback is crucial in refining and optimizing the explainability features of smart cars, making them more transparent and understandable to users.

7.3.5 Gathering user feedback

To gather user feedback effectively, developers can employ various methods and techniques. What follows are some common approaches used in the automotive industry.

7.3.6 Surveys and questionnaires

Surveys and questionnaires are a popular method for collecting user feedback. Developers can design surveys to gather information about user preferences, satisfaction levels, and suggestions for improvement. These surveys can be distributed to a wide range of users, including smart car owners, fleet operators, and even potential customers. The data collected from surveys can provide valuable insights into user needs and expectations.

7.3.7 User interviews and focus groups

User interviews and focus groups allow developers to have direct conversations with users to understand their experiences, opinions, and suggestions. These qualitative research methods provide in-depth insights into user perspectives and can help uncover valuable information that may not be captured through surveys alone. By conducting interviews and focus groups, developers can gain a deeper understanding of user needs and preferences, enabling them to make more informed design decisions.

7.3.8 User testing and observations

User testing involves observing users as they interact with smart cars in real-world scenarios. This method allows developers to observe user behavior, identify usability issues, and gather feedback on specific features or functionalities. By conducting user testing sessions, developers can gain firsthand insights into how users interact with the technology and identify areas for improvement.

7.4 ONLINE COMMUNITIES AND SOCIAL MEDIA

Online communities and social media platforms provide a platform for users to share their experiences, opinions, and suggestions. Developers can actively monitor these platforms to gather feedback and engage in discussions with users. This approach allows developers to tap into a larger user base and gain insights from a diverse range of perspectives. Iterative Design Process

User feedback is most valuable when it is used to drive an iterative design process. Iterative design involves continuously refining and improving the design of smart cars based on user feedback and testing. This process allows developers to address user needs and concerns, enhance usability, and optimize the overall user experience.

The iterative design process typically involves the following steps:

i. Collecting User Feedback

As discussed earlier, user feedback can be collected through various methods such as surveys, interviews, user testing, and online communities. It is essential to gather feedback from a diverse range of users to ensure a comprehensive understanding of user needs and preferences.

ii. Analyzing and Prioritizing Feedback

Once user feedback is collected, it must be carefully analyzed and prioritized. Developers should identify common themes, pain points, and areas for improvement. Feedback that aligns with the overall goals and objectives of the smart car project should be given higher priority.

iii. Designing and Implementing Changes

Based on the analysis of user feedback, developers can start designing and implementing changes to address the identified issues and improve the user experience. This may involve modifying the user interface, enhancing specific features, or optimizing the explainability of AI techniques.

iv. Testing and Evaluation

After implementing the changes, it is crucial to conduct testing and evaluation to assess their effectiveness. User testing sessions can be conducted to gather feedback on the redesigned features or interface. This feedback can then be used to refine the design further and address any remaining issues.

v. Repeating the Process

The iterative design process is cyclical, and the steps mentioned previously should be repeated multiple times. Each iteration builds upon the previous one, incorporating user feedback and continuously improving the design. This iterative approach ensures that smart cars evolve and adapt to meet the changing needs and expectations of users.

7.4.1 Incorporating explainable AI in user feedback

Explainable AI techniques can be incorporated into the user feedback process. Users can be provided with explanations of the AI system's decisions and recommendations, and their feedback on the clarity and usefulness of these explanations can be collected. This feedback can then be used to refine and enhance the explainability features of smart cars, making them more transparent and understandable to users.

In conclusion, user feedback and iterative design are essential components of smart car development. By actively seeking and incorporating user feedback, developers can create smart cars that are more user-friendly, efficient, and safe. The iterative design process ensures that smart cars continuously evolve and improve based on user needs and preferences. Incorporating explainable AI techniques in the user feedback process further enhances the transparency and comprehensibility of smart cars, making them more trustworthy and user-centric.

7.4.2 Safety considerations in smart cars

Safety is one of the most critical aspects of smart cars (Nikitas et al., 2020). As these vehicles become more advanced and autonomous, it is essential to ensure that they operate in a safe and reliable manner. In this section, we will explore the various safety considerations in smart cars and how explainable AI can contribute to enhancing safety.

7.4.3 Importance of safety in smart cars

The primary goal of any smart car system is to provide a safe and secure transportation experience for both the occupants of the vehicle and other road users. Safety considerations in smart cars encompass a wide range of aspects, including collision avoidance, pedestrian detection, lane keeping, and emergency braking, among others. By integrating advanced technologies and AI algorithms, smart cars can enhance safety by mitigating the risks associated with human error and improving overall driving performance.

7.4.4 Safety challenges in smart cars

While smart cars offer numerous safety benefits, they also present unique challenges. One of the main challenges is the complexity of the AI systems that power these vehicles. Smart cars rely on a combination of sensors, cameras, radar, and LiDAR to perceive the environment and make decisions in real time. However, the complexity of these systems can introduce potential vulnerabilities and safety risks. It is crucial to address these challenges to ensure the safe operation of smart cars.

7.4.5 Explainable AI for safety in smart cars

Explainable AI plays a vital role in addressing safety concerns in smart cars. By providing transparency and interpretability, explainable AI techniques enable users to understand how the AI system makes decisions and takes appropriate actions in safety-critical situations. What follows are some ways in which explainable AI can contribute to safety in smart cars

7.4.6 Decision explanation

Explainable AI techniques can provide insights into the decision-making process of smart cars (Michael, 2021). By explaining why a particular decision was made, such as applying emergency braking or changing lanes, users can have a better understanding of the system's behavior. This transparency allows users to trust the AI system and make informed decisions while driving.

7.4.7 Error detection and diagnosis

Explainable AI can help detect and diagnose errors or anomalies in the smart car system. By analyzing the internal workings of the AI algorithms, it becomes possible to identify potential issues that may compromise safety. For example, if a sensor malfunctions or a decision-making algorithm produces unexpected results, explainable AI can help pinpoint the problem and take corrective actions.

7.4.8 Safety validation and certification

Explainable AI techniques can assist in the validation and certification of smart car systems. Safety regulators and certification bodies require a thorough understanding of the AI algorithms and their impact on safety. By providing interpretable models and explanations, explainable AI can facilitate the evaluation and certification process, ensuring that smart cars meet the necessary safety standards.

7.4.9 Privacy and data protection

Safety in smart cars also extends to the protection of personal data and privacy (Gade et al., 2019). As smart cars collect and process vast amounts of data, it is crucial to ensure that this data is handled securely and in compliance with privacy regulations. Explainable AI can contribute to privacy and data protection by providing transparency in data handling and allowing users to have control over their personal information.

7.4.10 Collaborative safety

Collaborative safety is another aspect that can benefit from explainable AI in smart cars. By sharing information and insights about the driving environment and potential hazards, smart cars can work together to enhance safety. Explainable AI can facilitate this collaboration by providing interpretable models and explanations that enable smart cars to communicate and coordinate their actions effectively.

7.4.11 Human-machine interaction for safety

The interaction between humans and smart cars is crucial for ensuring safety (Zhu et al., 2018). Explainable AI can contribute to this interaction by providing understandable explanations to the users. By understanding the system's behavior and limitations, users can make informed decisions and take appropriate actions to ensure their safety and the safety of others on the road.

Safety considerations are of utmost importance in smart cars. Explainable AI techniques can play a significant role in enhancing safety by providing transparency, error detection, and validation capabilities. By understanding the decision-making process and potential risks, users can trust the AI system and make informed decisions while driving. Additionally, explainable AI can contribute to privacy protection, collaborative safety, and effective human-machine interaction. As smart cars continue to evolve, it is crucial to prioritize safety and leverage the power of explainable AI to ensure a secure and reliable transportation experience.

Explainable AI (XAI) has gained significant attention in recent years as a crucial aspect of developing intelligent systems, including smart cars. The ability to understand and interpret the decisions made by AI algorithms is essential for ensuring transparency, trust, and safety in the deployment of these systems. In the context of motor vehicles, XAI plays a vital role in addressing security challenges and enhancing the overall safety of smart cars.

7.4.12 Security challenges in smart cars

Smart cars, equipped with advanced technologies and AI algorithms, offer numerous benefits, such as improved safety, enhanced driving experience, and increased efficiency. However, these advancements also introduce new security challenges that must be addressed to ensure the integrity and reliability of smart car systems.

7.4.13 Cybersecurity risks

One of the primary security challenges in smart cars is the vulnerability to cyber-attacks (Hussain et al., 2021). As smart cars become more connected and autonomous, they rely heavily on communication networks and external systems, making them susceptible to various cybersecurity risks. Hackers can exploit vulnerabilities in the car's software, network connections, or even physical components to gain unauthorized access and control over the vehicle.

Cyber-attacks on smart cars can have severe consequences, including unauthorized access to personal data, manipulation of critical systems like braking and steering, and even remote hijacking of the vehicle. Therefore, it is crucial to develop robust security measures to protect smart cars from cyber threats.

7.4.14 Data privacy and protection

Smart cars generate and collect vast amounts of data, including personal information, driving patterns, and location data. This data is valuable and can be misused if not adequately protected. Ensuring data privacy and protection is essential to maintain user trust and prevent unauthorized access to sensitive information.

Smart car manufacturers and service providers must implement strong data encryption techniques, secure data storage practices, and strict access controls to safeguard the privacy of users. Additionally, clear policies and regulations should be in place to govern the collection, storage, and usage of data generated by smart cars.

7.4.15 Malicious attacks on AI systems

The integration of AI algorithms in smart cars introduces a new dimension of security challenges (Barredo Arrieta et al., 2020). Malicious actors can target the AI systems in smart cars to manipulate their behavior and cause harm. Adversarial attacks, where attackers intentionally manipulate input data to deceive AI algorithms, can lead to incorrect decisions and potentially dangerous situations.

Robust security measures need to be implemented to mitigate the risk of malicious attacks on AI systems. This includes techniques such as anomaly detection, intrusion detection systems, and continuous monitoring of the AI algorithms' performance. Additionally, explainable AI techniques can help identify and understand any vulnerabilities or biases in the AI models, enabling proactive measures to address them.

7.4.16 Supply chain security

Smart cars are complex systems that involve multiple components and software from various suppliers. Ensuring the security of the supply chain is crucial to prevent the introduction of compromised or malicious components into the smart car ecosystem. A compromised component can potentially compromise the entire system, leading to security breaches or vulnerabilities.

To address supply chain security challenges, smart car manufacturers should implement rigorous vetting processes for suppliers, conduct regular security audits, and establish secure communication channels with suppliers. Additionally, the use of tamper-resistant hardware and software verification techniques can help detect and prevent the use of compromised components.

7.4.17 Over-the-air updates

Over-the-air (OTA) updates have become a common practice in smart cars to deliver software updates and new features (Meske et al., 2022). While OTA updates offer convenience and flexibility, they also introduce security risks. Malicious actors can exploit vulnerabilities in the OTA update process to inject malicious code or gain unauthorized access to the vehicle's systems.

To ensure the security of OTA updates, smart car manufacturers should implement secure update mechanisms, including strong encryption, authentication, and integrity checks. Regular security audits and monitoring of the OTA update process are also essential to detect and prevent any potential security breaches.

7.4.18 XAI for security enhancement

Explainable AI techniques can play a significant role in enhancing the security of smart cars. By providing transparency and interpretability, XAI can help identify and understand potential security vulnerabilities in AI systems. XAI techniques such as feature importance analysis, rule extraction, and model-agnostic explanations can assist in identifying potential attack vectors and detecting anomalous behavior.

Furthermore, XAI can aid in detecting adversarial attacks by revealing the vulnerabilities and limitations of AI algorithms. By understanding how attackers can manipulate the input data to deceive the AI system, developers can develop robust defenses and countermeasures.

Security challenges in smart cars are a critical concern that needs to be addressed to ensure the safe and reliable operation of these vehicles. Cybersecurity risks, data privacy and protection, malicious attacks on AI systems, supply chain security, and OTA update security are among the key challenges that must be mitigated. The application of explainable AI techniques can significantly enhance the security of smart cars by providing transparency, identifying vulnerabilities, and aiding in the detection and prevention of security breaches.

7.4.19 Explainable AI for safety and security

Explainable AI (XAI) plays a crucial role in ensuring the safety and security of smart cars. As these vehicles become more advanced and autonomous, it is essential to understand how AI algorithms make decisions and explain those decisions. In this section, we will explore the application of explainable AI techniques in the context of safety and security in smart cars.

7.4.20 Enhancing safety with explainable AI

Safety is a paramount concern in the development and deployment of smart cars. The ability to explain the decisions made by AI systems can greatly enhance safety measures. By providing transparent and interpretable explanations, XAI can help identify potential risks and prevent accidents.

7.4.21 Real-time risk assessment

Explainable AI can be used to assess risks in real time by analyzing various data sources, including sensor data, traffic conditions, and historical accident data (Kabir et al., 2021). By employing interpretable models, such as decision trees or rule-based models, XAI can provide insights into the factors that contribute to potential risks. For example, if a smart car's AI system detects a pedestrian crossing the road, it can explain the decision-making process, highlighting the factors that led to the detection and the subsequent actions taken by the vehicle.

7.4.22 Error detection and diagnosis

Explainable AI techniques can also be employed to detect and diagnose errors in smart car systems. By providing transparent explanations, XAI can help identify the root causes of errors and enable developers to rectify them promptly. For instance, if an autonomous vehicle fails to detect a stop sign, XAI can explain by highlighting the features or conditions that led to the error, such as poor lighting or occlusion.

7.4.23 Safety-critical decision support

In safety-critical situations, smart cars may need to make split-second decisions that can have significant consequences. Explainable AI can provide decision support by explaining the rationale behind these critical decisions.

For example, if a smart car needs to decide between swerving to avoid an obstacle or maintaining its current path, XAI can provide an explanation by highlighting the factors considered, such as the speed and distance of the obstacle, road conditions, and the presence of other vehicles.

7.4.24 Strengthening security with explainable AI

Security is another crucial aspect of smart car development. As these vehicles become more connected and autonomous, they are vulnerable to cyberattacks and malicious activities. Explainable AI can help strengthen security measures by providing insights into potential vulnerabilities and detecting anomalous behavior.

7.4.25 Intrusion detection and prevention

Explainable AI techniques can be used to detect and prevent intrusions in smart car systems (Mankodiya et al., 2022). By analyzing network traffic and system logs, XAI can identify patterns and behaviors that deviate from normal operations. For example, if an AI system detects unauthorized access attempts or unusual data transfers, it can explain by highlighting the specific indicators of the intrusion.

7.4.26 Vulnerability assessment

Explainable AI can also be employed to assess the vulnerability of smart car systems to cyber-attacks. By analyzing the system architecture, communication protocols, and software components, XAI can identify potential weaknesses and provide explanations for the identified vulnerabilities. This information can then be used to strengthen the security measures and mitigate the risks.

7.4.27 Adversarial attack detection

Adversarial attacks, where malicious actors manipulate sensor inputs to deceive AI systems, pose a significant threat to smart cars. Explainable AI can help detect and mitigate these attacks by providing explanations for the decisions made by the AI system. By analyzing the input data and the decision-making process, XAI can identify anomalies and highlight adversarial manipulations. This information can then be used to develop robust defense mechanisms against such attacks.

7.4.28 Regulatory compliance and accountability

Explainable AI is not only crucial for safety and security but also for regulatory compliance and accountability in the smart car industry (Celino, 2020). As autonomous vehicles become more prevalent, there is a need for regulations and standards to ensure their safe and ethical operation. XAI can provide the necessary transparency and accountability to meet these requirements.

7.4.29 Compliance with safety standards

Explainable AI techniques can help smart car manufacturers demonstrate compliance with safety standards and regulations. By providing transparent explanations for the decision-making process, XAI can enable regulatory authorities to assess the safety measures implemented in the vehicles. This transparency can also facilitate the certification process for autonomous vehicles, ensuring they meet the necessary safety requirements.

7.4.30 Ethical decision-making

Smart cars often encounter ethical dilemmas on the road, such as deciding between protecting the occupants or avoiding harm to pedestrians. Explainable AI can provide insights into the ethical decision-making process by explaining the factors considered and the trade-offs made by the AI system. This transparency can help ensure smart cars adhere to ethical principles and societal norms.

7.4.31 Accountability and liability

Explainable AI can also play a crucial role in establishing accountability and liability in the event of accidents or malfunctions. By providing transparent explanations for the decisions made by AI systems, XAI can help determine the responsibility of different stakeholders, such as the vehicle manufacturer, the AI system developer, or the human operator. This accountability can facilitate the resolution of legal and insurance-related issues.

In conclusion, explainable AI is essential for ensuring the safety and security of smart cars. By providing transparent and interpretable explanations, XAI can enhance real-time risk assessment, error detection, decision support, intrusion detection, vulnerability assessment, and adversarial attack detection. Furthermore, XAI promotes regulatory compliance, ethical decision-making, and accountability in the smart car industry. As smart cars continue to evolve, the application of explainable AI techniques will be crucial in building trust and confidence in these advanced vehicles.

Explainable AI (XAI) has gained significant attention in recent years due to its potential to enhance transparency and trust in AI systems. In the context of motor vehicles, XAI can play a crucial role in ensuring the safety, reliability, and ethical use of smart cars. By providing understandable explanations for the decisions made by AI algorithms, XAI can help users, regulators, and stakeholders gain insights into the inner workings of smart cars. This section will explore the application of XAI in motor vehicles, focusing on privacy and data protection.

7.4.32 Importance of privacy and data protection in smart cars

Privacy and data protection are paramount concerns in the development and deployment of smart cars (Sado et al., 2020). These vehicles collect and process vast amounts of data, including personal information, driving behavior, and location data. It is essential to ensure that this data is handled securely and in compliance with privacy regulations to protect the rights and interests of individuals.

Smart cars rely on AI algorithms to make critical decisions, such as autonomous driving, route planning, and predictive maintenance. These algorithms require access to various types of data, including sensor data, GPS information, and historical driving patterns. However, the collection and use of this data must be done in a privacy-preserving manner to prevent unauthorized access, misuse, or unintended disclosure.

7.4.33 Privacy challenges in smart cars

Smart cars face several privacy challenges that must be addressed to safeguard user data. Some of the key challenges include:

i. Data Collection and Retention (Graefe et al., 2022)

Smart cars continuously collect and store data from various sensors and systems. The challenge lies in determining what data should be collected, how long it should be retained, and who has access to it. Striking the right balance between data collection for improving AI algorithms and respecting user privacy is crucial.

ii. Data Anonymization and Pseudonymization (Lorente et al., 2021)

To protect user privacy, it is essential to anonymize or pseudonymize the collected data. Anonymization involves removing or encrypting personally identifiable information (PII) from the data, while pseudonymization replaces identifiable information with pseudonyms. However, ensuring that the anonymization or pseudonymization techniques used are robust enough to prevent re-identification attacks is a challenge.

iii. Data Sharing and Third-Party Access (Clement et al., 2023)

Smart cars often rely on cloud-based services and external data sources for various functionalities. This necessitates data sharing with third parties, raising concerns about data security and privacy. Establishing secure data-sharing protocols and ensuring that third parties adhere to privacy regulations are critical challenges.

iv. Informed Consent and User Control

Users should have control over their data and be informed about how it is collected, used, and shared. Obtaining informed consent from users for data collection and processing is essential. However, designing user-friendly interfaces that clearly communicate data practices and obtaining meaningful consent can be challenging.

7.4.34 Role of explainable AI in privacy and data protection

Explainable AI can contribute significantly to addressing privacy and data protection challenges in smart cars. By providing transparent explanations for the decisions made by AI algorithms, XAI can help users understand how their data is being used and ensure that privacy is respected. Some ways in which XAI can enhance privacy and data protection in smart cars include:

i. Transparent Data Processing

XAI techniques can provide insights into how AI algorithms process and use data. By explaining the features and patterns that influence decision-making, users can gain a better understanding of how their data is being utilized. This transparency can help build trust and ensure that data processing is in line with privacy regulations.

ii. Detecting and Mitigating Bias

AI algorithms can inadvertently introduce biases in decision-making, which can have privacy implications. XAI techniques can help identify and mitigate these biases by providing explanations for the factors that contribute to decision outcomes. This can help ensure fair and unbiased treatment of individuals and protect their privacy rights.

iii. Reducing Overreliance on Sensitive Data (Liao et al., 2020)

Explainable AI can help identify the specific data features crucial for decision-making. By understanding which features are most influential, developers can design AI systems that rely less on sensitive data, thereby reducing privacy risks. This can be particularly important in cases where personal information needs to be protected.

iv. User Empowerment and Control (Doran et al., 2017)

XAI can empower users by providing them with understandable explanations for AI decisions. This transparency allows users to assess the privacy implications of data sharing and make informed choices about their data. By giving users control over their data, XAI can help protect their privacy and ensure compliance with privacy regulations.

7.4.35 Challenges in implementing XAI for privacy and data protection

While XAI holds promise for enhancing privacy and data protection in smart cars (Meteier et al., 2019), several challenges need to be addressed for its effective implementation:

i. Complexity of AI Algorithms

AI algorithms used in smart cars can be highly complex, making it challenging to provide simple and understandable explanations. Developing XAI techniques that can effectively explain the decisions made by complex algorithms without sacrificing accuracy is a significant challenge.

ii. Balancing Explainability and Performance

There is often a trade-off between the explainability of AI algorithms and their performance. Increasing the explainability of an algorithm may come at the cost of reduced accuracy or increased computational complexity. Striking the right balance between explainability and performance is crucial for the successful implementation of XAI in smart cars.

iii. Privacy-Preserving Explanations

Explanations generated by XAI techniques may inadvertently reveal sensitive information about individuals or their data. Ensuring that explanations do not compromise privacy while still providing meaningful insights is a challenging task. Developing privacy-preserving XAI techniques that can generate informative explanations without disclosing sensitive information is an active area of research.

iv. Regulatory Compliance (Arya et al., 2019)

Implementing XAI in smart cars requires compliance with privacy regulations such as the General Data Protection Regulation (GDPR) and other regional data protection laws. Ensuring that XAI techniques and systems adhere to these regulations can be complex, especially considering the evolving nature of privacy laws.

Privacy and data protection are critical considerations in the development and deployment of smart cars. Explainable AI can play a vital role in addressing privacy challenges by providing transparent explanations for AI decisions. By enhancing transparency, XAI can help build trust, empower users, and ensure compliance with privacy regulations. However, several challenges must be overcome to effectively implement XAI for privacy and data protection in smart cars. Future research and collaboration between industry, academia, and regulators are essential to address these challenges and realize the full potential of XAI in ensuring privacy and data protection in smart cars.

REFERENCES

A Historical Perspective of Explainable Artificial Intelligence—Confalonieri—2021—WIREs Data Mining and Knowledge Discovery—Wiley Online Library. (no date). Available at: https://wires.onlinelibrary.wiley.com/doi/10.1002/widm.1391 (Accessed: 13 December 2023).

Alufaisan, Y. et al. (2020) 'Does Explainable Artificial Intelligence Improve Human Decision-Making?' Available at: https://doi.org/10.31234/osf.io/d4r9t.

Arya, V. et al. (2019) 'One Explanation Does Not Fit All: A Toolkit and Taxonomy of AI Explainability Techniques', ArXiv, abs/1909.03012. Available at: https://consensus.app/papers/explanation-does-toolkit-taxonomy-explainability-arya/99491c79aa685082ad1edfa1ac8231fd/ (Accessed: 13 December 2023).

Barredo Arrieta, A. et al. (2020) 'Explainable Artificial Intelligence (XAI): Concepts, Taxonomies, Opportunities and Challenges Toward Responsible AI', Information Fusion, 58, pp. 82–115. Available at: https://doi.org/10.1016/j.inffus.2019.12.012.

Celino, I. (2020) 'Who Is This Explanation for? Human Intelligence and Knowledge Graphs for Explainable AI', pp. 276–285. Available at: https://doi.org/10.3233/SSW200024.

Clement, T. et al. (2023) 'XAIR: A Systematic Metareview of Explainable AI (XAI) Aligned to the Software Development Process', Machine Learning and Knowledge Extraction [Preprint]. Available at: https://doi.org/10.3390/make5010006.

Clinciu, M.-A. and Hastie, H. (2019) 'A Survey of Explainable AI Terminology', Proceedings of the 1st Workshop on Interactive Natural Language Technology for Explainable Artificial Intelligence (NL4XAI 2019), pp. 8–13. Available at: https://doi.org/10.18653/v1/W19-8403.

Doran, D., Schulz, S. and Besold, T.R. (2017) 'What Does Explainable AI Really Mean? A New Conceptualization of Perspectives', ArXiv [Preprint]. Available at: www.semanticscholar.org/paper/What-Does-Explainable-AI-Really-Mean-A-New-of-Doran-Schulz/a0ba972791a530641cec11a7b8de18a3dcaa45fb (Accessed: 13 December 2023).

Gade, K. et al. (2019) 'Explainable AI in Industry', Proceedings of the 25th ACM SIGKDD International Conference on Knowledge Discovery & Data Mining [Preprint]. Available at: https://doi.org/10.1145/3292500.3332281.

Graefe, J. et al. (2022) 'Human Centered Explainability for Intelligent Vehicles—A User Study', Proceedings of the 14th International Conference on Automotive User Interfaces and Interactive Vehicular Applications [Preprint]. Available at: https://doi.org/10.1145/3543174.3546846.

Hussain, F., Hussain, R. and Hossain, E. (2021) 'Explainable Artificial Intelligence (XAI): An Engineering Perspective', ArXiv, abs/2101.03613. Available at: https://consensus.app/papers/intelligence-engineering-perspective-hussain/3aa764b217535d9a86b26596c2ff39b8/ (Accessed: 13 December 2023).

Kabir, M. et al. (2021) 'Explainable Artificial Intelligence for Smart City Application: A Secure and Trusted Platform', ArXiv, abs/2111.00601. Available at: https://consensus.app/papers/intelligence-smart-city-application-secure-trusted-kabir/f128a7f220795455b20149d2d21892c7/ (Accessed: 13 December 2023).

Liao, Q. et al. (2020) 'Introduction to Explainable AI', Extended Abstracts of the 2020 CHI Conference on Human Factors in Computing Systems [Preprint]. Available at: https://doi.org/10.1145/3334480.3375044.

Lorente, M.P.S. et al. (2021) 'Explaining Deep Learning-Based Driver Models', Applied Sciences, 11(8), p. 3321. Available at: https://doi.org/10.3390/app11083321.

Mankodiya, H. et al. (2022) 'OD-XAI: Explainable AI-Based Semantic Object Detection for Autonomous Vehicles', Applied Sciences, 12(11), p. 5310. Available at: https://doi.org/10.3390/app12115310.

Meske, C. et al. (2022) 'Explainable Artificial Intelligence: Objectives, Stakeholders, and Future Research Opportunities', Information Systems Management, 39(1), pp. 53–63. Available at: https://doi.org/10.1080/10580530.2020.1849465.

Meteier, Q. et al. (2019) 'Workshop on explainable AI in automated driving: a user-centered interaction approach', Proceedings of the 11th International Conference on Automotive User Interfaces and Interactive Vehicular Applications: Adjunct Proceedings [Preprint]. Available at: https://doi.org/10.1145/3349263.3350762.

Michael, L. (2021) 'Explainability and the Fourth AI Revolution', ArXiv [Preprint]. Available at: www.semanticscholar.org/paper/Explainability-and-the-Fourth-AI-Revolution-Michael/4fbdaa79c59ce26c4c99e10bd7513ce1e2984fa6 (Accessed: 13 December 2023).

Natarajan, S. et al. (2020) 'AI-NAAV: An AI enabled Neurocognition Aware Autonomous Vehicle', 2020 IEEE Bangalore Humanitarian Technology Conference (B-HTC), pp. 1–6. Available at: https://doi.org/10.1109/B-HTC50970.2020.9297995.

Nikitas, A. et al. (2020) 'Artificial Intelligence, Transport and the Smart City: Definitions and Dimensions of a New Mobility Era', Sustainability [Preprint]. Available at: https://doi.org/10.3390/su12072789.

Phillips, P.J. et al. (2020) 'Four Principles of Explainable Artificial Intelligence'. Available at: https://doi.org/10.6028/NIST.IR.8312-draft.

Sado, F. et al. (2020) 'Explainable Goal-Driven Agents and Robots—A Comprehensive Review and New Framework', ArXiv, abs/2004.09705. Available at: https://consensus.app/papers/goaldriven-agents-robots-comprehensive-review-framework-sado/4b8de290a2d354f5a6b9d19dd877343f/ (Accessed: 13 December 2023).

Sovrano, F. and Vitali, F. (2021) 'An Objective Metric for Explainable AI: How and Why to Estimate the Degree of Explainability', ArXiv, abs/2109.05327. Available at: https://consensus.app/papers/metric-explainable-estimate-degree-explainability-sovrano/093a10dd7d7953019528c40d7f999324/ (Accessed: 13 December 2023).

Zhu, J. et al. (2018) 'Explainable AI for Designers: A Human-Centered Perspective on Mixed-Initiative Co-Creation', 2018 IEEE Conference on Computational Intelligence and Games (CIG), pp. 1–8. Available at: https://doi.org/10.1109/CIG.2018.8490433.

Chapter 8

Feature detection and feature visualization in smart cars utilizing explainable AI

Mandeep Kaur and Vinayak Goel

8.1 INTRODUCTION

In the field of smart cars, explainable AI plays a crucial role in enhancing transparency and trust in the decision-making process of these intelligent vehicles. One important aspect of explainable AI is understanding the importance of different features and visualizing them to gain insights into how the smart car makes decisions. Feature importance refers to the measure of the contribution of each feature in the decision-making process of a smart car. By understanding the importance of different features, we can gain valuable insights into how the smart car perceives and evaluates its environment. This knowledge can be used to improve the performance, safety, and reliability of smart cars.

The importance of feature importance lies in its ability to provide a clear understanding of which features have the most significant impact on the decision-making process. This knowledge can be used to identify potential biases or limitations in the smart car's decision-making algorithms. By analyzing feature importance, developers can ensure that the smart car's decisions are fair, unbiased, and aligned with human expectations.

8.1.1 Feature visualization

Feature visualization (Adadi and Berrada, 2018) is another important technique in the field of explainable AI for smart cars. It involves visually representing the learned features or patterns that the smart car uses to make decisions. By visualizing these features, one can gain a deeper understanding of how the smart car perceives and interprets its environment. One common approach to feature visualization is using heatmaps. Heatmaps provide a visual representation of the importance or relevance of different features in the decision-making process. For example, in the context of autonomous driving, a heatmap can show which areas of the environment are considered more important by the smart car's perception system. This information can be used to identify potential blind spots or areas where the smart car may

DOI: 10.1201/9781003502432-8

need additional sensors or improvements. Another approach to feature visualization is using saliency maps. Saliency maps highlight the most important regions or objects in an image contributing to the smart car's decision. By visualizing these salient regions, we can gain insights into the specific features or patterns that the smart car focuses on when making decisions. This information can be valuable for debugging and improving the performance of the smart car's perception system (Adadi and Berrada (2018).

8.1.2 Benefits of feature importance and feature visualization

Feature importance and feature visualization (Gerlings et al., 2020) are integral components of Explainable AI (XAI) that offer multifaceted benefits in enhancing the transparency and interpretability of machine learning models. Feature importance elucidates the significance of different input variables in influencing the model's predictions. This not only aids in comprehending the decision-making process but also facilitates the identification of key factors driving model outputs. The insights garnered from feature importance can guide model refinement, inform feature engineering strategies, and promote regulatory compliance by providing a clear rationale for the model's decisions. On the other hand, feature visualization translates complex model outputs into intuitive graphical representations, offering a visual understanding of the relationships within the data. This not only aids in pattern recognition and anomaly detection but also serves as a powerful tool for effective communication with non-technical stakeholders. Visualizations enable interactive exploration, fostering collaboration between humans and AI systems and facilitating the identification and resolution of potential issues through a more accessible and transparent representation of the model's behavior. In combination, feature importance and feature visualization contribute to the overarching goals of Explainable AI, fostering trust, facilitating communication, and ensuring responsible and ethical use of AI technologies.

The application of feature importance and feature visualization techniques in smart cars offers several benefits:

1. **Transparency:** By understanding the importance of different features and visualizing them, we can enhance the transparency of the smart car's decision-making process. This transparency is crucial for building trust between the smart car and its users.
2. **Debugging and Improvements:** Feature importance and visualization techniques can help identify potential biases, limitations, or areas for improvement in the smart car's decision-making algorithms. This knowledge can be used to debug and enhance the performance, safety, and reliability of smart cars.

3. **User Understanding:** Feature visualization techniques can help users understand how the smart car perceives and interprets its environment. This understanding can empower users to make informed decisions and interact more effectively with the smart car.

4. **Regulatory Compliance:** Feature importance and visualization techniques can assist in meeting regulatory requirements for transparency and accountability in the deployment of smart cars. By providing clear explanations of the decision-making process, smart car developers can ensure compliance with legal and ethical standards.

8.1.3   Challenges and limitations

While feature importance and feature visualization techniques offer valuable insights into the decision-making process of smart cars, there are also challenges and limitations to consider:

1. **Complexity:** Smart cars operate in complex and dynamic environments, making it challenging to determine the importance of different features accurately. The interactions between features and the context in which they occur can significantly impact their importance.

2. **Interpretability vs. Performance:** There is often a trade-off between the interpretability of the smart car's decision-making process and its performance. Highly interpretable models may sacrifice some level of performance, while more complex models may be less interpretable.

3. **Data Availability:** The effectiveness of feature importance and visualization techniques relies on the availability of high-quality and diverse training data. Limited or biased data can lead to inaccurate or misleading feature importance rankings.

4. **User Understanding:** While feature visualization techniques aim to enhance user understanding, there is a risk of overwhelming users with complex visualizations. It is essential to design user-friendly interfaces that effectively communicate the relevant information without overwhelming the user. Feature importance and feature visualization techniques are valuable tools in the field of explainable AI for smart cars. They provide insights into the decision-making process, enhance transparency, and empower users to understand and interact effectively with smart cars. However, challenges such as complexity, interpretability-performance trade-offs, data availability, and user understanding must be carefully addressed to fully leverage the benefits of these techniques. By overcoming these challenges, we can pave the way for safer, more reliable, and trustworthy smart cars in the future.

8.1.4 Local explanations and counterfactuals

In the previous section, we discussed the importance of feature importance and feature visualization in understanding the inner workings of smart cars. These techniques provide a global view of the model's decision-making process. However, sometimes, it is necessary to dive deeper and understand the local explanations for individual predictions. This is where local explanations and counterfactuals come into play.

8.1.5 Local explanations

Local explanations aim to provide insights into why a specific prediction was made by the smart car's AI model. Unlike global explanations, which provide an overview of the model's behavior, local explanations focus on a single instance or prediction. This is particularly useful when trying to understand why a certain decision was made in a specific context.

One popular technique for generating local explanations is LIME (Local Interpretable Model-Agnostic Explanations). LIME works by approximating the behavior of the AI model locally around the instance of interest. It does this by perturbing the features of the instance and observing the resulting changes in the model's predictions. By analyzing these changes, LIME can identify the features that had the most influence on the model's decision for that particular instance.

Local explanations can be visualized using techniques such as heatmaps or bar charts, which highlight the importance of each feature in the decision-making process. These visualizations provide a clear and intuitive understanding of the factors that contributed to a specific prediction.

8.1.6 Counterfactuals

Counterfactual explanations (Colley et al., 2022) take local explanations a step further by providing insights into what changes would need to be made to an instance to achieve a different prediction. In other words, counterfactuals answer the question, "What would need to be different for the model to make a different decision?" Counterfactual explanations are particularly useful in scenarios where the model's decision is not aligned with the user's expectations or preferences. By generating counterfactuals, users can understand the specific changes that would need to be made to the input features in order to achieve the desired outcome.

For example, let's say a smart car's AI model predicts that a certain road is safe to drive on, but the user disagrees and believes it is not safe. By generating counterfactual explanations, the user can understand what changes would need to be made to the road conditions (such as reducing the speed limit or adding additional signage) for the model to predict that the road is unsafe.

Counterfactual explanations can be generated using optimization techniques that aim to find the minimal set of changes required to achieve a different prediction. These techniques take into account the constraints and boundaries of the input features to ensure that the counterfactuals are realistic and feasible.

8.1.7 Benefits and applications

Local explanations and counterfactuals have several benefits and applications in the context of smart cars (Shin, 2021). Some of these include:

1. **Improved Trust and Transparency:** By providing local explanations and counterfactuals, smart cars can enhance trust and transparency between the AI system and the users. Users can understand why a certain decision was made and what changes would need to be made to achieve a different outcome, leading to increased confidence in the system.
2. **User Customization and Personalization:** Local explanations and counterfactuals allow users to customize and personalize the behavior of the smart car's AI system. By understanding the factors influencing the system's decisions, users can make informed changes to the input features to align the system's behavior with their preferences.
3. **Error Detection and Debugging:** Local explanations and counterfactuals can be used for error detection and debugging purposes. If the smart car's AI system makes a prediction that is clearly incorrect or unexpected, local explanations can help identify the specific features or factors that led to the erroneous prediction. This information can then be used to improve the system's performance and reliability.
4. **Regulatory Compliance and Accountability:** Local explanations and counterfactuals can play a crucial role in regulatory compliance and accountability. In situations where the smart car's AI system is involved in an accident or makes a decision that has legal implications, local explanations and counterfactuals can provide evidence and justification for the system's behavior.

Overall, local explanations and counterfactuals are powerful tools for understanding the inner workings of smart cars' AI systems at a granular level. They provide insights into the factors that influence the system's decisions and allow for customization, error detection, and regulatory compliance. By incorporating these techniques, smart cars can become more transparent, trustworthy, and user-centric.

8.1.8 Model-agnostic explanations

Model-agnostic explanations are a powerful tool in the field of explainable AI for smart cars (Kaptein et al., 2017). These techniques allow us to interpret the decisions made by any machine learning model, regardless of its complexity or underlying algorithm. In this section, we will explore the concept of model-agnostic explanations and their application in the context of motor vehicles.

8.1.9 Understanding model-agnostic explanations

Model-agnostic explanations aim to provide insights into the decision-making process of a machine learning model without relying on its internal structure. These techniques focus on understanding the relationship between the input features and the model's output rather than interpreting the inner workings of the model itself. By doing so, model-agnostic explanations offer a more transparent and interpretable view of the decision-making process.

One of the key advantages of model-agnostic explanations is their versatility. They can be applied to any machine learning model, including complex deep learning models, without requiring any modifications to the model architecture. This flexibility makes model-agnostic explanations particularly useful in the context of smart cars, where different models with varying levels of complexity may be employed for different tasks, such as object detection, lane detection, or decision-making.

8.1.10 Techniques for model-agnostic explanations

Model-agnostic explanations are essential in Explainable AI (XAI) as they provide a means to interpret the decisions of diverse machine learning models without relying on model-specific intricacies. Several techniques have been developed to achieve model-agnostic explanations, offering transparency and interpretability across a broad spectrum of algorithms. LIME (Local Interpretable Model-agnostic Explanations) perturbs input data and fits a locally interpretable model to explain predictions within specific regions of the input space. SHAP (SHapley Additive exPlanations) values, rooted in cooperative game theory, offer a comprehensive measure of feature importance by considering all possible feature subsets. Permutation feature importance involves the random shuffling of feature values to gauge their impact on model performance, providing a simple yet effective model-agnostic method. Counterfactual explanations generate instances with different predictions by making slight changes to input features, shedding light on model decision boundaries. Anchors, on the other hand, are interpretable rules that precisely define conditions under which a model's prediction is reliable. These techniques collectively empower users to understand and trust the decisions of a wide range of machine learning models, fostering transparency and accountability in AI applications. Several techniques have been developed to provide model-agnostic explanations for machine learning models. These techniques can be broadly categorized into two types: global explanations and local explanations.

8.1.11 Global explanations

Global explanations aim to provide an overall understanding of how the model makes decisions across the entire dataset (Shen et al., 2020). One popular technique for global explanations is feature importance, which measures the contribution of each input feature towards the model's output. Feature importance can be calculated using various methods, such as permutation importance, which evaluates the decrease in model performance when a feature is randomly shuffled.

Another technique for global explanations is feature visualization, which aims to visualize the relationship between the input features and the model's output. This can be achieved through techniques such as partial dependence plots, which show how the model's output changes as a specific feature varies while keeping other features constant.

8.1.12 Local explanations

Local explanations focus on understanding the model's decision for a specific instance or prediction (Ferreira and Monteiro, 2020). One popular technique for local explanations is the use of surrogate models, which are simpler and more interpretable models trained to approximate the behavior of the original model. Surrogate models can provide insights into the decision-making process of the original model by capturing its key features and decision boundaries.

Another technique for local explanations is using counterfactual explanations, which aim to identify the minimal changes in the input features required to change the model's decision. By generating counterfactual explanations, we can understand the specific factors that influence the model's decision for a particular instance and potentially identify areas for improvement or optimization.

8.1.13 Application of model-agnostic explanations in smart cars

Model-agnostic explanations have numerous applications in the field of smart cars, where transparency and interpretability are crucial for ensuring safety, trust, and regulatory compliance (Giacomo, 2019). Let's explore some of the key applications of model-agnostic explanations in the context of motor vehicles.

8.1.14 Safety and decision-making

Model-agnostic explanations can help improve the safety of smart cars by providing insights into the decision-making process of the models responsible for critical tasks such as collision avoidance or lane keeping. By understanding the factors that influence the model's decisions, engineers and regulators can identify potential vulnerabilities or biases and take appropriate measures to address them.

For example, using model-agnostic explanations, we can identify situations where the model may fail or make incorrect decisions, such as misclassifying pedestrians or failing to detect obstacles in certain lighting conditions. This information can be used to improve the model's performance and robustness, ensuring safer driving experiences.

8.1.15 Regulatory compliance and accountability

Model-agnostic explanations can also play a crucial role in regulatory compliance and accountability. In many countries, regulations require that the decisions made by autonomous vehicles be explainable and transparent. Model-agnostic explanations can provide the necessary insights to meet these regulatory requirements, allowing authorities and stakeholders to understand and verify the decision-making process of smart cars.

Using model-agnostic explanations, manufacturers and developers can demonstrate that their models make decisions based on valid and reliable factors rather than arbitrary or biased criteria. This transparency not only helps build trust among users and regulators but also ensures accountability in case of accidents or incidents involving smart cars.

8.1.16 User experience and trust

Model-agnostic explanations can significantly enhance the user experience and trust in smart cars. By providing clear and understandable explanations for the decisions made by the vehicle, users can have a better understanding of why certain actions are taken, leading to increased trust and confidence in the technology.

For example, imagine a smart car that explains why it decided to change lanes or brake suddenly. By providing model-agnostic explanations, the car can communicate its decision-making process to the driver, making the driving experience more transparent and understandable. This can help alleviate concerns and fears associated with autonomous driving and foster greater acceptance and adoption of smart cars.

Model-agnostic explanations are a valuable tool in the field of explainable AI for smart cars. These techniques provide transparent and interpretable insights into the decision-making process of machine learning models, regardless of their complexity or underlying algorithm. By applying model-agnostic explanations in the context of motor vehicles, we can enhance safety, regulatory compliance, user experience, and trust in smart cars, paving the way for a future where intelligent vehicles coexist harmoniously with humans on the roads.

8.1.17 Rule extraction and rule sets

Rule extraction and rule sets are powerful techniques used in the field of explainable AI to provide interpretable explanations for the decision-making process of smart cars (Hagras, 2018). These techniques aim to extract human-readable rules from complex machine learning models, allowing users to understand the reasoning behind the decisions made by the smart car's AI system.

8.1.18 Rule extraction techniques

Rule extraction techniques involve extracting rules from black-box models, such as deep neural networks, to create a simplified and interpretable representation of the model's decision-making process. These techniques aim to strike a balance between accuracy and interpretability, allowing users to understand the factors that influence the smart car's decisions.

One popular rule extraction technique is the "rule-based model" approach. This technique involves converting the learned decision boundaries of a complex model into a set of rules that can be easily understood by humans. The rules are typically represented in the form of "if-then" statements, where the "if" part represents the conditions that need to be met for a certain action to be taken, and the "then" part represents the action itself.

Another rule extraction technique is the "rule extraction from decision trees" approach. Decision trees are inherently interpretable models, and by extracting rules from decision trees, we can gain insights into the decision-making process of the smart car. The rules extracted from decision trees can be used to explain the reasoning behind the smart car's actions and provide transparency to the users.

8.1.19 Rule sets for decision-making

Rule sets are a collection of rules that work together to make decisions. In the context of smart cars, rule sets can be used to define the behavior and decision-making process of the AI system. These rule sets can be created manually by domain experts or automatically generated using rule extraction techniques.

One advantage of using rule sets is that they provide a transparent and interpretable representation of the decision-making process. Users can easily understand the rules and the conditions under which certain actions are taken by the smart car. This transparency helps build trust and confidence in the AI system, as users can verify and validate the rules based on their own knowledge and understanding.

Rule sets can also be updated and modified easily, allowing for iterative improvements in the decision-making process of the smart car. As new data and insights become available, the rule sets can be adjusted to incorporate the new information, ensuring that the smart car's behavior remains up-to-date and aligned with the user's preferences and requirements.

Furthermore, rule sets can be used to enforce safety and ethical considerations in the decision-making process of smart cars. By explicitly defining rules that prioritize safety and ethical guidelines, the smart car can make decisions that prioritize the well-being of the passengers, pedestrians, and other vehicles on the road.

8.1.20 Benefits and limitations of rule extraction and rule sets

Using rule extraction and rule sets in smart cars offers several benefits (Tambwekar and Gombolay, 2023). Firstly, these techniques provide transparency and interpretability, allowing users to understand the decision-making process of the smart car. This understanding can help build trust and confidence in the AI system, as users can verify and validate the rules based on their own knowledge and understanding.

Secondly, rule extraction and rule sets enable the customization and personalization of the smart car's behavior. By defining rules that align with the user's preferences and requirements, the smart car can make decisions tailored to the individual user's needs. This customization enhances the user experience and ensures that the smart car behaves in a way that is consistent with the user's values.

However, there are also limitations to the use of rule extraction and rule sets in smart cars. One limitation is the complexity of the decision-making process. Smart cars operate in dynamic and complex environments, where the rules may need to consider a wide range of factors and variables. Creating comprehensive rule sets that cover all possible scenarios can be challenging and time-consuming.

Another limitation is the trade-off between accuracy and interpretability. Rule extraction techniques aim to simplify complex models into interpretable rules, but this simplification may come at the cost of accuracy. The extracted rules may not capture all the nuances and complexities of the original model, leading to a potential loss of performance.

Furthermore, rule sets may not be able to handle situations that fall outside the predefined rules. In complex and unpredictable scenarios, the smart car may encounter situations not covered by the existing rules. In such cases, the smart car may need to rely on other decision-making mechanisms or fallback strategies to ensure safe and reliable operation.

Despite these limitations, rule extraction and rule sets provide valuable tools for enhancing the explainability and transparency of smart cars. By enabling users to understand and validate the decision-making process, these techniques contribute to developing trustworthy and user-centric AI systems in the field of smart cars.

REFERENCES

Adadi, A. and Berrada, M. (2018) 'Peeking Inside the Black-Box: A Survey on Explainable Artificial Intelligence (XAI)', *IEEE Access*, 6, pp. 52138–52160. Available at: https://doi.org/10.1109/ACCESS.2018.2870052.

Colley, A., Väänänen, K. and Häkkilä, J. (2022) 'Tangible Explainable AI—an Initial Conceptual Framework', in *Proceedings of the 21st International Conference on Mobile and Ubiquitous Multimedia*. New York, NY, USA: Association for Computing Machinery (MUM '22), pp. 22–27. Available at: https://doi.org/10.1145/3568444.3568456.

Ferreira, J.J. and Monteiro, M.S. (2020) 'What Are People Doing About XAI User Experience? A Survey on AI Explainability Research and Practice', in A. Marcus and E. Rosenzweig (eds). *Lecture Notes in Computer Science*. Cham: Springer International Publishing, pp. 56–73. Available at: https://doi.org/10.1007/978-3-030-49760-6_4.

Gerlings, J., Shollo, A. and Constantiou, I.D. (2020) 'Reviewing the Need for Explainable Artificial Intelligence (xAI)', pp. 1–10. Available at: https://doi.org/10.24251/HICSS.2021.156.

Giacomo, G.D. (2019) 'WhiteMech: White-Box Self-Programming Mechanisms', *2019 IEEE 18th International Conference on Cognitive Informatics & Cognitive Computing (ICCI*CC)*, pp. 3–3. Available at: https://doi.org/10.1109/ICCICC46617.2019.9146075.

Hagras, H. (2018) 'Toward Human-Understandable, Explainable AI', *Computer* [Preprint]. Available at: www.semanticscholar.org/paper/Toward-Human-Understandable%2C-Explainable-AI-Hagras/026e7c05af3f50daddafd34524e c67b2186f6628 (Accessed: 13 December 2023).

Kaptein, F. et al. (2017) 'The role of emotion in self-explanations by cognitive agents', *2017 Seventh International Conference on Affective Computing and Intelligent Interaction Workshops and Demos (ACIIW)*, pp. 88–93. Available at: https://doi.org/10.1109/ACIIW.2017.8272595.

Shen, Y. et al. (2020) 'To Explain or Not to Explain: A Study on the Necessity of Explanations for Autonomous Vehicles', *ArXiv*, abs/2006.11684. Available at: https://

consensus.app/papers/explain-explain-study-necessity-explanations-autono-mous-shen/ccb979c3a9df5982a8976daa432e116f/ (Accessed: 13 December 2023).

Shin, D. (2021) 'The Effects of Explainability and Causability on Perception, Trust, and Acceptance: Implications for Explainable AI', *The International Journal of Human-Computer Studies*, 146. Available at: https://doi.org/10.1016/j.ijhcs.2020.102551.

Tambwekar, P. and Gombolay, M. (2023) 'Towards Reconciling Usability and Use-fulness of Explainable AI Methodologies', *ArXiv*, abs/2301.05347. Available at: https://doi.org/10.48550/arXiv.2301.05347.

Index

Numbers in *italic* indicate a figure and numbers in **bold** indicate a table.

3D mapping, 18
4G communication technologies, 106, 119, 123
5G communication technologies, 53, 77, 106, 119, 123, 129
6G communication technologies, 53, 60, 123, 129

A

A*, 10
accessibility, 4, 61, 111, 125
accidents, 4–5, 16–20, 35, 50, 64, 74, 75, 78, 80–81, 83, 94, 108–109, 111, 118, 124, 137, 149, 151, 162, 165
   pedestrian, 78
   traffic, 17, 50, 74, 108
   vehicle, 75
accountability, 26, 33, 35, 39, 45–46, 52, 60–61, 74, 150–151, 160, 162, 164–165
accuracy, 9, 13–14, 16, 31, 35–37, 41, 55–56, 58, 61, 86, 88, 91, 94, 111, 154
   vs. interpretability, 61, 166–168
activation maximization, 25, 29, 33–34
active learning, 125
ADAF, 53
Adaptive Cruise Control (ACC), 2, 81–83, 124
Adaptive Dehazing (AD), 59
adaptive traffic signal control, 124
advanced driver assistance systems (ADAS), 124
adversarial attack detection, 150–151

AI/ML, 18, 76
Airbus, 85
alerts, 2, 78–79
   context-aware, 40
   fault, 125
   real-time, 40
   unnecessary, 135
AlexNet architecture, 6
algorithms
   AI, 25–26, 35, 38–40, 50, 52, 65, 76, 87–88, 128, 135, 138–141, 144–149, 151–154
   AI/ML, 76
   AI-based, 1
   computer vision, 15
   DBSCAN, 13
   decision-making, 9, 145, 158–159
   deep learning (DL), 9–12, 19
   Dijkstra, 10
   integrated cognitive, 108
   localization, 9
   machine learning (ML), 3, 9, 30, 50–51, 60, 76
   mapping, 9
   ML-based, 60
   probabilistic, 3
   RANSAC, 13
   State lattice, 10
   trust evaluation, 128
   vehicle, 60
   XAI, 10, 75, 88–92
Alljoyn, 120
alternative fuel vehicles, 124
ANFIS models, 56
APIs, 120, 129
Apple Home Kit, 120

artificial intelligence (AI), 1, 53, 60, 73,
    85, 100, 106, 112, 117, 125,
    128, 134
  algorithms, 25–26, 35, 38–40, 50, 52,
    65, 76, 87–88, 128, 135, 138–141,
    144–149, 151–154
  in autonomous vehicles, 3–6, 47
  black-box, 26
  integration of, 5, 20, 27, 29, 147
  malicious attacks on, 147–148
  systems, 5, 19, 25–30, 33–34, 36,
    39–40, 42, 45, 47, 53–54, 59, 66,
    76, 136–142, 144–146, 148–151,
    153, 159, 162, 166–168
  techniques, 9–12, 50, 79, 128, 143
  see also AI/ML; explainable artificial
    intelligence (XAI)
artificial neural networks (ANN), 84,
    87–88 108
AS-DBSCAN, 13
Association for Computing Machinery
    (ACM), 7, 46
attention heat maps, 58
Automated Guided Vehicles (AGV), 56
automated navigation technology, 56
automated robotics bus, 84
automation, 46, 95
  driving, 18, 46
  levels of, 1–3, 2, 52, 80
Automotive Safety Integrity Levels
    (ASILs), 19
autonomous driving (AD), 1, 2, 5, 9, 12,
    15–17, 19–20, 42, 45–46, 50, 51,
    54–56, 58–62, 64–66, 65, 79, 83,
    107, 139, 152, 158, 165
  vision-based, 54
autonomous driving systems, 16–17, 19,
    59–60
  integration of, 17
autonomous electric helicopter, 85
autonomous electric tram, 84
autonomous microbus, 84
autonomous underground vehicle, 84
autonomous underwater vehicle
    (AUV), 85
autonomous vehicles (AVs), 1–20,
    50–65, 73–95
  adoption of, 36, 39–40
  AI techniques and deep learning
    algorithms in, 9–12
  AI-driven decision making in, 6–7
  data integration in, 12–15

human-AI interaction in, 16–17
importance of AI in, 3–6
levels of autonomy of, 1–3, 2, 77, 82
perception system in, 13, 15–16, 15,
    20, 37, 158–159
protocol architecture, 52
safety and reliability in, 5, 16–20, 18,
    38–39, 46, 50
security, 125
sensor fusion and data integration in,
    12–15
XAI in, 34–35, 35, 45–47, 50–65,
    73–95
see also specific types of autonomous
    vehicles; smart cars

B

banking, 54, 74
Bayesian Convolutional LSTM, 6
Bayesian neural networks, 37–38
Berkeley DeepDrive eXplanation
    (BDD-X) dataset, 55, 55
best practices, 43–44, 46–47, 134
bias, 52, 54, 61, 73, 138–140, 148, 153,
    158–160, 165
Big Data, 76, 111
  analysis, 18, 106
black box models, 26, 57, 61–62
blind spots, 158–159
blockchain, 54, 56, 128
  construction, 56
  technology, 53
Brake Control Module (BCU), 83

C

cameras, 1, 9, 12–13, 15, 50, 53, 82,
    83–85, 102, 145
  smart, 84
  video, 80
cargo tracking, 125
CARLA driving benchmark, 58
central computing unit (CCU), 80
Cloud-based Internet of Vehicles
    (CIoV), 100, 101, 107–108, 112
cloud computing, 77, 106, 111–112
collision warning systems, 124–125
comprehensibility, 27, 42–43, 47,
    142, 144
computer-aided learning, 125
computer vision, 3, 9, 15, 33–34, 59
congestion prediction systems, 124

connected cars, 111
connected vehicles, 50, 76, 100,
    109–111, 116
Controller Area Network
    (CAN bus), 82
Convolutional Neural Networks
    (CNNs), 6, **8**, 13, 20, 58, 74–76,
    90–92, 94–95
Cooperative Collision Avoidance
    Systems (CCAS), 109
Cooperative Intelligent Transportation
    System (CITS), 100, 101
counterfactuals, 88, 161–164
cross-domain integration, 129
cybersecurity, 18, 62; risks 147–148
cyber threats, 5, 127, 147

D
data
    accident, 149
    analog, 123
    analysis, 4, 18, 58, 106, 129
    anonymization and
        pseudonymization, 152
    autonomous, 106
    availability, 160
    biased, 160
    cloud, 12
    collection and retention, 19,
        123–124, 152–153
    collector devices, 126
    distributed, 129
    encryption, 147
    exchange, 76, 106, 116, 122
    extraction, 123
    formats, 116, 129
    fusion, 129
    handling, 125, 146
    historical, 137, 149
    immutability, 56
    informed consent and user
        control, 153
    input, 33–34, 87–89, 147–148,
        150, 163
    integration, 12–15
    integrity, 125
    intelligence, 126
    interchange, 129
    location, 147, 152
    management, 20, 53, 129–130
    mining, 108, 134

multi-dimensional, 50
multimodal IoV, 129
normalization, 129
personal, 145, 147
privacy, 5, 145, 147–148, 152
processing, 61, 76, 130, 153
protection, 138, 145–146, 151–155
real-time, 1, 14, 45, 108, 124, 137
RELLIS3D, 14
security, 5, 152
sensitive, 61, 153
sensor(y), 3, 12–13, 20, 123, 128,
    137, 149, 152
sharing and third-party access, 116,
    126, 152–154
silos, 121
sources, 15, 52, 123, 149, 152
storage, 147
syntax, 120, 129
traffic, 12, 125, 136
transfer, 127, 150
transmission, 117, 119, 129
transparency, 46
user, 106, 138, 152
vehicle, 128
visual, 9, 15
see also privacy and data protection
DBSCAN algorithm, 13
debugging, 34, 159, 162
decision explanation, 145
decision-making, 3–4, 6, 9, 17, 31–32,
    35, 37, 41–43, 50, 52–54, 58,
    64–65, 135, 138, 153, 163
AI-driven, 4, 6, 20, 25
algorithms, 9, 145, 158–159
automated, 54, 74
biases in, 153
ethical, 17, 151
logic, 60
mechanisms, 168
path, 88
processes, 6, 9, 27, 30, 33–34, 36–39, 42,
    54, 56, 86, 135, 139, 141, 145–146,
    149–151, 158–161, 163–168
real-time, 6, 12, 38
rule sets for, 166–167
safety and, 165
systems, 73
transparency in, 139–140
see also decision explanation;
    decision support; decision
    trees (DT)

decision support, 137–139, 151
  safety-critical, 149–150
decision trees (DT), 30, 36, 58, 73, 149,
  166
decomposability, 89
dedicated short-range communications
  (DSRC), 123, 129
deep learning (DL), 6, 7, 8, 88, 95, 108
  algorithms, 9–12, 19
  approaches, 14
  architecture, 14
  methods, 130
  models, 19, 56–57, 163
  networks, 59
  systems, 58
  techniques, 6, 12, 16, 19–20
  technologies, 19
  see also deep learning computer
    vision (DLCV)
deep learning computer vision
  (DLCV), 59
deep neural networks (DNNs), 6, 31,
  33, 36, 60, 73–74, 77, 88, 166
Deep Q-Network, 56
Delimited Anti-Jamming approach, 108
DENSE dataset, 13–14
design processes, iterative, 138,
  143–144
device-to-device (D2D), 78, 120
Dijkstra Algorithm, 10
direct-to-device (D2D), 118
discrimination, 61
DL techniques, 6, 12, 20
  integration of, 20
Dyna, 65
dynamic route guidance, 124

E
edge computing, 53
edge devices, 123
edge intelligence (EI), 53
electrical vehicles (EVs) using XAI,
  134–155
  continuous improvement, 141
  decision explanation, 145
  error detection and diagnosis, 145,
    149
  explainable recommendations,
    137–140
  feature designing for smart electrical
    vehicles, 134–137

iterative design, 141
  malicious attacks on, 147–148
  privacy and data protection in,
    145–146
  safety in, 144–146, 149–150
  safety validation and
    certification, 145
  supply chain security, 148
  user concerns and misconceptions,
    140–142
  user education and training, 140
  user feedback, 141–143
  see also online communities and
    social media; smart cars
Electric Power Assisted Steering System
  (EPAS), 83
emergency brake assistance, 124
emergency services, 118
energy/fuel consumption/management,
  4–5, 56, 103, 124
Engine Control Module (ECU), 18, 82
ensemble models, 36
error detection and diagnosis, 145, 149
ethical considerations, 3, 46,
  138–140, 167
European Union General Data
  Protection Regulation (GDPR),
  61–62, 154–155
explainability, 27–39, 51–54, 59–62,
  62, 65–66, 73–74, 79, 88–89, 94,
  141–144, 168
  interpretability vs. transparency, 27, 28
  key concepts in, 27–29, 27
  measuring fidelity, comprehensibility,
    and trustworthiness, 42
  metrics for evaluating, 41–42
  model transparency, 27, 28
  performance vs., 35–37, 154
  tailoring metrics to specific use
    cases, 42
  trustworthiness, 27, 28–29
explainable artificial intelligence (XAI),
  25–47, 26
  algorithms, 10, 75, 88–92
  approaches to developing XAI
    models, 29–30
  challenges of implementing in
    autonomous vehicles, 34–35, 35
  error detection and diagnosis, 149
  evaluation and validation, 40–42, 41
  feature importance analysis, 32–33
  fundamentals, 25

handling uncertainty, 37–38
human-AI interaction, 39–40
incorporating in user feedback, 144
integration of in user interfaces,
    135–137
interpretability vs. transparency, 28
introduction to, 26
methods, 86–88
model transparency, 28, 30–31
performance and explainability,
    trade-offs between, 35–37
in privacy and data protection in,
    153–155
real-time risk assessment, 149
regulatory compliance, 45–46, 155
rule-based systems, 31–32
safety and reliability, 38–39
for safety and security, 149–150
for security enhancement, 148–149
SHAP (SHapley Additive exPlanations)
    and LIME (Local Interpretable
    Model-agnostic Explanations)
    methods, 25, 29, 32–33
significance of, 26–27
simulation and testing, 44–45
trustworthiness, 28–29
user studies, 43–44
visualization techniques, 33–34
see also explainable artificial
    intelligence (XAI) applications in
    autonomous vehicles
explainable artificial intelligence (XAI)
    applications in autonomous
    vehicles, 7, 73–95
AV components and design, 79–86
challenges of implementing and
    limitations, 34–35, 35, 61–64
current state of, 52–60
future trends, 64–66
integration of, 38–39, 46–47, 57,
    116, 135–136
Internet of Vehicles (IoV) network
    architecture, 77–79
IoV structure and need for XAI-IDS, 76
methods and algorithms, 86–92
models to improve overall system
    performance, 92–94
practical implementation of
    XAI-based models, 76–77
prospects and future directions,
    50–66

XAI frameworks, 76
XAI method for convolutional neural
    networks in self-driving cars,
    74–75
explainable recommendations, 137–138
building trust through, 140
Explainable Security (XSec), 62–63, 64
explanation completeness, 41
explanation fidelity, 41–42, 47

F

feature detection and feature
    visualization, 158–168
benefits and applications, 162
benefits and importance of, 159–160
challenges and limitations, 160
counterfactuals, 161–162
global explanations, 164
local explanations, 161, 164
model-agnostic applications, 164–165
model-agnostic explanations,
    163–164
regulatory compliance and
    accountability, 165
rule extraction and rule sets, 166–168
safety and decision making, 165
in smart cars utilizing XAI, 158–168
user experience and trust, 165–166
feature importance, 33, 61, 64, 87, 139,
    158–161, 163–164
see also feature importance analysis
feature importance analysis, 25–26, 29,
    32–33, 148
SHAP and LIME methods, 32–33
Federated Deep Reinforcement
    Learning (RL) model, 56
Federated Learning (FL), 58–60
of XAI models (FED-XAI), 59–60
feedback loops, 40
fidelity, 42
see also explanation fidelity
Fifth Generation Mobile Network (5G
    cellular), see 5G communication
    technologies
finance, 30, 32–33
Finland, 84
fleet tracking and management, 125
Ford Motor Company, 58
Forward Collision Warning (FCW),
    2, 81
fuel efficiency, 4

G

gaming, 65
Gaussian occupancy mapping, 14
Gaussian process, 14
gaze estimation, 55
GazeMobileNet model, 55
Global Positioning System (GPS), 12,
    15–16, 18, 50, 78, 80, 152
Google Weave, 120
GPS, *see* Global Positioning System (GPS)
ground segmentation, 14

H

hacking, 5
handover, 16–17
Hazard Analysis and Risk Assessment
    (HARA) process, 18–19
healthcare, 26–33, 54, 74, 102, 118–119
human-AI interaction, 16–17, 39–40
  in AVs, 16–17
    designing user-friendly XAI interfaces, 40
    ensuring positive user experience, 40
human-centric, 41, 54
human drivers, 1, 3–4, 6, 15–17, 39, 53
human-driving learning methods, 54–55
human error, 17, 50, 144
human factors, 16–17, 80
human-machine interface (HMI), 16, 139
hybrid AI models, 36

I

IEC 61508, 18
image recognition, 53
image segmentation, 33
Industrial Internet Consortium
    (IIC), 120
Industries 4.0, 120
Information and Communication
    Technologies (ICT), 100–101
information exchange, 118
infotainment, 100–101, 104, 109–111,
    124–125
Institute of Electrical and Electronics
    Engineers (IEEE), 7, 8, **11**, 46,
    110, 116
integration
  of AI, 5, 20, 27, 29, 147
  of autonomous driving systems, 17
  chassis, 52
  cross-domain, 129
  data, 12–15

of DL techniques, 20
IoV, 119, 125, 129
of probabilistic models, 38
of safety mechanisms, 39
sensor, 4, 14
of vehicle components, 80, 116
of vehicle security and safety, 18
of XAI, 38–39, 46–47, 57, 116,
    135–136
Intelligent Transportation System (ITS),
    84, 95, 100–101, 101, 104, 109,
    112, 116, 118, 122, 124–125, 129
  see also Cooperative Intelligent
    Transportation System (CITS)
Intelligent Transport System (ITS), 74,
    77, 101
Intelligent Vehicle Motion Planning
    (IVMP), 60
intelligent vehicles, 58, 122, 158, 166
interaction technologies, 52
Internet of Autonomous Vehicles
    (IoAV), 53
Internet of Energy (IoE), 104, 112
Internet of Everything (IoE), 118–119
Internet of Things (IoT), 18, 53, 84,
    100–102, 103, 104, 107, 110–111,
    116, 118–121, 129
  interoperability, 120–121
Internet of Vehicles (IoV), 53, 76
  AI-based, 112
  applications, 124–126
  applications and services, 84–85
  autonomous vehicle components and
    design, 79–83
  Cloud, 112
  communication system, 107
  current issues, 85–86
  directions, 126–130
  ecosystem, 121–124
  emerging applications for smart cities,
    100–112
  evolution of, 101
  future issues and challenges of,
    116–130
  future research interoperability, 119,
    121, 130
  future scope of, 111–112
  integration, 119, 125, 129
  issues and challenges of, 110–111
  layered architecture of, 104,
    106–107, 117, 122
  ML, 112

network architecture, 77–86
security challenges and requirements
    of, 127
see also Cloud-based Internet of
    Vehicles (CIoV)
interoperability, 107, 111, 116,
    119–121, 123, 126, 129–130
    cross-domain, 121
    cross-semantic, 121
    cross-syntactic, 121
    IoT, 120–121
    IoV, 119, 121, 130
    semantic, 120, 128
interpretability, xv, 27, 30–32, 35–36,
    53–54, 58, 60–62, 66, 86, 88–89,
    145, 148, 159, 163–164, 167
    vs. accuracy, 61, 166–168
    local vs. global, 54, 87–88
    vs. performance, 36, 160
    real-time, 35
    vs. transparency, 27–28, 27, 30–32, 89
interpretable neural networks, 54
inter-vehicle model, 78, 112
intra-vehicle model, 78
intrusion detection, 56, 76, 125, 147, 151
    and prevention, 76, 150
in-vehicle infotainment (IVI), 110
IoTivity, 120
ISO 26262, 18–19
iterative design process, 138, 143–144
iterative learning, 3

J
Japan, 84

L
Lane Change Assistant (LCA), 81
Lane Departure Warning (LDW), 2,
    81, 124
Lane Keeping Assist (LKA), 81, 83
language translation, 53
layer-wise relevance propagation (LRP),
    76–77, 87
liability, 5, 17, 151
Light Detection and Ranging (LiDAR),
    1, 9, 12–16, *15*, 18, 50, 53, 80, 82,
    82, 84, 128, 145
LIME (Local Interpretable Model-
    agnostic Explanations), 25, 29,
    32–33
linear regression, 30, 73, 88

localization, 12, 16, 52
    algorithms, 9
logistic regression, 30, 73
logistics optimization, 125
Long Short-Term Memory (LSTM), 6
    Bayesian Convolutional, 6
low-latency
    communication, 117
    links, 79
    networks, 129
    transmission, 53

M
machine-centric, 54
machine learning (ML), 3, 16, 100, 108,
    112
    algorithms, 3, 9, 30, 50–51, 60, 76
    models, 29, 35–36, 73–74, 77, 86, 89,
        93, 95, 159, 163–164, 166
machine-to-human (M2H), 118
machine-to-machine (M2M), 118
malicious attacks, 56, 147–148
mapping algorithms, 9
Markov Decision Process (MDP), 11, 65
    see also uncertain Markov Decision
        Process (uMDP); uncertain
        Partially Observable Markov
        Decision Process (uPOMDP)
mask generation, 92
metrics, 14, 58
    comprehensibility, 42
    for evaluating explainability, 41–42
    evaluation, 42, 47
    human-centric, 41
    quantitative, 41
    tailoring to specific use cases, 42, 47
    technical, 43
    trust, 58
microwave access (WiMAX), 123, 129
middleware, 120–121
military systems, 54, 74
Mobile Ad hoc Network (MANET),
    100–104, 103, 108, 118
mobility, 3–4, 20, 50, 103, 109, 111,
    121, 124
model-agnostic methods, 54, 93, 163
model inquiry, 92–93
model-specific methods, 54
model transparency, 25–31, 27, 33–34
    limitations and use cases, 30
    transparent models in XAI, 30
"Molly Problem," 64

N

National Highway Traffic Safety
    Administration (NHTSA), 46
National Institute of Standards (NIST), 76
natural language explanations, 40
network(s)
    architecture, 130
    automotive, 123
    Bluetooth, 78, 106, 123
    bottlenecks, 111
    cellular, 116
    communication, 102, 117, 147
    components, 130
    connections, 147
    connectivity, 120
    construction, 91
    decentralized, 116
    deep, 88
    deep learning, 59
    dynamic, 128
    generative adversarial, 130
    global, 112
    heterogeneous, 123
    infrastructure-less, 101–102
    IoT, 110
    IP, 78
    layers, 73–74, 76, 106–107, 120, 123
    low-latency, 129
    model, 90, 108
    neural, 35, 58, 74–76, 93
    nodes, 111–112, 122
    output, 92
    paradigm, 107
    quality of service, 124
    road, 118
    satellite, 106
    security, 128
    self-organized, 101
    sensor(y), 108–110, 126
    size, 91
    social, 110
    speed, 111
    structure, 107
    topology stability, 128
    traffic, 150
    vehicle, 110–111
    vehicular, 108, 117, 121, 129
    virtual, 120
    WAVE, 106, 123
    Wi-Fi, 106, 123
    wired, 102
    wireless, 102, 118–119

    wireless sensor (WSNs), 110, 126
    WLAN, 106
    see also 4G communication
        technologies; 5G communication
        technologies; 6G communication
        technologies; artificial neural
        networks (ANN); Bayesian
        neural networks; Controller
        Area Network (CAN bus);
        Convolutional Neural Networks
        (CNNs); deep neural networks
        (DNNs); Deep Q-Network;
        Internet of Vehicles (IoV);
        interpretable neural networks;
        Mobile Ad hoc Network
        (MANET); Region-based
        Convolutional Neural Networks
        (R-CNN); Software Defined
        Network (SDN)
non-transparent models, 31

O

object recognition, 33
obstacle avoidance, 53
oneM2M, 121
One-Shot Federated Learning, 58
online communities and social media,
    143–155
open-source technologies, 120
optimization, 56, 80, 164
    logistics, 125
    numerical, 6
    platforms, 125
    route, 124
    techniques, 10, 162
    traffic flow, 4
OR-based filtering, 13
over-the-air (OTA) updates, 4, 148

P

Park Assist (PA), 81, 82
Park Distance Control (PDC), 81
passenger safety, 38, 50
path planning, 9, 18, 53, 95
pedestrians, 3, 5, 9, 17, 19, 38–39, 74,
    101, 116, 122, 151, 165, 167
    safety of, 38, 50
pedestrian-to-pedestrian (P2P), 118
perception-action mapping, 51
perception systems, 13, 15–16, 15, 20,
    37, 158–159

performance, 4–5, 9–10, 13–14, 17,
    45–46, 58–61, 62, 65–66, 73, 76,
    84, 91, 94–95, 108, 118, 128, 140,
    147, 158–159, 163–165, 168
cognitive, 128
driving, 3, 58, 144
and explainability, trade-offs
    between, 35–37, 47, 154
gaze vector estimation, 55
human, 53
vs. interpretability, 36, 160
prediction, 87
strategies for achieving balance, 36
system, 44, 92–94, 162
pollution, 122
detection, 121
post hoc explanation methods, 54, 62,
    63, 64
Prediction-based Routing (PBR), 110
predictive analytics, 4
privacy, 11, 56, 101, 125, 130, 138,
    146–147, 151
challenges in smart cars, 152–153, 155
data, 5, 145, 147–148, 152
laws, 155
preservation, 60
regulations, 138, 146, 152–155
rights, 153
risks, 153
threats, 56
see also privacy and data protection
privacy and data protection, 138,
    145–147, 152–155
adversarial attack detection, 150
cybersecurity risks, 147
malicious attacks, 147–148
over-the-air (OTA) updates, 148
role of XAI in, 153–155
security challenges, 146–147
probabilistic algorithms, 3
probabilistic models, 37–38
public transportation, 84

Q

quality of service (QoS), 110, 117,
    124–125, 127, 129

R

Radio Detection and Ranging
    (RADAR), 1, 9, 12–16, 50, 53,
    80–83, 82, 145

Random Selection, 56
RANSAC algorithm, 13
real-time kinetic (RTK) sensors, 53
real-time model explanation
    generation, 38
real-time risk assessment, 149, 151
real-time traffic data/monitoring/
    updates, 117, 135–136
real-world testing, 44–45, 47
recognition modules, 53
Region-based Convolutional Neural
    Networks (R-CNN), 6, 94–95
regulatory compliance, 38, 45–47, 51,
    64, 66, 151, 154–155, 159–160,
    164, 166
and accountability, 150–151, 162, 165
industry standards and guidelines, 46
regulatory frameworks for XAI
    integration, 46
reinforcement learning (RL), 7, 9, 11,
    60, 66, 128
see also Federated Deep
    Reinforcement Learning (RL) model
reliability, 4–5, 9, 16–20, 18, 25, 29,
    38–39, 41, 43, 50, 58, 64, 139,
    147, 151, 158–159, 162
RELLIS3D dataset, 14
remote vehicle diagnostics, 124
resource management, 128
ride-sharing services, 122
roadside actuators (RAs), 106
roadside units (RSUs), 50, 76, 78, 106,
    111–112, 117, 122
robotics, 65, 84
Robot Operating System (ROS), 14
robustness, 16, 25, 29, 41, 45, 55, 60,
    140, 165
rule-based systems, 25–26, 29, 31–32,
    36, 38
rule-based approaches to XAI, 31–32
scalability and complexity, 32
rule extraction, 88, 148, 166–168
benefits and limitations of, 167–168
techniques, 166–167
rule sets, 32, 166–168
benefits and limitations of, 167–168
for decision-making, 166–167

S

SAE J3016, 1–3, 2, 46
safety, 3–4, 9, 16, 37–40, 42–43, 46–47,
    50–52, 56, 74, 79, 100–101, 104,

109, 112, 118, 124–125, 134, 137, 144–146, 150–151, 158, 164–167
in AI-driven AVs, 17–20, 34
analyses, 18
applications, 124–125
assessments, 46
of AVs, 5, 16–17, 18, 19–20, 36, 38, 46
benefits, 144
-centric, 109
collaborative, 146
compliance with standards, 151
-critical, 35, 38–39, 60, 145, 149–150
and decision-making, 165
ecosystem, 39
enhancing with XAI, 144, 146, 148–149
features, 125
functional, 18
human, 25
human-machine interaction for, 146
measures, 79, 140, 149, 151
mechanisms, 20, 39, 45
objectives, 19
parameters, 109
passenger, 38, 50
pedestrian, 38, 50
protocols, 20, 39
public, 17, 39, 116
regulators, 145
requirements, 41, 151
risks, 142, 145
road, 4, 13, 19, 77–78, 124
in smart cars, 144–146, 149, 159, 165
standards, 5, 36, 45, 47, 145, 151
system, 7, 84, 139
validation and certification, 145
in XAI, 38–39
see also safety and reliability; safety-critical
safety and reliability, 38–39
in AI-driven AVs, 17–20
in autonomous driving, 19
of AVs, 5, 16, 18, 38–39
integration of safety mechanisms, 39
in modern transportation systems, 50
safety considerations in XAI, 38–39
safety-critical, 35, 38–39, 60, 145
decision support, 149–150
saliency estimation, 92–94
saliency maps/mapping, 25, 29, 33–34, 54, 93–94, 159
scalability, 31–32, 127–128

security, 5, 18, 20, 53, 56, 60, 62, 74, 76, 95, 100–101, 104, 107, 110–112, 119–120, 123, 125–127, 129–130
of AVs, 18, 54, 56, 125
challenges, 79, 127, 146–148
challenges in smart cars, 146–148
enhancement with XAI, 148–150
explainable, 64
in EVs using XAI, 134–155
framework, 53
of IoV, 127
layer, 121, 122
loopholes, 74
operational, 18
network, 128
protocols, 103
telecommunication, 50
threats, 56, 102
vehicle, 18
vulnerabilities, 54
of XAI, 63, 66
see also cybersecurity; over-the-air (OTA) updates; supply chain
self-attention-based model, 59
self-driving
automobiles, 118
conditions, 57
dataset, 55
systems, 54–55
technology, 5
see also self-driving cars; self-driving vehicles (SDVs)
self-driving cars, 1, 3–5, 9, 74–75, 100
self-driving vehicles (SDVs), 9, 60, 79, 86
self-organizing neuro-fuzzy approach, 57–58
semantics, 129
semantic segmentation, 14, 55, 57, 57, 59–60
Semantic Web, 120; technologies 121
SenML, 121
sensor fusion, 4, 7, 9, 12–15
sensors, 1, 3–5, 9, 12–16, 18, 52–53, 78–85, 101–102, 106, 109, 123, 126, 145, 152, 159
parking, 109
pressure, 108
real-time kinetic (RTK), 53
see also cameras; Light Detection and Ranging (LiDAR); Radio Detection and Ranging (RADAR); sensor

fusion; ultrasonic sensors (US); video cameras
SHAP (SHapley Additive exPlanations), 25, 29, 32–33
simple object access protocol (SOAP) technology, 119–120
simulatability, 89
simulation and testing, 44–45
  real-world testing scenarios, 45
  simulated environments for XAI validation, 44–45
situational awareness, 17, 135; driver 54–55
smart cars, 111
  accountability and liability, 151
  adversarial attack detection, 150
  design principles for, 134–137
  feature detection and feature visualization in, 158–168
  importance of privacy and data protection in, 152
  interfaces/user interfaces, 134–137
  intrusion detection and prevention, 150
  malicious attacks on, 147–148
  over-the-air (OTA) updates, 148
  privacy and data protection in, 145–147, 152
  privacy challenges in, 152–153
  regulatory compliance and accountability, 150–151
  safety considerations in, 144–146
  safety standards, 151
  security challenges in, 146–147
  supply chain security, 148
  user interface design for, 134
  user-centric design, 138
  vulnerability assessment, 150
smart cities, 50, 51, 56, 84, 95, 116, 121–122, 124, 126, 130
  IoV in, 100–112
smart environments, 120
smart factories, 120
smart homes, 102, 119–120, 129
Society of Automotive Engineers (SAE), 1, 46
  see also SAE J3016
Software Defined Network (SDN), 77, 129
solar-powered autonomous vehicles (SAUVs), 85
speech recognition, 53

State lattice algorithms, 10
stereo depth generation, 56
Stop-and-Go Control (SAGC), 81
STRIDE threat model, 19
structured adversarial attacks, 63
supply chain, 124
  security, 148
system performance, 44, 92–94

T

traffic flow, 4, 124
  optimization, 4
traffic jams, 4, 50, 109
traffic laws, 5, 76
traffic management, 118, 121
  systems, 100, 117
traffic rules, 9, 51, 74, 105, **105**
transferability, 61–62, 66
transparency, 25, 27–29, 31–34, 36, 38–39, 45–47, 52–54, 58, 61–62, 74, 76, 89, 94, 134, 136, 138–141, 144–146, 148–149, 151, 153–155, 158–160, 162–168
  data, 46
  vs. interpretability, 27–28, 27, 30–32, 89
  model, 25–31, 27, 33–34
trust
  building, 5, 16, 30, 36–39, 137, 139–141, 151, 153, 155, 159, 165, 167
  building through explainable recommendations, 140
  community, 76
  fostering, 26, 30, 33, 159
  issues, 112
  management, 55, 58, 128
  mechanisms, 56
  metrics, 58
  public, 5, 37–38
  user, 34, 42–43, 46, 138, 147
  see also trustworthiness
trustworthiness, 25, 27, 28–29, 33, 42, 47, 52, 56, 59, 77, 94–95, 136, 141

U

ultrasonic sensors (US), 1, 12, 15–16, 50, 80
uncertain Markov Decision Process (uMDP), 85
uncertain Partially Observable Markov Decision Process (uPOMDP), 85

uncertain Partially Observable
     Stochastic Game (uPOSG), 85
uncertainty, 37–38, 47, 136
   epistemic, 19
   probabilistic models and uncertainty
     management, 38
   uncertainty in AV context, 37
U-Net mode, 56
United States, 46
Unmanned Aerial Vehicle (UAV), 56
user acceptance, 20, 40
user-centric, 43–44, 47, 60, 138–139,
     144, 162, 168
user concerns and misconceptions,
     140–142
   continuous improvement and
     feedback, 141
   gathering user feedback, 142
   importance of user feedback,
     141–142
   user education and training, 140
   user feedback and iterative design, 141
user customization and
     personalization, 162
user experience, 40, 43–44, 47,
     134–138, 141, 143, 167
   and trust, 165–166
user-friendly interfaces, 40, 47, 153, 160
user interfaces, 39, 134–136, 141, 143
   in-vehicle, 52
user privacy, 152
user studies, 43–44, 47
   conducting user-centric XAI
     evaluations, 43
   methodologies and best practices,
     43–44
user trust, xv, 34, 42–43, 46, 138, 147
user understanding, 43–44, 47, 160

V

vehicle diagnostic systems, 125
vehicle-to-barrier (V2B), 79
vehicle-to-building (V2B), 78, 117, 122
vehicle-to-cloud (V2C), 117, 122

vehicle-to-device (V2D), 117
vehicle-to-driver (V2D), 78, **105**
vehicle-to-everything (V2X), 46, 60, 76,
     78–79, 109, 112, 117, 123, 129
vehicle-to-grid (V2G), 78–79, 104,
     117, 122
vehicle-to-home (V2H), 78–79
vehicle-to-infrastructure (V2I), 50,
     78–79, 104, **105**, 117, 124
vehicle-to-pedestrian (V2P), 78, 104,
     105, 117
vehicle-to-roadside (V2R), 78–79, **105**,
     117–118, 122
vehicle-to-sensors (V2S), 78
vehicle-to-vehicle (V2V), 6, 50, 78, 104,
     105, 108–109, 117–118, 122, 124
vehicle traffic, 50
Vehicular Ad hoc Network (VANET),
     58, 100–101, 103–104, 103,
     109–110, 112, 116, 118
Vehicular Cloud Computing (VCC), 77
VeRiMi dataset, 58
video cameras, 80
visualization techniques, 25–26, 29,
     33–34, 159–160
   practical implementations, 34
   visualizing model decisions, 34
VPL modules, 53
vulnerability assessment, 150–151

W

weather conditions, 3, 5, 13–14, 55–56,
     59, 84, 106, 124, 135

X

XAI, *see* explainable artificial
     intelligence (XAI)

Y

Yolo V4, 55, 90–91, 94

Z

ZigBee, 78, 123
zone estimation, 55